The Notary's Manual

A guide for public notaries

Sanjay P. Gogia LL.M.

Notary Public (England & Wales)
Visiting Lecturer, University of Turin, Italy (International Trade Law)
Former Tutor, University of Cambridge (Notarial Practice) and
Tutor, (Notarial Practice) University College London

Published by Notary Training

"For notaries our name is our reputation"

Sanjay P. Gogia

**FOR MY PARTNERS, FRIENDS
& COLLEAGUES**

First Edition September 2014

Notary Training
www.notarytraining.co.uk

Printed in Great Britain by Berforts Information Press Ltd

CONTENTS

Rules and Regulations made by the Court of Faculties

BIOGRAPHICAL NOTE

Sanjay pursued a bachelor's degree in Law from Government Law College, Bombay and master's degree in Law from the University of Bombay and is admitted as an Advocate at the Bar Council of Delhi in India. He has worked with Dua Associates in their New Delhi office in the areas of business & commercial laws with an emphasis on advising foreign companies to establish a presence in India. Sanjay came to England to study law at the College of Law as a recipient of the British Chevening Scholarship, followed by qualifying as a Solicitor at Allen & Overy, London. Sanjay was a founding member of the India Group at Allen & Overy and was also instrumental in forming the British – Indian Lawyers Association under the flagship of The Law Society. He was admitted as a Solicitor of the Supreme Court of England and Wales in 1998. Sanjay qualified as a Notary Public in 2004 after successfully completing his Notarial Studies at the University of Cambridge. Prior to qualifying as a Notary Public Sanjay has also worked with Eversheds. He was leading the "India Desk" at Eversheds. Sanjay is also registered as an Indian Lawyer with the legal and judicial authorities in Monaco.

As a Notary Public Sanjay is involved in drawing, attesting, certifying and authenticating various kinds of deeds and documents including wills, commercial and intellectual property agreements, change of name certificates, statutory declarations and powers of attorney used in India and other parts of the world. He certifies documents for use in all jurisdictions and invariably advises clients on the wording and form of the document itself. He specialises in the preparation of notarial documents used in India and Indian consular offices in the UK. Sanjay is a former member of the "Notarial Qualification Board" and "Notarial Advisory Board" of the Faculty Office of the Archbishop of Canterbury which deals with notaries of England & Wales.

Sanjay is a former tutor at the Post Graduate course in Notarial Practice, University of Cambridge and a visiting lecturer to the University of Turin, Italy at LL.M in International Trade Law and a frequent contributor to various notarial publications. He has been a tutor in notarial practice at the University College London since September 2013.

PREFACE & ACKNOWLEDGEMENTS

Every notary is required to be professional. Notaries are usually held in high accountability and are relied upon by the public because of the high degree of responsibility which they exercise. For this reason, among others, each notary public needs a reliable manual at hand which he or she may turn for answers to the questions, problems and dilemma which from time to time present themselves. With such a need in mind it was the publisher's goal to prepare at best the various practice rules and relevant legislation permitted.

The text covers various topics which a Notary Public is likely to be concerned such as legalisation requirements of various countries and rules and regulations made by the Court of Faculties. I am grateful to the Faculty Office for permitting to publish the practice rules in this manual. I am thankful to the Legal Ombudsman and The National Archives for permitting to publish various texts. Finally my thanks to The Notaries Society for all their help, support and guidance.

Not a single book would ever be written without the help of Colleagues who have encouraged me to produce this manual. I am grateful to my business partner Anne McMahon and my mentor Michael Pulvermacher. I would also like to thank Dale Burgess for printing this manual and Gary McWilliam and his team at CDN for updates on legalisation requirements.

Suggestions from readers for further improvement of this manual in the subsequent editions will be most gratefully acknowledged.

Sanjay P. Gogia
September 2014

INTRODUCTION

A Notary Public ranks among the most distinct and ancient professions in England & Wales. Public Notaries are officers of the law and their primary responsibility is the preparation and authentication of legal documentation usually used overseas or at various foreign consulates in England and Wales. A notary's principal duty is to authenticate under seal and signature various documents executed in England and Wales. This is a function which is and has been from time immemorial well recognised by international law and custom among all countries. Notarised documents often form a vital part of international trade.

Apart from a few specialised duties, such as the issue of ship protests, protests of bills of exchange, and the certification of copies and translations, the English and Welsh notary is dependant for his/her status and livelihood on the fact that his/her intervention is required in order to authenticate and render effective legal documents executed here for use overseas. In other words, the execution of a notarial act by a notary in England and Wales involves, in the vast majority of cases, a document which is intended to take effect abroad.

There are currently around 800 practising notaries in England and Wales including the 38 Scrivener notaries. The majority are also solicitors or barristers but there are a good number who practise as notaries only. Scrivener notaries also deal with legal translation and the preparation of legal documents in other languages.

The Faculty Office has been exercising regulatory functions since its creation by The Ecclesiastical Licences Act 1533. The Master of the Faculties, the judicial officer in charge of the Faculty Office, is the approved regulator and appointing authority as set out in the Legal Services Act 2007. There are two members' associations, one for Scrivener notaries and one for General notaries. Scrivener notaries are full members of the International Union of Latin Notariat (UINL) whereas The Notaries' Society has observer status at UINL.

The Faculty Office has been working to maintain the independence and training of the notarial profession in order that the reputation of the profession is enhanced not only in England & Wales but throughout the world. In recent years this has seen the introduction of a two-year post-graduate level notarial practice course initially run by the Institute of Continuing Education at The University of Cambridge and currently by the Faculty of Laws at University College London. The character of the notary as an international legal officer is paramount in both civil and common law traditions.

The notarial profession is an independent one and the majority of the notaries are sole practitioners. Some work in partnership and others through a limited company but not as Alternative Business Structures ("ABS"). For notaries the ABS model will not be in the client's best interests and undermines professional independence because neutrality and independence are vital elements of the notary's role and function.

Chapter 1

ETHICS AND RULES OF PROFESSIONAL CONDUCT

As far as ethics and the rules of professional conduct in the notarial profession are concerned it seems to me that there are professional standards which come into play in our practising lives in three respects:

- the first is in the Faculty issued by the Faculty Office at the time of admission as a public notary;
- the second is the practising rules (principally The Notaries Practice Rules 2014);
- the third is the general professionalism and integrity with which a notary must conduct business as a legal professional.

1.   **The Notarial Faculty**
      A Notarial Faculty requires that a notary should "faithfully exercise the office of a public notary". A notary should make contracts or instruments for or between any party or parties requiring the same and s/he should not add or diminish anything without the knowledge and consent of such party or parties that may alter the substance of the fact. S/he should not make or attest any act, contract or instrument in which s/he knows there is violence or fraud and in all such things s/he should act uprightly and justly in the business of public notary according to the best of her/his skill and ability.

2.   **The Notaries Practice Rules 2014 ("the Rules")**
      Under Rule 4 of the Rules a notary shall:
      - uphold the rule of law and the proper administration of justice;
      - act with integrity;
      - maintain his/her independence and impartiality;
      - provide a prompt and proper standard of service for all clients;
      - act in a way that maintains public trust in the office of notary
      - comply with all legal and regulatory obligations and cooperate with the Master and any persons or body appointed by him/her in the exercise of the Masters regulatory functions;
      - operate his/her notarial practice in accordance with proper governance and sound financial and risk management principles; and

- operate his/her notarial practice in such a way as to provide equality of opportunity and respect for diversity.

Under Rule 7 of the Rules, a notary should not directly or indirectly obtain or attempt to obtain instructions for professional work or permit another person to do so on his/her behalf. Neither must s/he do anything in the course of practising as a notary, in any manner which compromises or impairs;
- the notary's independence or integrity;
- a person's freedom to instruct a notary of his/her choice;
- the notary's ability to act in the best interests of the client;
- the good repute of the notary or of the notarial profession;
- the notary's proper standard of work; or
- the notary's duty of care to persons in all jurisdictions who may place legitimate reliance on his/her notarial acts.

Rule 8 imposes a duty on the notary to inform the client, at the time of accepting instructions, of the right to make a complaint under the Conduct and Discipline Rules 2011 and/or the Legal Services Act 2007 as well as how to make such a complaint.

Under Rule 9, a notary shall not favour the interests of one client over those of another and shall not favour his own interests or those of any other person over those of his clients. Generally, a notary conducting a conveyancing transaction as a notary rather than as a solicitor, must not act for both seller and buyer in a transaction relating to property situated in England and Wales. A notary may exceptionally be permitted to act for both parties in situations specified in Rule 6A of the Rules 2014.

Under Rule 10, a notary must act impartially and, in particular, must not perform any notarial act which involves or may affect:
- his/her own affairs;
- the affairs of his/her spouse or partner or a person to whom the notary is engaged to be married;
- the affairs of a person to whom s/he is directly and closely related;
- the affairs of a person with whom s/he is in a professional partnership or by whom s/he is employed or from whom s/he receives a benefit by being provided with office accommodation or other facilities for his/her notarial practice;

- the affairs of a person who has appointed the notary to be his/her attorney which concern a matter within the scope of the power of attorney granted;
- the affairs of a trust of which s/he is a trustee or of an estate where s/he is a personal representative of the deceased;
- the affairs of a body corporate of whose board of directors or governing body s/he is a member;
- the affairs of an employee of the notary;
- the affairs of a partnership of which s/he is a member or of a company in which the notary holds shares either exceeding 5% of the issued share capital or having a market value exceeding such figure as the Master may from time to time specify.

Under Rule 18.1 a notary may charge a professional fee for all notarial work undertaken by him/her and the basis upon which that fee will be calculated or the fee to be charged for the work done, shall be made known in advance to any new instructing person. Unless otherwise permitted under rule 18.3 a notary is not permitted to share his/her professional fees with any person not entitled to act as a notary.

Any person following the proper procedure can make conduct complaints. The current procedure for all notaries who are members of The Notaries' Society is that such notary should first seek to address the complaint promptly on his own. However, if the matter cannot be resolved, then the complainant should write to the Secretary of the Notaries' Society. If the matter is still not resolved to the satisfaction of the complainant, then after a period of eight weeks from the date of making the initial complaint to the notary, the complainant can complain direct to the Legal Ombudsman. The notary will then be required to pay a non-refundable fee of £400 to the Legal Ombudsman in order for the complaint to be investigated.

3.   **Professional Conduct**
In common with lawyers in most parts of the world, solicitors and barristers in England & Wales have always been expected, by the general public and by their professional colleagues and others, to observe certain standards of professional conduct. Most General Notaries either practising as solicitors or have previously practised as solicitors and are therefore well versed in conduct rules of the Law Society.

Rule 5 provide that a notary shall at all times have regard to any code of code of practice approved by the Master from time to time. There is such a code of practice in the course of preparation which will be available in the not too distant future. My hope for the new code of practice is that it is not simply used for sound bites, but is regarded as the document with real substance, which brings about improvements and closer collaboration between notaries and their clients.

In addition the Legal Services Consumer Panel is encouraging the notarial profession via the Faculty Office to adopt a new British Standard which sets out requirements for identifying and responding to consumer vulnerability. The standard for inclusive service provision (BS 18477) was developed by consumer organisations, charities and governmental bodies to:

- encourage the use of fair, ethical and inclusive practices;
- show organisations how to identify vulnerable consumers and to treat them fairly to comply with the law;
- help organisations to understand what consumers have a right to expect from them;
- improve accessibility to services for all; and
- increase consumer confidence.

BS18477 was published in 2010 and can be used by service providers dealing with the public. As notaries, we should all be providing fair services which are accessible to all. Rule 8 of the Rules obliges every notary to inform the client/consumer about his/her complaints handling procedure. The Faculty Office and the Notaries' Society report that complaints from clients/consumers to date are generally about fees rather than any error or omission relating to the above principles. So far, BS 18477 does not encourage clients/consumers to be more active in terms of making complaints about conduct matters and seems unlikely to do so if notaries adopt and comply with BS 18477. However the increased regulation encouraged by the Legal Services Consumer Panel and imposed by the Legal Services Board through the Faculty Office inevitably raises the cost of regulation and therefore the cost of notarial practice which may be detrimental to the longer term interests of our clients/consumers. The already small number of notaries in practice may reduce further if these costs become disproportionate to the benefits which may be generated.

We are fast reaching a stage where the expectations of clients are increasing day by day. It is extremely important as a profession that we become stronger by adhering to the current rules of conduct and continuing to provide a prompt, efficient and cost effective professional service.

Chapter 2

RECORD KEEPING

Record-keeping is one of the most important functions of a notary. If there is any doubt as to whether or not s/he did a particular act, the notary must be able to give a clear answer.

A previous Master the late Sir John Owen introduced The Notaries (Records) Rules 1991 which provided that every public notary shall keep a permanent record of all notarial acts 'in accordance with good notarial practice'. At the time this was deemed to be, for provincial notaries in respect of public form documents, a record of the original or a complete copy of such documents. In the case of a private document, it meant that either a description of the document or an extract from such a document should be kept. For scrivener notaries, the rule was subsequently confirmed that public form documents should be issued in duplicate with one original to be kept in the protocol (and in exceptional cases a complete photocopy of the document could be kept instead). The protocol was to be preserved permanently. With regard to other documents, a record was to be kept in the protocol of the names of the parties and the nature of the document attested. This record was to be kept for six years.

Subsequent amendments to record-keeping rules (see the Notaries Practice Rules 2009 & 2014) have removed the differences between the record keeping requirements of scrivener notaries and general notaries, although many notaries (scriveners and general notaries) prefer to retain a duplicate original of a public form document rather than a photocopy, thereby replicating the practice of Civil Law notaries.

Guidance as to how records should be maintained by a Notary Public is given in the recent editions of "The General Notary". Whilst a tutor on the Notarial Practice course at the University of Cambridge and now at University College London, I have always directed students to the form of register given in "The General Notary" as I consider it absolutely imperative for notaries to keep proper records in a proper format. I give below the format for ease of reference.

Rule 23.1 of the 2014 Rules states that a notary shall keep proper records of his/her notarial acts. Rule 23.2 states that the records so kept shall be sufficient to identify:
- the date of the act;
- the person at whose request the act was performed;

16

- the person or persons, if any, intervening in the act and, in the case of a person who intervened in a representative capacity, the name of his principal;
- the method of identification of the party or parties intervening in the notarial act, and in the case of a party intervening in a representative capacity, any evidence produced to the notary of that party's entitlement so to intervene;
- the nature of the act and the fee charged.

I think the nature of the act should be slightly elaborated in addition to the above. For eg: brief particulars of the nature of the document "Power of Attorney by AB empowering CD to sell plot no.99 Main Street, Whitetown, Yellow County, Utopia" especially in cases where a copy of the document is not kept in private form.

Under Rule 23.3, where the notarial act is in the public form, the notary shall place an original of the act or a complete photographic copy of the same in a protocol, which shall be preserved permanently by the notary.

A digital or electronic storage system is now permitted provided that documents are stored in indelible or unalterable form.

Rule 23.4 states that records of acts not in public form, (kept in accordance with Rule 23.2), shall be preserved for a minimum period of twelve years and, for the avoidance of doubt, such preservation may also be by means of a suitable digital or other electronic system, which enables the storage of documents in an indelible and unalterable format. (Note: it is clear that strictly speaking the requirement is for the *record* of the act to be maintained for 12 years, but not necessarily a *copy* of the notarial act). However Rule 23.3 does requires a copy of a public form notarial act to be stored, in the form stated above. It is not sufficient for the purposes of Rule 23.3 to keep a mere record of a public form notarial act.

Currently Rule 25 states that when a notary ceases to practise as such then he shall arrange for his records to be transferred to notary in practice appointed by the retiring notary or his continuing notarial partners or alternatively another notary in practice approved by the Master and appointed by the persons having custody of the records (eg. personal representatives, or to an archive designated for the purpose under regulations made by the Master from time to time. The persons making such transfer shall give written particulars to the Registrar of the date of transfer and the person or archive to which the records were transferred. Records in electronic format will now be much easier to be so transferred and maintained.

It is pertinent to remember that records should always be kept up to date, as the Master or any person authorised by the Master may inspect such records at any time. This power is reserved to the Master under Rule 24 of the Rules. A reduction in the period of time during which records must be maintained, currently permanently, and ability for all records to be maintained in an indelible and unalterable electronic format would, in my opinion, make record-keeping more appropriate to the twenty-first century.

Protocol No.	Full name and address of person(s) or company requesting the act	Name and address of appearer(s) (if different)	Proof of identity and evidence of representative capacity (copied?[✓])	✓	Nature of act (copied? [✓]) and any matter to record	✓	Country: Legalisation Required?	Fee and Disbursements (paid? [✓])

Chapter 3

LEGAL OMBUDSMAN & SIGN POSTING

In the rapidly changing and competitive world of legal services, one of the best ways to ensure long-term success is through client satisfaction.

A recent survey into the use of legal services by the Legal Ombudsman found that 82% of consumers would choose a lawyer based on personal experience or recommendations from friends, relatives and work colleagues. Satisfied customers will be loyal; they will use your services again. Satisfied customers spread the word; they'll tell other people how much they like your business and value the service you offer. You won't have to invest as much time and energy (or money) bringing new people through your door.

Research done by the Legal Ombudsman shows that a good complaints process – one that is well explained and easy to follow – can increase customer confidence in a business, particularly if any problems that arise are addressed speedily and effectively. It demonstrates that the business has confidence in the service offered and a commitment to delivering those services to the highest standards.

According to the Legal Ombudsman using an internal complaints procedure, will help notaries and lawyers to improve their levels of customer service overall, to reduce the number of complaints finding their way to the Legal Ombudsman and to increase service standards across the profession. As well as reinforcing some of the practical and common sense approaches to good complaint handling, this chapter highlights some of the steps that can be taken to ensure the process works towards a positive outcome for all.

Before you receive a complaint
Having a clear complaints process in place will mean you are ready to deal with a complaint when the time comes. Some things to consider are:

- Appointing someone to act as a point of contact, to whom complaints should be sent in the first instance: this will avoid the possibility of complaints going unanswered due to a lack of ownership. Give their details on your correspondence and your website. Usually sole practitioners are themselves the first point of contact.

- Sometimes involving someone else early in the process may help. This will allow the complaint to be moderated, and gives you the benefit of a more objective viewpoint. In addition, complainants often appreciate having an objective opinion.

- The complaints process should be accessible to all, including vulnerable customers and those with special needs or requirements. You should be contactable by email, phone and letter. Complaints do not need to be made in writing. Be alert to any customer contact that looks like a complaint.

- If you are unable to resolve the complaint, you should inform your customer that they can take it to the Legal Ombudsman. This will usually happen after the option of the informal complaints procedure managed by the Notaries Society has been exhausted.

Ten simple steps recommended by the Legal Ombudsman under the headings:

Listen, Inform, Respond

Listen
1.   **Identify when a complaint is being made.** When a customer is unhappy with the service they receive, there are factors that could prevent them from making a formal complaint. They might feel intimidated or concerned that a complaint will affect their matter, or they may have special needs or requirements, which need accommodating in order to make your complaints process accessible and fair.

2.   **Understand the reason for the complaint.** Good practice takes into consideration the type of complaint that's being made. Try to spot the signs and 'softer' cues to establish early on what type of complaint is being made. For instance, although they may not mention the word 'complaint', a customer may indicate they're unhappy with the costs or that they're confused about the length of time a case is taking to proceed.

It may also be helpful to think about any underlying reasons for the complaint. Perhaps a customer is anxious about the progress of their case, hasn't fully understood the legal process or is working to a limited budget. Take these things into account as the complaint progresses.

Inform

3. **Acknowledge the complaint within two working days of receipt.** Good practice requires a timely acknowledgement of a complaint. The experience of consumers in other sectors shows that a response within two working days increases their confidence in a complaint handling process.

4. **Provide a map of options.** Rather than just asking the customer what they want to do next, provide options. For example, you could offer formal and informal routes to resolving their complaint. For instance, if the issue relates to greater clarity over costs, you might simply need to provide the customer with a more detailed breakdown of their bill. In this way, the complaint could be dealt with quickly and informally. On the other hand, if the complaint is about whether you have followed their instructions regarding the work it may require a more formal route in which both parties provide written evidence to support their arguments.

5. **Spell out implications.** Reassure the customer that they won't be charged for complaining. Be clear and upfront about how long it will take to investigate the complaint and that you have eight weeks within which to resolve it. Additionally, some customers may be concerned that raising a formal complaint will prejudice or disrupt their matter. You should explain what, if any, impact the complaint will have on the work being done as early as possible.

6. **Use clear, comprehensible language and neutral tone.** Clarity in any communication is vital to a considered and effective complaints procedure. Avoid jargon and emotive or provocative language.

Respond

7. **Share your findings.** Once you have conducted a thorough investigation, and have established all the facts required to make a decision, share the findings and your conclusion with your customer. Include as much detail as is necessary for the customer to understand how and why you have reached a decision.

8. **If you find that you provided poor service** acknowledge what went wrong and offer the customer a suitable remedy, along with a full explanation of what happened. The remedy should be proportionate to the level of poor service. For example, if there was a small administrative error that didn't adversely impact their matter but which caused minor inconvenience, an apology might be more appropriate. If, on the other hand, they've been overcharged,

it would be sensible to apologise, refund the amount and perhaps pay a small amount of compensation.

9. **If you decide you offered a reasonable service** provide a full and clear explanation about how you reached that decision and show evidence where possible.

10. **Signpost the customer to the Legal Ombudsman.** If you can't agree on a resolution to the complaint you must signpost your customer to us.

Mandatory Information for General Notaries to be given to all Notarial Clients under Section 8 of The Notaries Practice Rules 2014

My notarial practice is regulated by the Faculty Office of the Archbishop of Canterbury:

The Faculty Office
1, The Sanctuary
Westminster
London, SW1P 3JT
Tel: 020 7222 5381
Email: faculty.office@1thesanctuary.com
Website: www.facultyoffice.org.uk

If you are dissatisfied about the service you have received, please do not hesitate to contact me. If I am unable to resolve the matter you may then complain to the Notaries Society of which I am a member, who have a Complaints Procedure which is approved by the Faculty Office. This procedure is free to use and is designed to provide a quick resolution to any dispute.

In that case please write (but do not enclose any original documents) with full details of your complaint to:-

Secretary of The Notaries Society
Old Church Chambers
23 Sandhill Road
St James
Northampton, NN5 5LH
Email secretary@thenotariessociety.org.uk
Tel: 01604 758908

If you have any difficulty in making a complaint in writing, please do not hesitate to call the Notaries Society/the Faculty Office for assistance.

Finally, even if you have your complaint considered under the Notaries Society Approved Complaints Procedure, you may at the end of that procedure, or after a period of eight weeks from the date you first notified me that you were dissatisfied, make your complaint to the Legal Ombudsman*, if you are not happy with the result:

Legal Ombudsman
PO Box 6806
Wolverhampton, WV1 9WJ
Tel: 0300 555 0333
Email: enquiries@legalombudsman.org.uk
Website: www.legalombudsman.org.uk

If you decide to make a complaint to the Legal Ombudsman you must refer your matter to the Legal Ombudsman within six months from the conclusion of the complaint process.

*certain kinds of commercial entities are not eligible to make a complaint to the Legal Ombudsman – please refer to the Legal Ombudsman Scheme Rules or consult the Faculty office.

Mandatory Information for Scrivener Notaries to be given to all Notarial Clients under Section 8 of The Notaries Practice Rules 2014

This notarial practice is regulated by the Master of the Faculties through the Faculty Office of the Archbishop of Canterbury:

The Faculty Office
1, The Sanctuary
Westminster
London, SW1P 3JT
Tel: 020 7222 5381

If you are dissatisfied about the service you have received from myself please do not hesitate to contact me with your instructions.

If I am unable to resolve the matter you may then complain to The Scriveners Company, which has a role in the regulation of scrivener notaries. Please write (but do not enclose any original documents) with full details of your complaint to the following address:

The Clerk
The Scriveners Company
HQS Wellington
Temple Stairs
Victoria Embankment
London, WC2R 2PN
Email: clerk@scriveners.org.uk

The Company will arrange for your complaint to be considered by a panel of 3 individuals who will be independent of the Scrivener Notary against whom the complaint has been made. The procedure is free to use and is designed to provide a quick resolution to any dispute. If you have any difficulty making a complaint in writing, please do not hesitate to telephone the Clerk of the Company for assistance on:

Tel: 020 7240 0529

If you remain dissatisfied you may make a complaint to the Legal Ombudsman at the end of the Scriveners Company's Complaints Procedure or after eight weeks have elapsed from the date on which you made your complaint to me:

Legal Ombudsman
PO Box 6806
Wolverhampton, WV1 9WJ
Tel: 0300 555 0333
Email: enquiries@legalombudsman.org.uk
Website: www.legalombudsman.org.uk

Chapter 4

TERMS & CONDITIONS OF PRACTICE

Terms and conditions of the client agreement should be carefully drafted by Notaries to ensure that the instructions received and work to be carried out are clear. It is usually helpful to have pre-drafted terms and conditions which can provide notaries with a secure, legal foundation to protect their rights in dealing with clients. If disputes or problems arise, these will be readily resolved if clients can make reference to clearly written terms and conditions.

So, what else are terms and conditions good for? How should one go about drawing them up? It is important to limit the risk, not the business. Terms and Conditions should be an essential part of a notary's practice. Not only are they a good risk management tool, they protect the notary's interests in the event of a dispute with a client by clarifying key elements of the business relationship in which the notary is engaged. It forms the basis of the contract which should be in writing. If you have an oral agreement, you may forget to include some elements and there could be disagreement or misunderstanding about some matters e.g. the parameters of the notary's involvement, release of documents or payment of fees. With a written agreement, all the terms and conditions should be crystal clear at any point in time.

One should not take it for granted that the threads of a business relationship are strong enough to withstand any crisis. The fact is that disagreements can, and do, arise especially if a close personal relationship is intertwined with a business one. If a notary agrees everything verbally, s/he may not always mention the things that seem to be obvious or apparently familiar. It is these issues that usually create trouble in the future if and when you need to enforce any agreement made. Written contracts are of course much better evidence and therefore much easier to enforce should you end up in court.

Written terms and conditions can help a notary in three important ways:

1.   They clarify key issues which helps to settle disputes and so reduce the possibility of a formal claim being made against you.

2.   They can help keep the cost of your Professional Indemnity insurance down. Insurance companies look to insure businesses that carry out good risk management which includes issuing written

Terms and Conditions. Poor risk management leads to claims, and more expensive Professional Indemnity cover.

3.   They enhance your professional image. A client meeting which includes written Terms and Conditions shows that you take your business seriously.

Terms and Conditions don't have to be lengthy or complex. One page on the back of a quote can often suffice and, as long as you can prove that you've presented the client with your terms of business, you don't necessarily need them to return a signed copy although this would be preferable.   The client is then less able to argue that they were not accepted. Terms and Conditions should be drawn up by a professional with knowledge and sufficient experience about notarial business and the relevant notarial practice rules.

If you are a sole practitioner notary, it is very important that you get into the habit of always using written terms and conditions. This is because you probably don't have deep pockets should you be sued. If you use written terms and conditions, it is also far less likely that you will end up in court - your clients will be much more inclined to work with you to find a solution and try to work things out.

Under Rule 8 of the Notarial Practice Rules 2014 a Notary must inform a client in writing how to complain in a form prescribed by the Master "from time to time". Also under Rule 15.1 a notary must make the basis of his/her charges known in advance. The Rule does not say that this should be communicated in writing but without any doubt this would be sensible as it provides a clear point of reference should there be any query about costs.

Whilst the basis of charge may not be the only provision in terms and conditions, most clients might think it the most important one. For the notary, surely a key reason for ensuring clients agree to terms and conditions is to ensure that the notary's liability is limited (to the extent permitted by law and by using a well-drafted limitation of liability clause) to a figure that matches the Master's requirement for a minimum level of PI cover (currently £1,000,000). Such clauses are used by most solicitors too. Even though there is no history of litigation against notaries in England & Wales, and next to nothing in the way of disciplinary proceedings, there is no reason to be complacent and it is very sensible to have written terms and conditions.

I set out below some sample standard terms and conditions which may be used. Advice can always be sought from a commercial specialist well versed in such documents.

Draft Terms & Conditions

1. HOURS OF BUSINESS: My office hours are 09:30 to 17:30 from Monday to Friday. In appropriate cases I can arrange to see you outside my usual office hours, or away from the office. In such cases I would charge a reasonable fee for travelling time plus the cost of my travel.

2. RESPONSIBILITY: A Notary's first duty is to the transaction as a whole. Notarial acts are relied upon by clients, third parties and foreign governments and officials worldwide. Unless otherwise agreed in writing, a Notary's responsibility is limited to the Notarial formalities and does not extend to advice on or drafting of documentation or in relation to substantive legal input on the matter under consideration. I do not give foreign law advice.

3. FEES: My present hourly rate is £180 and my minimum fee is £60. I reserve the right to vary these rates in respect of extremely urgent work or work done outside ordinary office hours or at the weekend.

4. PAYMENT: My charges are normally payable on presentation (usually at the meeting) by cash, cheque or by immediate BACS transfer. Notarised documents will not normally be released until all fees and disbursements have been paid in full.

5. DISBURSEMENTS: You are responsible for all payments which I make on your behalf. Typical examples are legalisation fees paid to the Foreign and Commonwealth Office and/or an Embassy, legalisation agents' fees, Companies Registry fees, courier fees and special delivery postage charges. However I shall not incur these expenses without first obtaining your consent to do so.

6. DOCUMENTATION TO BE PREPARED: I may need more than one appointment to finalise the matter, particularly if it is necessary for me to prepare all or some of the documentation.

7. PROOF OF IDENTITY: Identification of individuals and proof of residential address is required. This is usually by way of a current passport, photo card driving licence or national identity card and a

recent gas, electricity or other bill or bank statement. Exceptionally, other proof may be acceptable.

If you act on behalf of a company, I will need to establish that it exists and that the signatory has authority to represent it. I generally conduct my own checks at the Companies House. In some cases I may ask you to produce a certificate of incorporation, good standing certificate or other similar evidence.

8. WRITTEN TRANSLATION: In cases where I do not have knowledge of the language in which the document is written, official translations may be required before and/or after execution of the documentation.

9. LIABILITY: I carry professional indemnity liability cover of £1,000,000 which is the minimum level of cover specified by the Master of the Faculties. I therefore limit the level of my liability to you to £1,000,000 unless you are injured or die as a result of my negligence, in which case my liability is without limit.

10. COMPLAINTS: I aim to provide all clients with an efficient and high standard of service. However, in the unlikely event that you should wish to complain, then you should follow the complaints procedure set out below. Notaries are regulated by the Faculty Office of the Archbishop of Canterbury: The Faculty Office, 1, The Sanctuary, Westminster, London SW1 3JT, Telephone: 020 7222 5381, Email: faculty.office@1thesanctuary.com, Website: www.facultyoffice.org.uk

If you are dissatisfied about the service you have received, please do not hesitate to contact me. If I am unable to resolve the matter then you may complain to the Notaries Society of which I am a member, who have a Complaints Procedure which is approved by the Faculty Office. This procedure is free to use and is designed to provide a quick resolution to any dispute.

In that case please write (but do not enclose any original documents) with full details of your complaint to: The Secretary of The Notaries Society, Old Church Chambers, 23 Sandhill Road, St James, Northampton NN5 5LH, Email: secretary@thenotariessociety.org.uk, Tel: 01604 758908

If you have any difficulty making a complaint in writing, please do not hesitate to call the Notaries Society/the Faculty Office for assistance.

Finally, even if you have your complaint considered under the Notaries Society Approved Complaints Procedure, you may at the end of that procedure, or after a period of eight weeks from the date you first notified me that you were dissatisfied, make your complaint to the Legal Ombudsman*, if you are not happy with the result:

Legal Ombudsman, P.O. Box 6806, Wolverhampton, WV1 9WJ,
Tel: 0300 555 0333, Email: enquiries@legalombudsman.org.uk,
Website: www.legalombudsman.org.uk

If you decide to make a complaint to the Legal Ombudsman you must refer your matter to the Legal Ombudsman within six months from the conclusion of the complaint process.

*certain kinds of commercial entities are not eligible to make a complaint to the Legal Ombudsman – please refer to the Legal Ombudsman Scheme Rules or consult the Faculty office.

11. RECORDS: At the end of the matter, a formal entry of the main details of your transaction together with copies of the notarised document may be kept. In particular, when notaries are requested to certify documents such as public deeds, the above details will also be kept in their notarial protocols.

12. DATA PROTECTION: I use the information you provide primarily for the provision of my services to you and for related purposes including: updating and enhancing client records, analysis to help us manage our practice, statutory returns, legal and regulatory compliance.

13. MONEY LAUNDERING: Notaries are obliged under the Money Laundering Legislation to take measures to protect against fraud and forgery. To ensure that I comply with this you acknowledge and agree that. I may make all such enquiries as I deem necessary or appropriate in order to comply with my duty, and you will provide me with such documents and information as I may request. Your failure to do so will entitle us to terminate my engagement and cease acting for you forthwith.

14. EQUALITY AND DIVERSITY: I am committed to promoting equality and diversity in all of its dealings with clients and third parties.

15. THE RELEVANT LAW: The law which governs my contract with you is English Law and it is agreed that any dispute relating to my services shall be resolved by the English courts.

Signature: ....

For and on behalf of: ....

Date: ....

Chapter 5

NOTARIAL INSPECTIONS

The LSB has been urging the Faculty Office that more has to be done by putting clients first. In a report ("Developing Regulatory Standards") published in December 2012 the LSB asked the Faculty Office to be more proactive in terms of inspections and interventions. Sadly in recent years public trust in traditional institutions – e.g. in the medical, legal, banking and political sectors has been seriously eroded.

The Faculty Office has introduced new regulations known as The Notaries' (Inspections) Regulations 2014. It is intended that the records and practices of around 20 to 25 notaries will be inspected every year. The inspection will be conducted by practising notaries who with more than 10 years' standing. At this stage the Faculty Office does not intend to do spot checks and notice of 7-14 days is likely to be given. The inspection will be carried out using a pro-forma questionnaire approved by the Master from time to time. The inspecting notary will also provide a written summary of his findings in a report to the Master.

The Master shall give such directions as he thinks fit which may include ordering a further inspection or inspections or the carrying out of training or supervision of the notary's practice, or aspects of it, and for such period or periods, as he may direct. Where the inspecting notary's report discloses matters which may amount to an allegation of notarial misconduct, as defined by rule 2.1 of the Notaries' (Conduct and Discipline) Rules 2011, then the Registrar of the Faculty Office shall proceed to appoint a Nominated Notary to investigate the allegation pursuant to rule 5 of those Rules. Where an inspection of a notary's accounts is ordered pursuant to Rule 12 of the Notaries' Accounts Rules 1989 (as amended) the provisions of that Rule shall apply together with such directions as may be given by the Master or Registrar in the particular case and the procedure set out in Regulations 6-9 shall be followed. The Master has approved the following questionnaire for inspections:

1. What is your assessment of the notary's general availability to see clients and the suitability of the premises used for such purposes? Please comment with reference to issues such as location, accessibility (for the disabled), proximity to public transport, privacy, records storage, etc.

2. What is your assessment of the means by which the notary's practice is published? Please refer to the notary's website where appropriate.

3. To what extent do the notary's records comply with the requirements in Rule 23 of the Notaries Practice Rules 2014? You may require production of a document from the protocol at random. Was a record made of the proof of identity provided by the client?

4. Check that the notarial bank account paying-in slip or ledger corresponds with the amount of fees recorded in the notarial register. Bear in mind that some practitioners will be using other payment methods, such as BACS, debit cards, e-billing, etc.

5. How does the notary provide regulatory information to clients, such as details at the outset on how a complaint may be made?

6. Is there evidence that notarial acts have been completed in a timely manner and correspondence answered and calls returned promptly?

7. In relation to new clients, does the notary provide in advance details of the fee or the basis on which the fee will be calculated, in accordance with rule 18.1 of the Notaries Practice Rules 2014?

8. Are clients charged a fee which accords with this information? If the fee was calculated on a time basis, was the time spent properly recorded?

9. Do the names and addresses and passport details (if any) on the document match with the proof or proofs of identity provided? This may necessitate checking the document itself, and inquiring how issues of non-matching are dealt with.

10. If the notary did not deal personally with legalisation, is there evidence that the notary gave the client advice as to the possible need for legalisation and whether the country concerned would normally require legalisation of the notary's seal and signature?

11. With reference to the work being undertaken by the notary, do you consider the notary's skills and knowledge are adequate, having regard in particular to Rule 4 of the Notaries' Practice Rules 2014? Please consider in particular the correct form applicable to documents and the procedure for execution, the notary's linguistic

ability, the special needs of particular clients (arising from disability dependency, etc.).

12. What is your assessment of the notary's approach to continuing professional education and ensuring that requisite skills are up to date? In particular, has the notary maintained an up to date CPE record showing points obtained up to the inspection date for the current year?

13. Is there a record of complaints received and action taken in respect of them? It is not part of your function to investigate the adequacy of any action taken.

14. Is there anything in the register or protocol which appears to disclose a breach of the Notaries' Practice Rules 2014 or the Notaries' Practice Rules 2009?

15. Is there any other aspect of the notary's practice or records which appears to give cause for concern?

16. Is there any aspect of the notary's practice that you consider to be instructive to other practitioners or otherwise commendable?

Notarial Inspections can be a daunting prospect; however with an understanding of the practice rules, coupled with proper procedures and processes in place to ensure compliance, they should not be seen as daunting but instead a positive experience. The new inspection regime also provides assurance to both the wider profession and the public that the Faculty Office is protecting their interests by reducing risk through inspection and intervention and ensuring the advice and guidance issued to the profession is up to date.

The Inspectors want to help promote high standards and are happy to give advice where procedures merely need to be tightened up. Accordingly the preparation for an inspection should not have to start when you receive the notification of an Inspection, but is an ongoing process to ensure that you are up to date with your knowledge of the Practice Rules and that your systems and processes are compliant.

The Questionnaire approved by the Master is also an information gathering exercise to understand how the profession is practising. One should ensure that you all the required notarial records are up to date. This helps the inspection run more smoothly and prevents any delay at the outset. Most of the records are those routinely prepared by notaries during their day to day work as required under Rule 23 of the Notaries Practice Rules 2014.

New Rule 4 now requires a notary to exercise his office at all times in accordance with general principles. Under article 4 of the Notaries Practice Rules 2014 a notary shall uphold the rule of law and the proper administration of justice, act with integrity, maintain his independence and impartiality, provide a prompt and proper standard of service for all clients, act in a way that maintains the trust in the office of notary which the public may reasonably expect and comply with all the legal and regulatory obligations and cooperate with the Master and any persons or body appointed by him in the exercise of the Master's regulatory functions.

A notary is required to provide to any new client a copy of the form of words prescribed by the Master from time to time which explains that the client has a right to make a complaint under the Notaries' (Conduct and Discipline) Rules 2011 and details of how to make such a complaint.

There are no major restrictions for a notary to publicise his practice. However Rule 14 lays down the requirements for publicity. A notary may advertise his practice in any manner and through any medium with the exception of unsolicited telephone calls or unsolicited visits to persons or organisations provided that the general principles in Rule 4 are upheld. These are

- uphold the rule of law and the proper administration of justice;
- act with integrity;
- maintain his/her independence and impartiality;
- provide a prompt and proper standard of service for all clients;
- act in a way that maintains public trust in the office of notary
- comply with all legal and regulatory obligations and cooperate with the Master and any persons or body appointed by him/her in the exercise of the Masters regulatory functions;
- operate his/her notarial practice in accordance with proper governance and sound financial and risk management principles; and
- operate his/her notarial practice in such a way as to provide equality of opportunity and respect for diversity.

Also the client's freedom to instruct a qualified person of the client's choice should not be unduly restricted, the notary's good reputation for integrity and professional standards of work should not be damaged and finally the notary should comply with any relevant non-statutory code of advertising standards and practice currently in force. The Advertising Standards Authority (ASA) is the self-regulatory organisation of the advertising industry in the United Kingdom. The ASA is a non-statutory organisation and so cannot interpret or enforce legislation. However, its code of advertising practice broadly reflects legislation in many respects. The ASA is not funded by the British Government, but by a levy on the advertising industry. Its role is to "regulate the content of advertisements, sales promotions and direct marketing in the UK" by investigating "complaints made about ads, sales promotions or direct marketing", and deciding whether such advertising complies with its advertising standards.

In recent years it has been seen that some notaries describe themselves as exclusively associated with a region of England and Wales e.g. "Nottingham Notary". The Faculty Office no longer appoints district notaries and such geographical associations or restrictions should no longer happen. Rule 19 of the Notaries Practice Rules 2014provides that the name of a firm of notaries shall consist only of the name or names of one or more present or former principals as a firm name in use on 1st January 1989 or the name of a firm of qualified legal practitioners of which a notary is a partner or one approved by the Master in writing. These rules also apply to domain names used by notaries. Any notary starting to use an internet domain name for the purpose of promoting his notarial practice after 1st December 2009 shall comply with Rule 19.

An inspector may investigate whether the notary has complied with Rule 22 of the Notaries Practice Rules 2014 in relation to Continuing Professional Education. The current requirement is that each notary must obtain 6 points in each practice year of which at least 3 points must be through an accredited activity but the balance can be earned at the rate of 1 point per hour spent on an unaccredited activity eg. reading a relevant publication such as The Notary. However a notary does not require CPE in the first two years. Instead, a newly qualified notary is required to attend an Education day in each of the first two years – these are approved by the Master.

Under Rule 23.3, where the notarial act is in the public form, the notary shall place an original of the act or a complete photographic copy of the same in a protocol, which shall be preserved permanently by the notary. A digital or electronic storage system is now permitted provided that documents are stored in indelible or unalterable form. Rule 23.4 states that records of acts not in public form, kept in accordance with Rule 23.2, shall be preserved for a minimum period of twelve years and, for the avoidance of doubt, such preservation may be by means of a suitable digital or other electronic system, providing for the storage of documents in an indelible and unalterable format.

One of the best ways to inform the client about various regulatory information is by way of terms and conditions discussed in the previous chapter which may include fees, client identification, complaints, liability, professional indemnity insurance, legalisation and any other issues which arise from time to time.

Every notarial practice should have an internal complaints procedure as most of these should be dealt in the first instance. It is extremely important that necessary steps should be taken by each notary in preparing and managing a good notarial practice. A great statesman once said "If you fail to prepare, be prepared to fail". Benjamin Franklin

RULES AND REGULATIONS MADE BY THE COURT OF FACULTIES

Notaries (Inspections) Regulations 2014

Notaries Practice Rules 2014

Notaries (Qualification) Rules 2013

Notaries (Practising Certificates) Rules 2012

Notaries (Conduct and Discipline) Rules 2011

Notaries (Continuing Professional Education) Regulations 2010

Notaries (Supervision Fees) Regulation 2010

Notaries (Conduct and Discipline) Rules 2009

Notaries (Post-Admission) Rules 2009

Notaries Practice Rules 2009

Notaries (Advisory Board) Rules 2008

Notaries (Qualification) (Amendment) Rules 2008

Notaries (Miscellaneous Provisions) Rules 2002

Notaries Practice Rules 2001

Notarial Appeals and Hearings Rules 2000

Notaries (Access to Justice Act) (Consequential Provisions) Rules 1999

Notaries (Qualification) Rules 1998

Public Notaries (Conduct and Discipline) Rules 1993

Order of the Master made Pursuant to the Notaries (Records) Rules on the 4th March 1992

Notaries (Post-Admission) Rules 1991

Notaries (Records) Rules 1991

Notarial Rules and Orders (Ratification and Citation) Rules 1991

Public Notaries (Practising Certificates) Rules 1991

Notaries' Accounts (Deposit Interest) Rules 1989

Notaries Accounts Rules 1989

Notaries' Practice Rules 1989

Notaries Trust Accounts Rules 1989

Notaries (Notification of Address) Rules 1982

Notaries (Practising Certificates) Rules 1982

Notarial Contingency Fund Rules 1981

NOTARIES (INSPECTIONS) REGULATIONS 2014

These Regulations are made pursuant to Rule 24 of the Notaries Practice Rules 2014 and Rule 12 of the Notaries Accounts Rules 1989 (as amended) & Rule 11 of the Notaries Trust Accounts Rules 1989.

The Regulations to be known as The Notaries (Inspections) Regulations 2014.

1. The Registrar will select annually the notaries whose records and practices shall be inspected pursuant to these Regulations. The number of such inspections shall be determined annually by the Master.

2. The inspections shall be carried out by an inspector selected by the Registrar from a panel of inspectors appointed for the purpose by the Master. Inspectors shall be notaries who have been in practice as notaries and have held a practicing certificate continuously for not less than 10 years.

3. The Registrar shall ensure, so far as practicable, that the inspector and the notary whose practice is to be inspected are in different geographical locations, are not known to each other personally, and that there is no likelihood of a professional or commercial conflict of interest arising between them.

4. A notary whose records and practice is to be inspected shall be given notice of such inspection by the Registrar of not less than seven days.

5. The inspector shall be entitled to a fixed fee for each inspection carried out, such fee to be set by Order of the Master from time to time, together with reasonable expenses of travel and accommodation to be assessed by the Registrar.

6. The inspection shall be carried out using a pro-forma questionnaire to be approved by the Master from time to time. The inspector shall also prepare a written summary of his findings in a report for the Registrar.

7. The notary whose records and practice is to be inspected shall co-operate with the inspector in providing access to such records files accounts ledgers and other papers ("the inspected documents") as shall be requested to enable the inspector to complete the questionnaire and report. The inspector shall at all times respect the confidentiality of the inspected documents and shall not disclose information concerning the inspected documents or the clients of the notary save to the Master or Registrar as may be necessary. Any breach of this Regulation shall be deemed to be Notarial Misconduct for the purposes of the Notaries (Conduct and Discipline) Rules 2011.

8. Following the inspection, the inspector shall within 14 days file a copy of his report and the completed questionnaire with the Registrar and send a copy of both documents to the notary.

9. The notary shall have 14 days from the receipt of the copy report and questionnaire to file any comments he or she may have on the report and questionnaire with the Registrar and with the inspector.

10. The Registrar may then seek any clarification which he considers necessary from the inspector and/or the notary before sending the completed questionnaire, the report and the notary's comments (if any) to the Master.

11. The Master may give such directions as he thinks fit which may include (but without limitation) ordering a further inspection or inspections of the notary's practice, a requirement to undertake further training or the supervision by a notary appointed by the Master of the notary's practice, or aspects of it, for such period as may be directed by the Master.

12. Where the inspector's report discloses matters which may amount to an allegation of Notarial Misconduct, as defined by Rule 2.1 of the Notaries (Conduct and Discipline) Rules 2011, then the Registrar shall proceed to appoint a Nominated Notary to investigate the allegation pursuant to Rule 5 of those Rules. In that case the report shall be referred to the Master in accordance with Regulation 10 and the Master shall give such directions under Regulation 11 as he thinks fit but excluding those matters which are the subject of the allegation of Notarial Misconduct. The inspector may not be appointed as Nominated Notary in such a case.

13. Where following an inspection under these Regulations a further inspection of a notary's accounts is ordered pursuant to Rule 12 of the Notaries Accounts Rules 1989 (as amended) the provisions of that Rule shall apply together with such directions as may be given by the Master or Registrar in the particular case.

14. Where following an inspection under these Regulations a further inspection of a notary's trust accounts is ordered pursuant to Rule 11 of the Notaries Trust Accounts Rules 1989 the provisions of that Rule shall apply together with such directions as may be given by the Master or Registrar in the particular case.

C R George

The Right Worshipful Charles R George, Q.C.
Master
    10 April 2014

NOTARIES PRACTICE RULES 2014

WE CHARLES RICHARD GEORGE One of Her Majesty's Counsel Commissary or Master of the Faculties of the Most Reverend Father in God JUSTIN PORTAL by Divine Providence Lord Archbishop of Canterbury Primate of All England and Metropolitan in exercise of the powers conferred by section 4 of the Public Notaries Act 1843 and section 57 of the Courts and Legal Services Act 1990 and of all other powers Us enabling hereby make the following Rules:

PART I: PRELIMINARY

1.   Citation and Commencement
1.1   These rules may be cited as the Notaries Practice Rules 2014.

1.2   These rules shall come into force on 1st May 2014 save for rule 20 which shall come into force on a date to be appointed by the Master by Order made under these rules.

2.   Interpretation
2.1   In these rules:-
"approved regulator" has the meaning given to it in section 20 of the Legal Services Act 2007;

"arrangement" means any express or tacit agreement between a notary and another person whether contractually binding or not;

"client" includes any person who has instructed a notary to carry out a reserved legal activity within the meaning of section 12 of the Legal Services Act 2007;

"firm" includes a sole practitioner and professional partnership (which expression shall include a limited liability partnership and any other body corporate) the members of which are authorised to conduct legal practice as such;

"holding company" and **"subsidiary company"** have the meanings assigned to them by the Companies Act 2006, and two companies are "associated" where they are subsidiary companies of the same holding company;

"the Master" means the Master of the Faculties;

"notarial act" means any act that has validity by virtue only of its preparation performance authentication attestation or verification by a notary and includes any such act carried out by electronic means;

"notary" includes a firm of notaries;

"performance" includes execution completion and carrying out;

"person" includes a body corporate or unincorporated association or group of persons;

"principles" means the general principles set out in rule 4;

"qualified legal practitioner" means
(i)   a person qualified to provide legal services to the public in England and Wales; or
(ii) a person qualified to provide legal services to the public under the laws of any other jurisdiction who practises as such in England and Wales;

"the Registrar" means the Registrar of the Court of Faculties;

2.2   for the purposes of these rules:

2.2.1   a notary's practice includes the preparation and performance of notarial acts and any other service undertaken as a notary whether or not such service may only be undertaken by a notary;

2.2.2   for the avoidance of doubt the Interpretation Act 1978 applies to these rules as it applies to an Act of Parliament;

2.2.3   reference to any other rules or regulations which govern the practice of a notary in England and Wales and made by the Master shall include any rules and regulations made in substitution therefore;

2.2.4   words importing the masculine gender shall include the feminine gender and words importing the singular shall where the context so admits include the plural and vice versa

PART II: PRACTICE AS A NOTARY

3.   **Oath of Office and Recognition of Notarial Acts**
3.1   A notary shall exercise the office of public notary in accordance with the Oath or Declaration made by him at the time of the grant of his Notarial Faculty as set out in section 7 of the Public Notaries Act 1843 and shall offer appropriate notarial services to any person lawfully and reasonably requiring the same.

3.2   A notary in possession of a valid practising certificate issued pursuant to the Notaries (Practising Certificate) Rules 2012 may issue notarial acts in the public or private forms intended for use in England and Wales and in any other jurisdiction.

4. General Principles

4.1 Without prejudice to rule 3.1 above a notary shall exercise his office at all times in accordance with the principles set out below and these rules shall be read in accordance with such principles.

4.2 A notary shall:

4.2.1 uphold the rule of law and the proper administration of justice;

4.2.2 act with integrity;

4.2.3 maintain his independence and impartiality;

4.2.4 provide a prompt and proper standard of service for all clients;

4.2.5 act in a way that maintains the trust in the office of notary which the public may reasonably expect;

4.2.6 comply with all legal and regulatory obligations and cooperate with the Master and any persons or body appointed by him in exercise of the Master's regulatory functions;

4.2.7 operate his notarial practice in accordance with proper governance and sound financial and risk management principles; and

4.2.8 operate his notarial practice in such a way as to provide equality of opportunity and respect for diversity.

5. Code of Practice

5.1 A notary shall at all times have regard to any code or codes of practice approved by the Master from time to time.

5.2 Failure to comply with this rule may amount to "Notarial Misconduct" as defined by rule 2 of the Notaries (Conduct and Discipline) Rules 2011.

6. Bankruptcy

A notary who is bankrupt may not practice as a notary on his own behalf or as the sole member of a professional partnership until he is discharged from bankruptcy, provided that this rule shall not prevent him from practicing as the employee of another notary.

7. Obtaining Instructions

A notary shall not directly or indirectly obtain or attempt to obtain instructions for professional work or permit another person to do so on his behalf, or do anything in the course of practising as a notary, in any manner which compromises or impairs or is likely to compromise or impair any of the following:

7.1 the principles;

7.2 a person's freedom to instruct a notary of their choice;

7.3 the notary's ability to act in the best interests of the client;

7.4 the good repute of the notary or of the notarial profession;

7.5 the notary's proper standard of work;

7.6   the notary's duty of care to persons in all jurisdictions who may place legitimate reliance on his notarial acts.

8.   Duty to inform instructing person of right to complain

8.1   When a notary accepts instructions for professional work or changes the terms on which he is acting he must provide the client with a copy of a form of words prescribed by the Master from time to time (the "prescribed form of words") which explains that the client has a right to make a complaint under Part II of the Notaries (Conduct and Discipline) Rules 2011 and how to make such a complaint.

8.2   The prescribed form of words may be provided to the client electronically.

9.   Conflicts of Interest

9.1   Conflicts of Interest (General)

9.1.1   In the conduct of his practice a notary shall not favour the interests of one client over those of another and shall not favour his own interests or those of any other person over those of his clients.

9.2   Conflicts of Interest (Conveyancing Transactions)

9.2.1   A notary conducting a conveyancing transaction in the capacity of a solicitor, or a licensed conveyancer, or member of another professional body with an approved regulator, is subject to the rules and any guidance relating to (a) conflicts of interest and (b) relations with third parties laid down by the approved regulator of that professional body, and should comply with such rules and have regard to any such guidance accordingly.

9.2.2   A notary conducting a conveyancing transaction in the capacity of a notary must not act for both seller and buyer in a transaction relating to property situated in England and Wales unless:

(a)   the notary is satisfied that no conflict of interest exists or is likely to arise during the course of the transaction, whether or not the transaction is between parties at arm's length; and

(b)   both parties are established clients in that they have instructed the notary on previous occasions; or

(c)   the consideration does not exceed £10,000 in an individual transaction; and

(d)   both clients are informed of the advantages of separate representation before they give their written consent to the notary acting for both of them; and

(e)   both parties consent in writing.

9.2.3 For the avoidance of doubt this rule shall apply to a notary acting for one party in his capacity under rule 9.2.1 and another party in his capacity under rule 9.2.2.

9.3   Relations with third parties
9.3.1 A notary shall not communicate directly by any means whatsoever with any other party to a conveyancing transaction where that party is represented by a lawyer except:
    (a)   to obtain information about the name and address (including e-mail address) of that lawyer; or
    (b)   with the consent of that lawyer; or
    (c)   after notifying the lawyer of the intention to contact the party direct because the other party's lawyer has refused or without good reason failed to pass on messages or to reply to communications; or
    (d)   in exceptional circumstances where it is impracticable to contact that party's lawyer; provided that any communication under (a) to (d) of this rule shall be in writing.
9.3.2 A notary who is dealing with any unrepresented party to a conveyancing transaction must not take unfair advantage of that party, and where it is necessary for practical reasons to communicate orally with an unrepresented party the notary should immediately thereafter make a written note of the communication and should as soon as possible confirm the substance of it in writing to the unrepresented party.

9.4   Conflicts of Interest (notarial activities other than conveyancing transactions)
9.4.1 In respect of notarial activities other than conveyancing transactions, a notary may act for both parties to a transaction but only if:
    (a)   each party has consented in writing to the notary so acting; and
    (b)   the notary is satisfied that there is no conflict of interest between the parties.
9.4.2 For the avoidance of doubt a notary does not act for both parties to a transaction merely by preparing or authenticating a notarial act in his capacity as a public certifying officer even though that act may concern two or more parties.

10.   Duty to Act Impartially in respect of Notarial Acts
A notary must act impartially and in particular must not perform any notarial act which involves or may affect:
10.1   his own affairs, including matters in which he is personally interested jointly with another person;

10.2   the affairs of his spouse or partner or a person to whom the notary is engaged to be married (for the purpose of this sub-rule, "partner" means a person with whom the notary cohabits or with whom he has a sexual relationship and includes a partner of the same sex);

10.3   the affairs of a person to whom he is directly and closely related;

10.4   the affairs of a person with whom he is in a professional partnership or by whom he is employed or from whom he receives a benefit by being provided with office accommodation or other facilities for his notarial practice;

10.5   the affairs of a person who has appointed the notary to be his attorney which concern a matter within the scope of the power of attorney granted;

10.6   the affairs of a trust of which he is a trustee or of an estate where he is a personal representative of the deceased;

10.7   the affairs of a body corporate of whose board of directors or governing body he is a member;

10.8   the affairs of an employee of the notary;

10.9   the affairs of a partnership of which he is a member or of a company in which the notary holds shares either exceeding five percent of the issued share capital or having a market value exceeding such figure as the Master may from time to time specify.

11. Employed Notaries

11.1   Save as permitted by rule 11.2 a notary who is the employee of a non-notary shall not perform any notarial act as part of his employment or do or perform any notarial act for his employer or his employer's holding, associated or subsidiary company.

11.2   A notary may act for a person who is also the client of the qualified legal practitioner or firm of qualified legal practitioners by which he is employed but he shall take all proper and reasonable steps in the exercise of his notarial practice to maintain his independence of his employer and in particular he shall:

     11.2.1   ensure that his independence and integrity as a notary is fully recognised in writing in any contract of employment entered into by him; and

     11.2.2   annually send to his employer a written statement of professional independence in a form approved by the Master from time to time, and shall declare in his application for a notarial practising certificate that he has complied with this rule.

12. Language

12.1   Notarial acts shall normally be drawn up in the English language.

12.2   A notary may upon request or in appropriate circumstances prepare a notarial act in a language other than English if he has sufficient knowledge of the language concerned.

12.3   A notary may not authenticate by means of a notarial act a document drawn up in a language other than English unless he has satisfied himself as to its meaning but this does not prevent a notary from authenticating the execution or signature of a document in any language.

12.4   A notary may not certify the accuracy of a translation that has been made by someone other than himself unless he has knowledge of the language sufficient to satisfy himself as to the accuracy of the translation but this does not prevent a notary from attesting a translator's affidavit or authenticating a verification.

13. Undertakings

13.1   Any notary giving an undertaking, whether oral or in writing, shall be personally liable for that undertaking, and the implementation of any such undertaking is required as a matter of conduct. Save in exceptional cases a failure by a notary to honour an undertaking will constitute Notarial Misconduct as defined in rule 2 of the Notaries (Conduct and Discipline) Rules 2011.

13.2   An undertaking given by a notary in writing or confirmed in writing shall be signed by the notary giving it.

14. Publicity

A notary may advertise his practice and seek to obtain directly or indirectly clients and business in any manner and through any medium whether informative or promotional with the exception of unsolicited telephone calls or unsolicited visits to persons or organisations provided that:

14.1   the principles are upheld;

14.2   the client's freedom to instruct a qualified person of the client's choice is not thereby unduly restricted;

14.3   the notary's good reputation for integrity and professional standards of work is not thereby damaged;

14.4   he complies with any relevant non-statutory code of advertising standards and practice currently in force;

but nothing in this rule shall be construed as authorising the use of the word "notary" or any word designating or indicating notarial services in any publicity for activities which are not of a notarial nature.

15. Scrivener Notaries

No notary shall describe himself professionally as a Scrivener or a Scrivener notary unless he holds the qualifications to practise as a Scrivener notary from time to time prescribed by the Incorporated Company of Scriveners.

16. Introductions and Referrals

When a notary enters into an arrangement with another person for the introduction of clients to the notary or by the notary to the other person he must ensure:

16.1 that the client is informed in writing of the arrangement and of any commission or other benefit the notary may be receiving or pay;

16.2 that he either obtains the client's written agreement as to the destination of the commission or accounts to the client for the commission;

16.3 that he remains able to advise the client independently in accordance with these rules and continues to do so regardless of his own interests.

17. Offering Services other than as a Notary

17.1 Where a notary by himself or with any other person operates, actively participates in or controls any business, other than a notary's practice, the notary shall ensure:

17.1.1 that the name of that business has no substantial element in common with the name of any practice of the notary;

17.1.2 that the words "notary", "notaries," "attorney(s)" or "lawyer(s)" or any words designating or indicating a notarial or legal practice are not used in connection with the notary's involvement with that business;

17.1.3 that any client referred by any practice of the notary to the business is informed in writing that, as a customer of that business, he does not enjoy any protection attaching to the client of a notary, and that where that business shares premises or reception staff with any practice of the notary, every customer of the business is informed in writing that, as a customer of that business, he does not enjoy the protection attaching to the client of a notary.

17.2 Rule 17.1 does not apply to the practice of a qualified legal practitioner.

18. Fees

18.1 A notary may charge a professional fee for all notarial work undertaken by him, and the basis upon which that fee will be calculated or the fee to be charged for the work done, shall be made known in advance to any new client.

18.2   Subject to rule 18.3 below a notary shall not share or agree to share his professional fees with any person not entitled to act as a notary; provided that this rule shall not prohibit the payment of any allowance or allowances, sum or sums of money, that are or shall be agreed to be made or paid to the widows or children of any deceased notary or notaries, by any surviving partner or partners of such deceased notary or notaries.

18.3   A notary who also practises as a qualified legal practitioner either in a professional partnership or as an employee may share professional fees provided that:

18.3.1   his professional partners or employer are also qualified legal practitioners;

18.3.2   the notary shall keep accounts which enable the income and expenditure arising from his practice as a notary to be distinguished from the income and expenditure arising from his practice or employment as a qualified legal practitioner; and

18.3.3   shall furnish the Faculty Office with such additional information as to his professional partnership and accounting arrangements or his employment as may be prescribed in rules or orders of the Master.

19.   Name of a Firm of Notaries

19.1   The name of a firm of notaries shall consist only of:

19.1.1   the name or names of one or more present or former principals together with conventional references to the firm and to such persons;

19.1.2   a firm name in use on 1st January 1989;

19.1.3   the name of a firm of qualified legal practitioners of which a notary is a partner; or

19.1.4   one approved in writing by the Master.

19.2   Any notary starting to use an internet domain name for the purpose of promoting his notarial practice after the 1st December 2009 shall comply with one or more of the requirements in 19.1.1 to 19.1.4 of this rule.

20.   Investment Business
[This rule came into force by Order of the Master made on 20 August 2014]

20.1   In this rule "appointed representative", "investment" and "regulated activity" have the meanings assigned to them by the Financial Services and Markets Act 2000 and the Financial Services and Markets Act 2000 (Regulated Activities) Order 2001 as extended by the Financial Services Act 2012.

20.2   A notary shall not in connection with any regulated activity:

       20.2.1   have an exclusive arrangement with a provider of financial services nor with a provider of financial services advice (whether of independent advice or restricted advice or both) under which the notary could be constrained to recommend, introduce or refer clients or effect for them (or refrain from so doing) transactions or contracts:

            a.   in some investments or markets but not others;
            b.   with some persons or companies but not others;
            c.   through the agency of some persons or companies but not others.

       20.2.2   be an appointed representative.

20.3   Notwithstanding any provision in rule 17 a notary shall not by himself or with any other person set up, operate, actively participate in or control any separate business which is an appointed representative.

20.4   For the avoidance of doubt a notary shall comply with this rule in connection with regulated activity carried on within England and Wales and in any other jurisdiction

21.   Supervision of a Notary's Office

21.1   A notary shall take reasonable steps to ensure that every office where he practises is and can be seen to be:

       21.1.1   open, save exceptionally and for a good reason, during normal office hours for the provision of appropriate notarial services to members of the public; and

       21.1.2   properly supervised. In particular a notary shall ensure that he or another notary holding a Practising Certificate shall spend sufficient time at such office to ensure adequate control of the staff employed there and afford requisite facilities for consultation with clients. Such notary may be a principal, employee or consultant of the firm or a locum tenens.

21.2   In determining whether or not there has been compliance with the requirement as to supervision in rule 21.1, account shall be taken of, inter alia, the arrangements for the principals to see or be apprised of incoming communications.

21.3   Where the operation or supervision of a notary's office in accordance with this rule is prevented by illness, accident or other sufficient or unforeseen cause for a prolonged period, suitable alternative arrangements shall be made without delay to ensure compliance.

21.4   In cases where a notary is not in attendance on days when his office is normally open to the public, he shall make adequate arrangements to ensure the provision of notarial services to persons requiring the same.

22.   Continuing Professional Education

22.1   After commencing practice and having satisfactorily completed the required period of supervision, a notary shall, within every such successive period as shall be determined by the Master, participate in such programmes, courses or seminars approved by the Master as may be necessary to acquire the number of credit points determined by the Master.

22.2   Upon determination by the Master of the periods and number of credit points, they shall be included in regulations made by the Master under this rule from time to time.

PART III: RECORDS AND INSPECTIONS

23.   Duty to Keep Records

23.1   A notary shall keep proper records of his notarial acts in accordance with this rule.

23.2   The records so kept must clearly identify:
23.2.1   the date of the act;
23.2.2   the person at whose request the act was performed;
23.2.3   the person or persons, if any, intervening in the act and, in the case of a person who intervened in a representative capacity, the name of his principal;
23.2.4   the method of identification of the party or parties intervening in the notarial act, and in the case of a party intervening in a representative capacity, any evidence produced to the notary of that party's entitlement so to intervene;
23.2.5   the nature of the act;
23.2.6   the fee charged.

23.3   In the case of a notarial act in the public form, the notary shall place an original of the act or a complete photographic copy of the same in a protocol which shall be preserved permanently by the notary and for the avoidance of doubt such preservation may be by means of a suitable digital or other electronic system providing for the storage of documents in an indelible and unalterable format.

23.4   Records of acts not in public form kept in accordance with rule 23.2 shall be preserved for a minimum period of twelve years and for the avoidance of doubt such preservation may be by means of a suitable digital or other electronic system providing for the storage of documents in an indelible and unalterable format.

23.5 A notary who preserves records by means of a digital or other electronic system in accordance with rules 23.3 and 23.4 shall notify the Registrar of any username and password required for access to such digital or electronic system and the Registrar shall keep such information confidential.

23.6 A copy of a notarial act or of the record of a notarial act preserved in accordance with rules 23.3 and 23.4 shall, upon payment of a reasonable fee, be issued upon the application of any person or authority having a proper interest in the act unless prevented by order of a competent court.

23.7 Any question as to whether a person has a proper interest in an act for the purposes of rule 23.6 shall be determined by the Master.

24. Inspections of Records and Practice

24.1 A notary's premises, records and practice may be inspected from time to time on behalf of the Master and as directed by him

24.2 The records which may be inspected in accordance with rule 24.1 shall include all documents in the notary's possession relating in any way to his practice as a notary, whether or not they also relate to non-notarial matters, and shall include documents stored by means of a digital or other electronic system.

24.3 Copies of documents inspected in accordance with rule 24.1 may be taken for onward transmission to the Master where requested by the person carrying out the inspection.

24.4 Inspections shall be carried out in accordance with regulations to be made by the Master from time to time under this rule.

25. Notaries Ceasing to Practise

25.1 When a notary ceases to practise as such then he, or failing him his continuing notarial partners or the person having possession or custody of the records maintained by him pursuant to rule 23, shall arrange for such records to be transferred:

25.1.1 to another notary in practice appointed by him or by his continuing notarial partners;

25.1.2 to another notary in practice appointed, with the approval of the Master, by the persons having possession or custody of the records; or

25.1.3 to any archive designated for the purpose under regulations made by the Master from time to time;

and the persons making such transfer shall give written particulars to the Registrar of the date of transfer and the person or archive to which the records were transferred.

25.2 The provisions of rules 23 and 24 shall apply to a notary or archive to which the records of any notary are transferred pursuant to this rule as they apply to the notary himself.

26 Application to Ecclesiastical Notaries

The provisions of this Part shall apply to notaries appointed for ecclesiastical purposes only subject to the following modifications:

26.1 The requirement of rule 23 to keep a record of notarial acts shall apply only to such ecclesiastical acts as law or custom requires to be performed in the presence of a public notary and recorded in writing.

26.2 Any act or transaction properly recorded in the Act Book of any Archbishop or Bishop, or in the Minute Book of any Cathedral Chapter, shall be deemed to have been properly recorded in accordance with rule 23.

26.3 Rule 25 shall not apply to ecclesiastical notaries, but upon a person ceasing for any reason to hold the office in respect of which he was appointed an ecclesiastical notary, any records kept by him pursuant to this Part shall be transferred to the succeeding holder of that office (being an ecclesiastical notary) upon his appointment.

PART IV: MISCELLANEOUS

27 Waivers

The Master shall have power to waive any of the provisions of these rules in any particular case or classes of case for the purpose expressed in such waiver, and to revoke such waiver.

28 Repeals and Savings

28.1 Subject to rule 28.2 the Notaries Practice Rules 2009, with the exception of Rule 17 thereof, are hereby revoked.

28.2 Rule 28.1 does not absolve any notary from the duty to comply with the Notaries Practice Rules 2009 prior to the coming into force of these rules and records maintained by a notary in accordance with Rules 20-23 of the Notaries Practice Rules 2009 prior to the coming into force of these rules shall continue to be so maintained by him and rules 23.5, 23.6, 24, 25 and 26 of these rules shall apply to such records.

C R George

___

The Right Worshipful Charles R George, Q.C.
Master   **10 April 2014**

NOTARIES (QUALIFICATION) RULES 2013

WE CHARLES RICHARD GEORGE One of Her Majesty's Counsel Commissary or Master of the Faculties of the Most Reverend Father in God Justin Portal by Divine Providence Lord Archbishop of Canterbury Primate of All England and Metropolitan in exercise of the powers conferred by section 4 of the Public Notaries Act 1843 and section 57 of the Courts and Legal Services Act 1990 and of all other powers Us enabling hereby make the following Rules:

PART I: PRELIMINARY

1.   **Citation and Commencement**
     1.1   These rules may be cited as the Notaries (Qualification) Rules 2013

     1.2   These rules shall come into force on the 1st day of December 2013

2.   **Interpretation**
     In these rules:
     'the Board' means the Qualifications Board established under rule 6;

     'the Company' means the Incorporated Company of Scriveners of London;

     'Degree' means a qualification awarded following a post secondary course of at least three years' duration (or of an equivalent duration part time) at a university or an establishment of higher education or an establishment of similar level;

     'the Directive' means the Directive 2005/36/EC of the European Parliament and of the Council of 7th September 2005 as amended from time to time;

     'the Faculty Office' means the Registry of the Court of Faculties;

     'the Master' means the Master of the Faculties;

     'the Notarial Practice Course' means a course approved from time to time by the Master comprising the prescribed subjects set out in paragraphs 9, 10 and 11 of schedule 2;

     'the Office Practice Course' means a course approved from time to time by the Master comprising the matters set out in schedule 5; and

     'the Registrar' means the Registrar of the Court of Faculties.

PART II: GENERAL PROVISIONS AS TO ADMISSION

3   **Qualification for Admission as a Notary Public**
No person shall be admitted as a notary public to practise in England and
Wales unless such person:

3.1   Is at least 21 years of age and has satisfied the requirements of
these rules;

3.2   Has taken the oath of allegiance and the oath required by Section 7
of the Public Notaries Act 1843; and

3.3   Is, except where such application is made under rule 4
(ecclesiastical notaries) or rule 8 (European Economic Area
notaries) either a solicitor of the Senior Courts of England and
Wales, or a barrister at law or holds a Degree.

4   **Ecclesiastical Notaries**
Any person appointed as registrar of either of the provinces of Canterbury
or York, as registrar to the Archbishop of Wales, as legal adviser to the
General Synod to the Church of England, as legal secretary to the
Governing Body of the Church in Wales, as registrar of any diocese in
England or Wales, as an officer of the ecclesiastical court in Jersey or
Guernsey, or as the deputy to any such officer, may apply for admission as
a notary public for ecclesiastical purposes only, upon satisfying the Master
of the fact of such an appointment.

5   **General Notaries**
Any person who satisfies the requirements of rule 3 and who has obtained
the qualifications required under Part III of these rules may apply for
admission as a general notary to practise in England and Wales.

PART III: QUALIFICATIONS

6   **Qualifications Board and Fees for Applications**
6.1   There shall be established a Qualifications Board constituted in
accordance with schedule 1.

6.2   The functions of the Board shall be:
6.2.1   To advise the Master whether a degree or other qualification
should be approved by him for the purpose of these rules.
6.2.2   To advise the Master on the standard of the qualifications of
any person applying for admission as a general notary under
these rules.
6.2.3   To advise the Master on the qualifications and experience of
persons applying for recognition that they are eligible for
admission as a general notary under rule 8.
6.2.4   To advise any other body concerned with the administration
or regulation of the notarial profession in England and

Wales or any part of it on matters relating to qualifications and experience.

6.3 The Master may by Order delegate to the Board any of his functions under these rules relating to the approval or recognition of degrees, qualifications and experience.

6.4 The Master may from time to time by Order prescribe fees or the maximum fees which may be charged in respect of any application to the Master under these rules and such fees may be applied by the Faculty Office towards meeting the expenses of the Board but subject thereto the expenses of the Board and of its members shall be paid from and such fees shall form part of the general notarial income of the Faculty Office.

7 Practical Qualifications

7.1 Any person wishing to be admitted as a general notary under rule 5 shall have undertaken and attained a satisfactory standard in a course or courses of studies covering all of the subjects listed in schedule 2.

7.2 Whether a particular course of studies satisfies the requirements of these rules and whether a person has obtained a satisfactory standard in that course shall be determined by the Master after seeking the advice of the Board.

7.3 The Master after seeking the advice of the Board may by Order direct that the award of a particular qualification meets the requirements of these rules as to some or all of the subjects listed in schedule 2.

7.4 The Master may as a condition of making a direction under rule 7.3 require the body by which the qualification is awarded to issue those pursuing a course of studies leading to that qualification with such information about the notarial profession, these rules and other rules made by the Master and the Company as the Master may specify.

7.5 The Master may by Order add any subjects to the list in schedule 2 or remove any subjects from that list or alter any of the provisions of that schedule but before doing so he shall consult the Board.

8 Notaries of the European Economic Area

8.1 This rule applies to a person who:
 (a) holds the office of notary public in a member state of the European Economic Area other than the United Kingdom, or
 (b) holds all the qualifications and has completed all the practical training necessary for appointment or admission to

that office in such a member state but has not yet been so appointed or admitted.

8.2 Any person to whom this rule applies may apply to the Master for recognition that he is qualified for the purposes of rule 10.1 for admission as a general notary to practise anywhere in England and Wales and such application shall be made to the Faculty Office in such form and accompanied by such information as the Master may from time to time by Order prescribe.

8.3

8.3.1 Any person applying to the Master for recognition under this rule shall satisfy the Master, in consultation with the Board, that:

(a) he can demonstrate a knowledge sufficient for a notary to practise in England and Wales in those subjects contained in schedules 3 and 4 either through examinations set by such institution or body recognised by the Board for the purpose taken within the last 5 years in those subjects, or from the applicant's own practical experience of the areas of law covered by those subjects; and

(b) he can demonstrate a competence in Notarial Practice with respect to the practice of a notary in England and Wales, and in particular the matters listed in paragraph 11 of schedule 2.

8.3.2 Where an applicant is unable to demonstrate the requisite knowledge or experience set out in 8.3.1 above, he may be required:

(a) to take an aptitude test by way of an examination or examinations in such form and set by an institution or body recognised by the Board as may be prescribed from time to time by the Master; or

(b) undertake a period of supervision under a qualified and admitted notary for such period as may be specified by the Master not exceeding 3 years and such period may include a requirement to undertake further training and assessment.

8.4 The Master shall after consultation with the Board examine any application made under this rule in accordance with the procedures set out in articles 13 and 14 of the Directive.

8.5 Where an application is made to the Master under rule 8.2 he shall determine the application as soon as possible and communicate the outcome to the applicant in a reasoned decision within four months of the production of all the certificates and documents relating to the applicant referred to in article 3 of the Directive.

8.6 If the Master refuses an application under rule 8.2 or has not determined the application within the time prescribed by rule 8.5 the Master shall be deemed to have refused an application for a faculty and the applicant may pursue the remedy provided for in the Ecclesiastical Licences Act 1533 and mentioned in section 5 of the Public Notaries Act 1843.

9   Notaries of Scotland and Northern Ireland
9.1 This rule applies to a person who holds the office of notary public in Scotland or Northern Ireland.

9.2 A person to whom this rule applies wishing to be admitted as a general notary for England and Wales shall have satisfied the requirements of rule 7 with such exemptions in any particular instance as the Master shall determine after seeking the advice of the Board.

PART IV: PROCEDURE FOR ADMISSION

10   Application for Admission
10.1 A person qualified for admission as a notary under these rules shall apply in writing to the Faculty Office on such form as the Master may from time to time specify.

10.2 The application shall be accompanied by:
   (a) A certificate of fitness in such form as the Master may from time to time prescribe to be given by a notary public to the effect that the applicant is known to him and that having made due enquiry to the best of his knowledge and belief the applicant is a fit and proper person to be created a notary public; and
   (b) A certificate of good character in such form as the Master may from time to time prescribe to be given by a person who is qualified under paragraph 10.3 testifying to the good character, honesty, reliability, diligence and trustworthiness of the applicant and stating that the person giving the certificate knows of no reason why the applicant should not be created a notary public;
   (c) Evidence that the applicant has successfully completed the Notarial Practice Course within a period not exceeding two years prior to the date of the application provided that this requirement shall not apply to an applicant under rule 8.2 who has demonstrated to the satisfaction of the Master his knowledge and competence in accordance with rule 8.3, the application to be accompanied by evidence that such demonstration was within the same period.

10.3 A person is qualified to give the certificate of good character required by paragraph 10.2(b) of this rule if he is a person of good standing and character, he has known the applicant for a period of not less than five years, he is not related to the applicant by blood, marriage or adoption, and he is not a professional partner, employer or employee of the applicant.

10.4 In the case of a person qualified under rule 4 the certificate of fitness shall further state that the applicant is conformable to the doctrine and discipline of the Church of England as by law established (or, in the case of a person qualified only by reason of holding an ecclesiastical appointment in Wales, the doctrine, discipline and constitution of the Church in Wales).

10.5 The certificate of fitness and the certificate of good character may be given in the case of a person qualified under rule 8 by suitably qualified persons in the applicant's Home state and in the case of a person qualified under rule 9 by suitably qualified persons in Scotland or Northern Ireland as appropriate.

10.6 The application shall be accompanied by such fee as the Master may from time to time prescribe.

11 Publicity, Refusal of Applications and Admissions

11.1 The Master may give, or require an applicant to give, such publicity to an application made under rule 10 as in the circumstances appear to the Master to be necessary.

11.2 Any representations made to the Master following such publicity shall be notified to the applicant, and the Master shall consider any response thereto made by the applicant before deciding whether a faculty shall be granted.

11.3 Any decision by the Master to refuse an application under rule 10 shall be notified to the applicant by the Registrar in writing to enable the applicant to pursue (if so advised) the remedy provided for in The Ecclesiastical Licences Act 1533 and mentioned in Section 5 of the Public Notaries Act 1843.

11.4 Upon the Master deciding to grant an application under rule 10, the Registrar shall cause a faculty to pass the seal in accustomed form. The applicant shall appear personally before the Registrar to make the oaths mentioned in rule 3.2 and the Registrar shall then admit him by delivering the faculty to him and causing his name to be entered upon the roll of notaries. The Master may appoint a Commissioner to act in place of the Registrar for this purpose.

11.5 Before admitting the applicant in accordance with rule 11.4 the Registrar shall be satisfied that the applicant has successfully completed the Office Practice Course.

PART V: REPEALS AND SAVINGS

12   The following Rules are hereby revoked:

12.1   The Notaries (Qualification) Rules 1998

12.2   The Notaries (Qualification) (Amendment) Rules 2008

12.3   Rule 10 of the Notaries (Access to Justice Act) (Consequential Provisions) Rules 1999

13   Subject to any further Order of the Master, the certificates of fitness and of good character prescribed by the Master's Orders of 27th August 1992 and 13th September 1993 respectively shall be the certificates prescribed for the purposes of rule 10.2. (a) and (b) of these rules.

Dated this 28th day of November 2013

Signed   C R GEORGE
              MASTER

SCHEDULE 1

QUALIFICATIONS BOARD

1 The Board shall comprise not more than 10 persons appointed by the Master after consultation with the Company, the Society of Scrivener Notaries and the Notaries Society and such other persons or bodies as the Master may consider appropriate.

2 The Master shall appoint one member of the Board to be Chairman for such period as the Master may determine.

3 Members of the Board, including the Chairman, shall hold office for such period as the Master may determine and may be removed from office by the Master at any time.

4 The Registrar shall act as Clerk to the Board or may appoint or nominate another person to act as Clerk in his place.

5 The Board shall meet as often as may be necessary and in any event not less than once each year.

6 The Board may delegate any of its functions under these rules to a subcommittee comprising not fewer than three of its members.

SCHEDULE 2

PRESCRIBED SUBJECTS

1. **Public & Constitutional Law**
   - The nature and sources of constitutional law
   - Conventions
   - The sovereignty of parliament
   - Introduction to the objectives and structure of the European Union
   - Human Rights and Freedom of Expression
   - Administrative Law

2. **The Law of Property**
   - The definition of "land" and the distinction between real and personal property
   - The nature of legal and equitable interests
   - Registered and unregistered land
   - Estates and interests in land: freehold, leases, mortgages, easements, covenants relating to land, licences
   - Principles relating to the transfer of legal estates and interest in land, and contracts enforceable in equity
   - Trusts of land, joint tenancies and tenancies in common

3. **The Law of Contract**
   - Formation of a contract: offer, acceptance, consideration, intention to create legal relations
   - Contents of a contract: express and implied terms
   - Exemption clauses and unfair terms
   - Vitiating factors: duress, undue influence, non-disclosure, misrepresentation, mistake
   - Discharge of contracts: performance, agreement, breach, frustration
   - Remedies: damages, specific performance, injunction

4. **The Law of the European Union**
   - Evolution of the European Union
   - The institutions of the European Union
   - The law making process
   - Sources and hierarchy of law in the European Union
   - The supremacy of European Union law
   - Overview of the substantive law of the European Union

5. **Equity and the Law of Trusts**
   - Equity and equitable principles
   - Formation of trusts: the three certainties; the beneficiary principle
   - Formal requirements to create a trust
   - Legality of a trust: perpetuities and accumulations
   - Completely and incompletely constituted trusts
   - Implied, resulting and constructive trusts
   - Trusts of land
   - Charitable trusts
   - Appointment, retirement and removal of trustees
   - Trustees' powers and duties
   - Rights of beneficiaries under a trust
   - Variation of trusts
   - Remedies for breach of trust

6. **Conveyancing**
   - Land registration and third-party rights
   - Conflicts of interest, undertakings and professional negligence
   - Contract: formation and enforceability
   - Deducing and investigating title
   - Pre-contract searches and enquiries
   - Mortgages
   - Planning considerations
   - Exchange of contracts
   - Pre-completion searches steps, completion and post-completion
   - Investigation of Title - registered and unregistered
   - Delayed completion and remedies
   - Leasehold properties

- Commonhold

7. The Law and Practice of Companies and Partnerships
- Company formation
- Articles of association
- Shares and debentures
- The members of a company, including rights of minority shareholders
- Company directors and other officers
- Administration
- Winding up
- Formation of partnerships
- Relationship between partners, including partners as agents
- Dissolution
- Limited Liability Partnerships

8. Wills Probate and Administration
- The nature and validity of wills
- Intestacy
- Planning and drafting a will
- Construction of wills
- Taxation and accounts for taxation purposes
- Applying for the grant
- Family provision claims
- Duties and powers of personal representatives
- Completion of the administration
- Beneficiaries' rights and remedies

9. Roman Law as an Introduction to Civil-Law Systems
- The different areas of law: property, obligations, family, agency, succession
- The use of written instruments in Roman practice - the tabellio and the notarius
- The reception of Roman law in medieval Europe and its continuing relevance to modern civil-law jurisdictions
- The civil-law courts in England
- The role of Roman law in the development of the English common law
- The development of the modern European notariat

10. Private International Law
- The structure and elements of private international law
- EU and common law rules on jurisdiction
- Recognition and enforcement of judgments under EU law and the common law
- Authentic instruments
- Arbitration and alternative dispute resolution

- Choice of law rules: contractual and non-contractual obligations, moveable and immoveable property, insolvency, marriages and civil partnerships, and succession
- The meaning and use of nationality, domicile and habitual residence as connecting factors
- Characterisation and the distinction between rules of substance and rules of procedure
- The role of public policy and mandatory rules
- The pleading and proof of foreign law

11. Notarial Practice
- The legislation and rules governing notarial practice
- Personal identity and capacity
- Corporate identity and capacity
- The law of agency and powers of attorney
- Execution of documents and deeds by individuals and bodies corporate
- Forms of notarial act
- Affidavits and statutory declarations
- The noting and protest of bills of exchange
- Document security and record-keeping
- Apostilles and consular legalisation
- The regulation of notarial services
- Appointment, supervision, and continuing professional education
- Professional standards and the Conduct and Discipline Rules

SCHEDULE 3

PRESCRIBED SUBJECTS (Rule 8.3)
(details of subjects as in Schedule 2 above)

1. Public/Constitutional Law

2. The Law of Property

3. The Law of Contract

4. The Law of the European Union

5. Equity and the Law of Trusts

6. Conveyancing

7. The Law and Practice of Companies and Partnerships

8. Wills, Probate & Administration

SCHEDULE 4

PRESCRIBED SUBJECTS (Rule 8.3)
(details of subjects as in Schedule 2 above)

PART 1

A.   Roman Law as introduction to Civil Law systems
B.   Private International Law

PART 2

Notarial Practice (including Bills of Exchange)

In Part 1 of this Schedule, the applicant may be required either to have passed an examination in these subjects, or to have undertaken supervised practice in these subjects under a qualified and admitted notary or otherwise satisfied the Master of his proficiency by practice as a notary in another member state.

In Part 2, the applicant shall have satisfied the Master either by examination or by supervised practice under a qualified and admitted notary in these areas.

SCHEDULE 5

OFFICE PRACTICE COURSE

- The practical aspects of preparing notarial acts, including the function of a newly qualified notary's supervisor and the use of other resources

- The application in practice of the Notaries Practice Rules

- Consular legalisation and apostilles

- Record-keeping, with particular reference to notarial acts in the public form, and accounts

- Client care and handling complaints

- The Conduct and Discipline Rules

NOTARIES (PRACTISING CERTIFICATES) RULES 2012

WE CHARLES RICHARD GEORGE One of Her Majesty's Counsel Commissary or Master of the Faculties of the Most Reverend Father in God Rowan Douglas by Divine Providence Lord Archbishop of Canterbury Primate of All England and Metropolitan in exercise of the powers conferred by section 4 of the Public Notaries Act 1843 and section 57 of the Courts and Legal Services Act 1990 and of all other powers Us enabling hereby make the following Rules:

1. **Citation and Commencement**
   1.1   These Rules may be cited as the Notaries (Practising Certificates) Rules 2012.

   1.2   These Rules shall come into force on 1st October 2013.

2. **Interpretation**
   In these Rules

   "the Master" means the Master of the Faculties

   "the Registrar" means the Registrar of the Court of Faculties

   "the Court" means the Court of Faculties

   "the Faculty Office" means the Registry or Office of the Court of Faculties

   "the Commissary" has the meaning assigned by the Notarial Appeals and Hearings Rules 2000

   the Contingency Fund" means the fund established under the Notarial Contingency Fund Rules 1981 (as amended)

   "a Notary" means a Public Notary whose name appears on the Roll of Notaries of England and Wales maintained by the Faculty Office

   "Notarial Act" means any act that has validity by virtue only of its preparation, performance, authentication, attestation or verification by a Notary, and includes any such act carried out by electronic means

   "Practising Certificate Year" means the 1st day of November in a calendar year until the 31st day of October in the following calendar year

   "Reserved Legal Activity" has the meaning set out in the Legal Services Act 2007

   "Specified Profession" and "Relevant Body" have the meanings set out in Rule 10 and the Second Schedule of the 2011 Rules

66

"a Finding" means a decision or decisions of the Relevant Body of a Specified Profession

"the 1998 Rules" means the Notaries (Qualifications) Rules 1998 or any subsequent amendment or replacement thereof

"the 2011 Rules" means the Notaries (Conduct & Discipline) Rules 2011 or any subsequent amendment or replacement thereof.

3. **Duty to hold a practising certificate**

    3.1   A Notary practising as such within England and Wales must at all times hold a practising certificate issued out of the Faculty Office save for those Notaries appointed for Ecclesiastical purposes only pursuant to Rule 4 of the 1998 Rules.

    3.2   No Notary empowered to practise within England and Wales may do or perform any Notarial Act or any other Reserved Legal Activity which a Notary is authorised to perform unless in possession of a valid practising certificate save for those Notaries appointed for Ecclesiastical purposes only pursuant to Rule 4 of the 1998 Rules.

    3.3   Practising as a Notary without a valid practising certificate is an offence unders Section 14 of the Legal Services Act 2007 and Notarial Misconduct for the purposes of Rule 2.1 of the 2011 Rules.

    3.4   A practising certificate as a Notary shall be valid and have effect for a single Practising Certificate Year subject to the exceptions set out in Rules 3.5 and 3.6 and the provisions of Rule 4.4 below.

    3.5   Where a Notary has been admitted during a Practising Certificate Year his or her first practising certificate shall be dated on the day he or she was duly admitted and received their notarial faculty and run until the 31st day of October following.

    3.6   In all other cases the date shall be determined by the Registrar in the circumstances of the case and having regard to the information provided by the Notary as to his or her insurance and practice arrangements.

    3.7   Notwithstanding the provisions of Rule 4.1 below, if a Notary fails to apply to renew or has not received his or her renewed practising certificate by the 31st day of December in a Practising Certificate Year they shall no longer be authorised to practise as a Notary and shall have their details removed from the list of practising Notaries published on the website of the Faculty Office.

4.   **Application**

4.1   The application for a practising certificate as a Notary shall be in such form as the Master may direct by Order from time to time and, save for any Notary to whom Rule 3.5 or 3.6 above applies, shall be lodged with the Faculty Office no later than the commencement of the relevant Practising Certificate Year.

4.2   The application shall be accompanied by:

4.2.1   the payment of such fee for the issue of a practising certificate as the Master may direct by Order from time to time;

4.2.2   the payment of such sum as a contribution to the Contingency Fund as the Master may direct by Order from time to time;

4.2.3   evidence of the insurance cover held by the Notary in compliance with the provisions of either Rule 6 or Rule 7 of these Rules;

4.2.4   a copy of the CPE Training Record maintained by the Notary for the preceding Practising Certificate Year pursuant to the Notaries (Continuing Professional Education) Regulations 2012;

4.2.5   if required pursuant to Rule 11A of the Notaries Accounts Rules 1998 (as amended), an Accountant's Report as therein defined; and

4.2.6   if required pursuant to Rule 8.2 of the Notaries Practice Rule 2009, confirmation that the Notary has sent to his or her employer a written statement of professional independence together with such other documentation as the Master may direct by Order or request from time to time.

4.3   Where a Notary is also a member of a Specified Profession he or she shall lodge with the Faculty Office a copy of their annual practising certificate or other evidence of their entitlement to practise as such within 21 days of receipt of the same from the relevant issuing authority.

4.4   Where a Notary has lodged an application for the renewal of his or her practising certificate in accordance with Rule 4.1 above but has not received the renewed practising certificate then the practising certificate issued for the immediately preceding Practising Certificate Year shall remain valid for the purpose of Rule 3.2 until 31st December in the new Practising Certificate Year or for the period until he or she receives the renewed practising certificate whichever shall be the shorter.

5.   **Form of practising certificate**

A practising certificate as a Notary shall be issued in such form as the Master may direct by Order from time to time.

6. Insurance

6.1 All Notaries in practice as such within England and Wales (save for those Notaries appointed for Ecclesiastical purposes only pursuant to Rule 4 of the 1998 Rules) shall at all times hold insurance covering their notarial practice for the following:

    6.1.1 insurance against civil liability for professional negligence incurred by the Notary in connection with his or her practice as a Notary; and

    6.1.2 insurance against financial loss suffered by a third party in consequence of any dishonest or fraudulent act or any omission by the Notary in connection with his or her practice as a Notary.

6.2 The minimum level of insurance cover in respect of 6.1.1 and 6.1.2 above shall be fixed from time to time by Order of the Master and shall come into force on the 1st day of November immediately following.

7. Where a Notary practises also as a member of a Specified Profession and as a member of such profession holds insurance cover in respect of Rule 6.1.1 and 6.1.2 and provided that the Registrar is satisfied that such insurance cover will extend to the holder's practice as a Notary then the requirements of Rule 6 shall have been satisfied.

8. If the insurance cover held by a Notary in accordance with Rules 6 or 7 above ceases at any time after 1st November in any Practising Certificate Year he or she shall forthwith provide the Registrar with details of the replacement policy or policies of insurance and if the Registrar is not satisfied that the replacement insurance cover is sufficient to comply with the said Rules 6 or 7 the practising certificate as a Notary shall cease to have effect immediately.

9. Restriction of practising certificate

9.1 The Registrar may on the issue of any practising certificate under these Rules, having regard to the provisions of these Rules and of any general direction given by the Master, restrict or endorse the certificate as to the matters in which the holder is entitled to practise as a Notary and the wording of the certificate or endorsement shall be as the Registrar shall direct.

9.2 Any Notary whose practising certificate has been restricted or endorsed as above may appeal to the Master against the imposition of such a restriction or endorsement by giving notice to the Faculty Office of such appeal within 14 days of the Registrar's decision.

9.3 Any appeal made by a Notary under Rule 9.2 may be heard by the Master in person or may be disposed of on the basis of written representations if the Notary so agrees.

9.4 Upon hearing such an appeal under Rule 9.3 the Master may either

9.4.1 direct the Registrar to issue a practising certificate to the Notary without condition or endorsement;

9.4.2 direct the Registrar to issue a practising certificate to the Notary containing conditions or endorsements imposed by the Master as he sees fit; or

9.4.3 dismiss the appeal.

9.5 Where a practising certificate held by a Notary has been suspended or restricted pursuant to Rule 6.5 of the 2011 Rules any appeal to the Master or application to the Commissary in respect of such restriction or endorsement shall be referred to the Court.

9.6 Where a practising certificate held by a Notary has been suspended or restricted pursuant to Rule 9.1 of the 2011 Rules any application to review the Order (as therein defined) under Rule 11 of the 2011 Rules shall be referred to the Court.

9.7 In the event that a Notary fails to provide the information required pursuant to Rule 4.2 above a practising certificate will not be issued. A Notary may appeal against the decision of the Registrar not to issue a practising certificate and the time limit in Rule 9.2 above shall apply. The appeal shall be conducted in accordance with Rules 9.3 and 9.4 above.

10. Where a Notary is a member of a Specified Profession and the Relevant Body of which has made a Finding against that Notary and such Finding discloses evidence of gross misconduct the Registrar may make an order ("an Interim Order") to suspend the Notary's practising certificate or restrict or limit the Notary's practice pending the conclusion of the procedures set out in Rule 10.4 or 10.5 of the 2011 Rules.

11. Where the Registrar has made an Interim Order the Notary may appeal to the Master and the procedure set out in Rule 6.5 of the 2011 Rules shall apply *mutatis mutandis* save that if disciplinary proceedings have been commenced in the Court of Faculties against the Notary any application shall be made to the Commissary.

12. **Revocations**

12.1 The following Order of the Master and Rules are hereby revoked:

- Order of the Master dated 16th June 1982
- The Public Notaries (Practising Certificates) Rules 1982
- The Public Notaries (Practising Certificates) Rules 1991
- The Public Notaries (Practising Certificates)(Amendment) Rules 1993
- The Public Notaries (Practising Certificates)(Amendment) Rules 1995

- The Public Notaries (Practising Certificates)(Amendment) Rules 1999

12.2 Any practising certificate issued pursuant to the rules which are hereby revoked for the Practising Certificate Year ending 31st October 2013 shall remain valid until that date or as provided in Rule 4.4. above.

Dated this 21st day of December 2012

Signed   C R GEORGE
                MASTER

NOTARIES (CONDUCT AND DISCIPLINE) RULES 2011

WE CHARLES RICHARD GEORGE One of Her Majesty's Counsel Commissary or Master of the Faculties of the Most Reverend Father in God Rowan Douglas by Divine Providence Lord Archbishop of Canterbury Primate of All England and Metropolitan in exercise of the powers conferred by section 4 of the Public Notaries Act 1843 and section 57 of the Courts and Legal Services Act 1990 and of all other powers Us enabling hereby make the following Rules:

PART I PRELIMINARY

1.   Citation and Commencement
1.1   These rules may be cited as the Notaries (Conduct and Discipline) Rules 2011

1.2   The rules come into force on the 1st day of May 2011

2.   Interpretation
2.1   In these rules:-
'1993 Rules' means the Public Notaries (Conduct and Discipline) Rules 1993.

'2009 Rules' means the Notaries (Conduct and Discipline) Rules 2009.

'Approved Procedure' means a complaints resolution procedure approved under rule 3 of these rules, rule 3 of the 1993 Rules, or rule 3 of the 2009 Rules.

'Commissary' and **'Deputy Commissary'** have the meanings assigned by the Notarial Appeals and Hearings Rules 2000.

'Client' includes any person who has instructed a notary to carry out a reserved legal activity within the meaning of section 12 of the Legal Services Act 2007 and any person who has placed legitimate reliance on a Notarial Act.

'Competent Complainant' means:-
(i)   A Nominated Notary,
(ii)   The Incorporated Company of Scriveners or a member of that Company nominated by it, or
(iii)   A Client where the complaint relates to Notarial Misconduct arising from notarial acts or other professional services performed by the notary in question.

'The Court' means the Court of Faculties.

'The Contingency Fund' means the fund referred to in the Notarial Contingency Fund Rules 1981.

'Designated Society' means the Incorporated Company of Scriveners, the Notaries Society, the Society of Scrivener Notaries and such other bodies as the Master may from time to time designate for the purposes of these rules.

'Firm' has the meaning assigned in rule 2 of the Notaries Practice Rules 2009.

'The Master' means the Master of the Faculties.

'Nominated Notary' means a notary appointed by the Registrar under rule 4 of these rules.

'Notarial Act' has the meaning given in rule 2 of the Notaries Practice Rules 2009.

'Notarial Misconduct' means:-
(i)   Fraudulent conduct,
(ii)   Practising as a notary public without a valid Practising Certificate or in breach of a condition or limitation imposed on a Practising Certificate, or
(iii)   Other serious misconduct which may include failure to observe the requirements of these rules or of the Notaries Practice Rules 2009 or falling seriously below the standard of service reasonably to be expected of a public notary.

'Panel' means not less than four notaries each of whom has held a Notarial Practising Certificate for a minimum of ten years.

'The Registrar' means the Registrar of the Court of Faculties.

'Scrivener Notary' means a notary who holds the qualifications to practise as a scrivener notary from time to time prescribed by the Incorporated Company of Scriveners of London or who did hold such qualifications before being struck off the Roll of Notaries or suspended from practice by an order of the Court and a notary who does not hold such qualifications but is employed by or is otherwise professionally associated with a Scrivener Notary or a firm of Scrivener Notaries.

'Specified Profession' and **'Relevant Body'** have the meanings specified in rule 10

'The First Schedule', **'the Second Schedule'** and **'the Appendix'** mean respectively the First Schedule, the Second Schedule and the Appendix to these rules.

2.2   References in these rules to a "notary" are references to a notary enrolled on the Roll of Notaries maintained by the Court.

73

2.3　The Interpretation Act 1978 applies to these rules as it applies to an Act of Parliament.

PART II: COMPLAINTS

3.　Complaints Resolution Procedures

3.1　The Master may from time to time approve by written notice a complaints resolution procedure produced by a Designated Society and may at any time by written notice withdraw approval of any procedure.

3.2　An Approved Procedure may include provision:-

3.2.1　for the informal resolution of disputes between members of the public and notaries concerning notarial acts done by a notary or the conduct of a notary's practice,

3.2.2　for the informal resolution of disputes between members of the public and notaries concerning the charges made by notaries for notarial services,

3.2.3　for dealing with complaints referred to a Designated Society by the Registrar about the conduct or practice of a notary who is a member of that Designated Society,

and for such other matters as the Master may from time to time specify.

3.3　Where a dispute with or complaint against a notary is dealt with in accordance with an Approved Procedure it shall be a duty of the notary to cooperate with the Designated Society in the operation of the procedure.

3.3.1　A notary shall comply with any reasonable action proposed by the Designated Society at the conclusion of the Approved Procedure.

3.3.2　A notary shall offer the client an alternative remedy which is reasonable in the circumstances of the complaint if he does not accept on reasonable grounds the conclusion of the Designated Society.

3.3.3　An apology, an offer of treatment or other redress shall not of itself amount to an admission of Notarial Misconduct.

3.4　A notary shall give the Office of Legal Complaints all such assistance requested by that Office in connection with the investigation, consideration or determination of complaints under the ombudsman scheme established under section 115 of the Legal Services Act 2007 as he is reasonably able to give.

3.5　Where a dispute with or complaint against a notary is received by the Registrar and there is no Approved Procedure available to deal with the complaint, the Registrar shall refer the matter to a member of a Panel of notaries appointed for this purpose by the Registrar to carry out the functions set out in Rule 3.2.

3.5.1   the notary carrying out these functions shall be entitled to a fixed fee to be specified by the Master from time to time which shall be payable by the notary complained against,

3.5.2   the notary carrying out these functions may not be appointed a Nominated Notary under Rule 4 in relation to the same dispute or complaint.

4.   Nominated Notaries

A Nominated Notary appointed by the Registrar under these rules shall be a notary (but not a Scrivener Notary) who holds a Notarial Practising Certificate and has held such a Certificate for not less than five years.

5.   Functions of Nominated Notaries

5.1   A Nominated Notary may be appointed by the Registrar to investigate an allegation of Notarial Misconduct referred to him by the Registrar and, if he thinks fit, to prepare and prosecute disciplinary proceedings against a notary in the Court in accordance with the provisions of these rules and to carry out such other functions as may be provided in these rules.

5.2   A Nominated Notary appointed under this rule shall be independent of and not personally acquainted with the notary who is the subject of the allegations of Notarial Misconduct to be investigated.

5.3   If the Registrar is unable to identify a Nominated Notary who fulfils the requirements in Rule 5.2 the Master shall appoint an independent person, who may or may not be a notary, to act in place of a Nominated Notary for the purposes of Rule 5.1, and that person shall carry out all functions conferred on a Nominated Notary by these rules.

5.4   Where a Nominated Notary investigates an allegation of Notarial Misconduct referred to him by the Registrar but such investigation does not lead to the issue of disciplinary proceedings in the Court the Nominated Notary shall be entitled to be paid such fixed fee as may have been previously authorised by the Registrar or such fee as the Registrar may determine should be paid for work properly done after considering a bill and other representations submitted by the Nominated Notary and such fee shall be paid by the Registrar out of the Contingency Fund.

6.   Referral of Allegations by Registrar

6.1   Where the Registrar receives evidence or an allegation concerning the conduct or practice of a notary which in his opinion does not amount to an allegation of Notarial Misconduct or where the precise nature of the allegation is unclear he shall refer the matter to a Designated Society or a notary appointed under Rule 3.5, to be dealt with in accordance with an Approved Procedure.

6.2 Where the Registrar receives evidence or an allegation concerning the conduct or practice of a notary (other than a Scrivener Notary) which appears to him to amount to an allegation of Notarial Misconduct he shall appoint a Nominated Notary to investigate the allegation pursuant to rule 5 of these rules.

6.3 Where the Registrar receives evidence or an allegation concerning the conduct or practice of a Scrivener Notary which appears to him to amount to an allegation of Notarial Misconduct he shall refer the allegation to the Incorporated Company of Scriveners.

6.4 Upon the referral of such an allegation to the Incorporated Company of Scriveners it shall be investigated by that Company under arrangements made by it and approved by the Master and if it thinks fit the Incorporated Company of Scriveners or a member of the Company nominated by it shall prepare and prosecute disciplinary proceedings in the Court against the Scrivener Notary in question in accordance with the provisions of these rules and the Incorporated Company of Scriveners or the member so nominated shall be regarded as a Nominated Notary for the purposes of rule 9.5 of these rules.

6.5 Where the Registrar receives evidence concerning a notary which amounts to *prima facie* evidence of gross misconduct, the Registrar, if he is satisfied that it is required for the protection of the public, may make an interim order to suspend the notary from practice or restrict or limit or impose conditions on the notary's practice pending the conclusion of disciplinary proceedings under Part III of these rules, save that the notary may appeal to the Master against the Registrar's decision within seven days of the issue of that interim order and on such appeal the Master shall have the same power as the Registrar has under this rule 6.5. The Registrar's power under this rule 6.5 shall not be exercisable after the end of the twenty-one day period specified in paragraph 4 of Part II of the First Schedule. Any interim order made under this rule 6.5 may be discharged or varied by the Commissary on application made to him after the end of that twenty-one day period.

7. **Referral of Allegations by Designated Societies**
Where an allegation against a notary comes to the attention of a Designated Society (whether or not in the course of the operation of an Approved Procedure) and it appears that such allegation amounts to an allegation of Notarial Misconduct the Designated Society shall refer the allegation to the Registrar for consideration in accordance with rule 6.2 or rule 6.3 of these rules as appropriate.

PART III: DISCIPLINARY PROCEDURE

8. **Disciplinary Proceedings in the Court of Faculties**

8.1   A complaint of Notarial Misconduct may be made to the Court by any Competent Complainant.

8.2   Where:

8.2.1   Evidence or an allegation concerning the conduct or practice of a notary has been received by the Registrar and he has not appointed a Nominated Notary to investigate the allegation or referred the allegation to the Incorporated Company of Scriveners (as the case may be) under rule 6.2 or rule 6.3 of these rules within 28 days of receiving the allegation, or

8.2.2   The Registrar has appointed a Nominated Notary or referred the evidence or allegation to the Incorporated Company of Scriveners and the Nominated Notary or the Incorporated Company of Scriveners has determined not to make a complaint of Notarial Misconduct to the Court in respect of the allegation or has not so made a complaint within 112 days of his appointment or the referral of the allegation (as the case may be);

then a complaint of Notarial Misconduct in respect of that allegation may be made to the Court by any notary who holds a Notarial Practising Certificate and such notary shall be deemed to be a Competent Complainant for the purposes of these rules.

8.3   Where a complaint against a notary has been made to the Court under rule 8.1 and the notary has been struck off or suspended from legal practice by a Relevant Body, as defined in rule 10, following a finding of misconduct, the Court may of its own initiative, or on the application of the complainant, suspend the notary from practice or make an order restricting or limiting or imposing conditions on the notary's practice pending the determination of the complaint, provided that the Court first considers any representations which the notary wishes to make about any such suspension or order.

8.4   The procedure set out in Part II of the First Schedule shall apply to all complaints of Notarial Misconduct made to the Court.

8.5   The forms set out in the Appendix with such variations or additions thereto as the Master may from time to time approve shall be used in all proceedings before the Court to which these rules relate.

9. **Disciplinary Sanctions**

9.1   Where the Court after hearing a complaint of Notarial Misconduct against a notary finds that it has been proved it may:

9.1.1   Order that the notary be struck off the Roll of Notaries,

9.1.2   Order that the notary be suspended from practice as a notary for a specified period or until certain conditions have been met or indefinitely,

9.1.3   Impose conditions as to the future scope or conduct of the notarial practice of the notary or conditions relating to the monitoring or supervision of his practice and direct that his Practising Certificate be endorsed or the endorsement on his Solicitor's Practising Certificate be marked accordingly,

9.1.4   Impose conditions as to the training that the notary must complete or further examination or examinations that he must pass before he may continue or resume practice as a notary, or

9.1.5   Order that the notary be admonished.

9.2   In addition to imposing any of the penalties listed in sub-rule 9.1 above the Court may order that unless the notary:-

9.2.1   Indemnifies any Client of the notary whom the Court finds to have suffered actual loss as a result of the Notarial Misconduct in question and;

9.2.2   Pays a monetary sum not exceeding £10,000 (or such higher sum as the Master may from time to time specify for the purpose of these rules) such sum to be paid to whomsoever the Court may direct,

the notary shall be struck off the Roll of Notaries.

9.3   Subject to rule 9.5 it shall be within the discretion of the Court to order:

9.3.1   That the costs of either party to the complaint be paid by the other party,

9.3.2   That the costs of the Court be paid by either party or by both parties (whether in equal or unequal shares),

9.3.3   That the costs of either party or of the court shall be paid from the Contingency Fund, and;

9.3.4   That a party against whom an order for Costs is made shall, instead of paying those costs to the other party or the Court, pay them into the Contingency Fund.

9.4   Any order for costs may be in a fixed sum assessed by the Court as representing or being a contribution towards the reasonable costs of the party concerned or may be for costs to be taxed.

9.5   The Court shall not make any order for costs against a Nominated Notary who shall in all cases be entitled to an order for costs in his favour such costs to be paid from the Contingency Fund.

9.6   Where an order is made for costs to be taxed the costs shall be taxed by the Registrar on such basis and in accordance with such scale applicable in the High Court or the County Court as the Court may direct.

10.   Specified Professions and Relevant Bodies

10.1   For the purposes of these rules a 'Specified Profession' means a profession specified in the Second Schedule and in respect of a Specified Profession 'Relevant Body' means the disciplinary body named for that profession in the Second Schedule.

10.2   The Master may by order add to or amend the Second Schedule.

10.3   It shall be the duty of any notary who is also a member of a Specified Profession and against whom a complaint has been made to the Relevant Body, and where such complaint has been found by that body to be substantiated, to report such finding forthwith to the Registrar (whether or not a penalty is imposed by the Relevant Body and without regard to the nature of such penalty).

10.4   Where it comes to the attention of the Registrar that a Relevant Body has found a complaint against a notary (other than a Scrivener Notary) to be substantiated, the Registrar shall appoint a Nominated Notary to investigate the matter and if he thinks fit to prepare and prosecute disciplinary proceedings as if he were acting under rule 5.

10.5   Where it comes to the attention of the Registrar that a Relevant Body has found a complaint against a Scrivener Notary to be substantiated, the Registrar shall refer the matter to the Incorporated Company of Scriveners for investigation in accordance with rule 6.4.

10.6   In proceedings under these rules the written decision of a Relevant Body shall be evidence of the facts stated in that decision.

11.   Application for Review

11.1   Where as a result of an Order made under these rules or the 1993 Rules or the 2009 Rules a notary:

11.1.1   has been struck off the Roll of Notaries other than pursuant to proceedings under rule 10 of the 1993 Rules, under rule 10 of the 2009 Rules, or under rule 10 of these rules, and a period of not less than twelve months has elapsed since the date of striking off,

11.1.2   has been suspended from practice for a period exceeding twelve months or for an indefinite period and a period of not less than twelve months has elapsed since the date of the suspension,

11.1.3   has had conditions imposed as to the future scope or conduct of his notarial practice, or conditions relating to the monitoring or supervision of his practice, or

11.1.4   has been struck off the Roll of Notaries pursuant to proceedings under rule 10 of the 1993 Rules, or under rule 10 of the 2009 Rules, or under rule 10 of these rules, and has since been restored to the Roll of Solicitors, or, where relevant, the equivalent record of practitioners maintained by a Specified Profession,

the notary may apply to the Court to review the Order.

11.2   In the case of an application under rule 11.1.1, rule 11.1.2 or rule 11.1.4 above it shall be for the notary to prove to the satisfaction of the Court that circumstances have changed since the Order was made and that it is not contrary to the public interest or the interest of the notarial profession that the order be reviewed and, in the case of a petition under rule 11.1.3, it shall be for the notary to prove to the satisfaction of the Court that as a result of a change in circumstances the conditions imposed are no longer necessary or desirable in the public interest.

11.3   The procedure set out in Part III of the First Schedule shall apply to an application brought under this rule.

11.4   On receiving an application brought under this rule by a notary other than a Scrivener Notary the Registrar shall appoint a Nominated Notary to act as respondent to the application and on receiving an application brought under this rule by a Scrivener Notary the Registrar shall appoint the Incorporated Company of Scriveners to act as respondent to the application.

11.5   Except in exceptional circumstances the costs of the respondent to an application brought under this rule and of the Court shall be paid by the applicant regardless of the outcome; in all other respects the provisions of rule 9.3 shall apply mutatis mutandis.

11.6   Upon hearing an application brought under this rule the Court may:
11.6.1   In the case of an application under rule 11.1.1 or 11.1.4 order that the notary be restored to the Roll of Notaries either immediately or on some specified future date;
11.6.2   In the case of an application under rule 11.1.2 order that the suspension be lifted either immediately or on some specified future date;
11.6.3   In the case of an application under rule 11.1.3 order that the conditions imposed be lifted or that different conditions be imposed;
11.6.4   Impose such conditions upon any order or require such undertakings to be given by the petitioner as it thinks fit, or
11.6.5   dismiss the application.

12.   First Schedule and Appendix

12.1   The provisions of Part I of the First Schedule shall apply to all proceedings under these rules.

12.2   It shall be within the discretion of the Registrar to grant to a party to proceedings before the Court such extension to any of the time limits contained in the First Schedule as appears to him to be reasonable.

12.3   Forms 3, 5, 6, and 8 set out in the Appendix shall be issued by the Registrar under the seal of the Court but any omission to affix the seal of the Court shall not invalidate a form or any proceedings to which it relates.

13.   Revocation, Savings and Consequential Amendments

13.1   Subject to rule 13.2 the 2009 Rules are hereby revoked.

13.2   Where any proceedings before the Court had been commenced under the 2009 Rules prior to the coming into force of these rules the 2009 Rules shall continue to have effect in respect of those proceedings.

13.3   In rule 3.3 of the Notaries (Prevention of Money Laundering) Rules 2007 "Notaries (Conduct and Discipline) Rules 2009" is omitted and "Notaries (Conduct and Discipline) Rules 2011" substituted therefor.

THE FIRST SCHEDULE

PART I: PRELIMINARY

1. References in this Schedule to forms are to the forms set out in the Appendix, references in Part II to the complainant and the respondent are to the person bringing a complaint and the notary against whom a complaint is brought respectively and references in Part III to the applicant and the respondent are to the notary applying for review and the person or body appointed to act as respondent to the application respectively.

2. Any notice or document required by this Schedule to be delivered to the Registrar shall be delivered to him at the Court of Faculties, 1 The Sanctuary, Westminster, London SW1P 3JT and shall be deemed to be delivered on the day on which it is actually received by the Registrar.

3. Any notice or document required by this Schedule to be served by the Registrar may be served by sending it by ordinary first class post or document exchange to such address as may have been specified by the party concerned as his address for service or if no such address has been specified for a notary to the address appearing for him on the Roll of Notaries, and any notice or document so sent shall be deemed to have been served on the second working day after dispatch by post or document exchange.

4. The hearing of a complaint or application under these rules shall take place at such venue as the Commissary may direct and each party shall be entitled to be present and to be represented by a notary, a solicitor or counsel.

PART II: PROCEEDINGS UNDER RULE 8

1. A complaint of Notarial Misconduct shall be made by a written complaint in form 1 and shall be supported by an affidavit in form 2.

2. The written complaint and affidavit in support shall be delivered to the Registrar.

3. On receiving a written complaint and affidavit in support the Registrar shall issue the complaint and serve a copy of each document together with notice of proceedings in form 3 on the respondent.

4. Within twenty-one days of service of the notice of proceedings on him the respondent shall deliver to the Registrar an answer to the complaint in form 4 and on receipt of an answer the Registrar shall serve a copy on the complainant.

5.	Within forty-two days of service of the notice of proceedings on him the respondent shall, if he intends to contest the proceedings, deliver to the Registrar an affidavit in reply to the complaint and on receipt of such affidavit the Registrar shall send a copy to the complainant.

6.	If the respondent fails to deliver an answer within the time prescribed by paragraph 4 the Registrar shall appoint a date for the hearing of the complaint and give notice to both parties in form 5.

7.	If the respondent delivers an answer within the time prescribed the Registrar shall refer the papers to the Commissary who shall make such directions for the future conduct of the complaint as he thinks fit including directions:-
	7.1	for the filing and service of further evidence including the affidavit evidence of witnesses,
	7.2	for the preparation and disclosure of lists of documents and for the inspection of such documents,
	7.3	for a preliminary hearing to consider any point of law or procedure which may be raised by the proceedings or to consider the making of further directions,
	7.4	for the hearing of the complaint and the attendance of witnesses at the hearing,
	and the Registrar shall serve a copy of the Commissary's directions and notice of any hearing (which shall be in form 5) on each party.

8.1	If a party to the complaint requires the deponent to any affidavit filed to attend at the hearing of the complaint he shall give notice to the Registrar and to the other party not less than fourteen days before the date appointed for the hearing.

8.2	If a deponent who has been so required to attend the hearing does not attend the onus shall be on the party seeking to rely on the affidavit evidence of that witness to show why the affidavit should be accepted in evidence.

9.1	The procedure adopted at the hearing shall take such form as the Court thinks fit in all the circumstances of the case but shall ensure that both parties are given an opportunity to state their case to the Court and to cross-examine any witnesses giving evidence in person at the hearing.

9.2	Subject to the provisions of paragraph 8 the complaint shall be decided on the basis of the affidavits filed.

9.3	At any time prior to the conclusion of a hearing the Court may, if it thinks it expedient to do so, adjourn the hearing and give such further directions as it thinks fit.

10. After hearing the complaint the Court may give its decision at the hearing or reserve judgment and the Registrar shall give notice to the parties of the Court's Order in form 6.

11.1 If the complainant wishes to apply to the Court for an order suspending the respondent from practice or restricting or limiting or imposing conditions on the respondent's practice pending the determination of the complaint he shall make the application in form 7, and shall lodge an affidavit in support of the application.

11.2 Subject to paragraph 11.8, on receiving an application in form 7 and affidavit in support the Registrar shall serve a copy of each document on the respondent and appoint a date for the hearing of the application (which shall be not less than ten days after the date on which the documents are served on the respondent) and shall give notice to the parties in form 8.

11.3 If the respondent wishes to oppose the application he shall, within fourteen days of its service upon him, deliver to the Registrar an affidavit in response and the Registrar shall serve a copy of the response on the complainant.

11.4 When the application has been determined by the Court the Registrar shall give notice to the parties of the Court's order in form 6.

11.5 Unless the Court orders otherwise the costs of the parties to the application shall be reserved to the hearing of the substantive complaint.

11.6 An application under this paragraph shall be heard by the Commissary or a Deputy Commissary alone and when the application has been heard by the Commissary or a Deputy Commissary the Commissary or (as the case may be) the Deputy Commissary in question shall not sit on the hearing of the substantive complaint.

11.7 At the hearing of an application under this paragraph the Court may, if it considers it appropriate to do so, give directions under paragraph 7 for the hearing of the substantive complaint.

11.8 Where it appears to him to be necessary for the protection of the public the Commissary or Deputy Commissary to whom an application under this paragraph is referred may direct such modifications to the procedure as he thinks fit including the making of an interim order to suspend the respondent from practice or restrict or limit or impose conditions on the respondent's practice pending the hearing of the application pursuant to paragraph 11.2.

PART III: APPLICATION FOR REVIEW UNDER RULE 11

1.   An application under rule 11 of these rules shall be made in form 9 and shall be accompanied by an affidavit or affidavits setting out in full the grounds of the application and the evidence in support.

2.   Upon receiving an application and affidavits in support the Registrar shall issue the application and serve a copy of each document on the Nominated Notary (or, as the case may be, the Incorporated Company of Scriveners) appointed as respondent under rule 11.4 and the Registrar shall also serve on both parties notice of hearing of the application in form 10.

3.   Where the Order which the applicant is seeking to review was made as a result of a complaint brought by a person who was a Competent Complainant as a person who had been a Client of the notary the Registrar shall also send copies of the above documents and notice and any affidavit delivered under paragraph 4 to the complainant who shall be entitled to attend the hearing and (if the Court so permits) to address the Court.

4.   The function of the respondent shall be to ensure that the applicant is put to proof of his case and to bring to the attention of the Court all such facts and matters as the respondent thinks should be before the Court and if the respondent wishes to present to the Court an affidavit or affidavits in reply to the application he shall deliver the same to the Registrar not less than twenty-eight days before the date of the hearing and the Registrar shall forthwith serve copies on the applicant.

5.   At the hearing the Court shall consider all documents and evidence which were before the Court before making the order which the applicant is seeking to review and shall consider the affidavits filed in support of and any affidavits filed in answer to the application and the applicant may give evidence in person. The Court shall also consider representations made to it by the parties.

6.   After hearing the petition the Court may give its decision at the hearing or reserve judgment and the Registrar shall give notice to the parties of the Court's Order in form 6.

THE SECOND SCHEDULE

Specified Profession	Relevant Body
Solicitor of the Senior Courts of England and Wales	The Solicitors Disciplinary Tribunal
Barrister in England and Wales	A Panel or Disciplinary Tribunal operated by the Bar Standards Board
Legal Executive	The Investigating Committee or the Disciplinary Tribunal of the Institute of Legal Executives
Licensed Conveyancer	The Investigating Committee established under section 24 of the Administration of Justice Act 1985 or the Discipline and Appeals Committee established under section 25(1) of that Act
	The body responsible for exercising disciplinary regulation over the avocat or other legal practitioner in the country in question

APPENDIX

Form 1: Written Complaint
IN THE COURT OF FACULTIES
In the Matter of [AB] a notary and
In the matter of the Notaries (Conduct and Discipline) Rules 2011
To the Registrar
I, the undersigned [CD] of [address] do hereby make complaint that the said [AB] of [address] has been guilty of Notarial Misconduct within the meaning of the said rules in that he/she has …(insert summary of allegation(s) of misconduct).
....

Details of my complaint are contained in the affidavit which accompanies this written complaint.
DATED this …………. day of ………….. 20...
Signed
Address for service

Form 2: Affidavit in support of Written Complaint
IN THE COURT OF FACULTIES
In the matter of [AB] a notary and
In the matter of the Notaries (Conduct and Discipline) Rules 2011
I [CD] of [address] make oath and say as follows:-
1.   I am a Competent Complainant within the meaning of the said rules as [specify how the deponent is a Competent Complainant].
2.   I make this affidavit in support of my written complaint against the above named [AB] a notary of [address]
3.   [Here state the facts concisely in numbered paragraphs and show the complainant's means of knowledge.]

Form 3: Notice of Proceedings
IN THE COURT OF FACULTIES
In the matter of [AB] a notary and
In the matter of the Notaries (Conduct and Discipline) Rules 2011
TO: [AB] a notary of [address]
TAKE NOTICE that a written complaint has been received by the Court alleging that you have been guilty of Notarial Misconduct. A copy of the complaint and the affidavit supporting it are attached to this notice.
You are required:-
1.   Within twenty-one days of service of this notice upon you to deliver to me an answer to the complaint in the form prescribed by the above rules, and
2.   If you intend to contest these proceedings, to deliver to me within forty-two days of service of this notice upon you a affidavit in reply to the complaint.
If you fail to comply with these requirements I will proceed to appoint a date for the hearing of the complaint.
All communications should be addressed to "The Registrar, The Court of Faculties, 1 The Sanctuary, Westminster, London SW1P 3JT".
DATED this ……… day of ………………. 20...

Form 4: Answer to Complaint
IN THE COURT OF FACULTIES
In the matter of [AB] a notary and
In the matter of the Notaries (Conduct and Discipline) Rules 2011
To the Registrar
I, [AB] in answer to the complaint of [CD], say that:-
1.   I intend to contest the complaint OR I do not intend to contest the complaint [and I consent to being struck off the Roll of Notaries] [delete as applicable]
2.   My address for service is
DATED this ……… day of ……………… 20...

Form 5: Notice of Hearing
IN THE COURT OF FACULTIES
In the matter of [AB] a notary and
In the matter of the Notaries (Conduct and Discipline) Rules 2011
To the above named respondent [AB] of [address] and to the complainant [CD] of [address]
TAKE NOTICE that this complaint will be heard by the Court on ……………..….
day   the ………………… day of ……………….. at [time of day] at
……………………………………. when you are required to attend.
If you do not attend the hearing may proceed in your absence.
DATED this ……… day of ……………… 20...
Signed
Registrar

Form 6: Order
IN THE COURT OF FACULTIES
In the matter of [AB] a notary and
In the matter of the Notaries (Conduct and Discipline) Rules 2011
To the above named [respondent/petitioner] [AB] of [address] and to the [complainant/respondent] [CD] of [address]
The Court having heard this [complaint] [application] on the ……. day of ………………… 200..
THE COURT ORDERS as follows:-
DATED this ……… day of ……………… 20...
Signed
Registrar

Form 7: Application for Suspension etc pending determination of Complaint
IN THE COURT OF FACULTIES
In the Matter of [AB] a notary and
In the matter of the Notaries (Conduct and Discipline) Rules 2011
To the Registrar
I, the undersigned complainant [CD] of [address] apply to the Court for an order that pending the determination of this complaint [the said respondent [AB] of [address] be suspended from practice as a notary] *OR* [the practice of the said respondent [AB] of [address] be restricted or limited as follows: *[specify*

restrictions or limitations] OR [the following conditions be imposed on the practice of the said respondent [AB] of [address]: [*specify conditions*]]

The grounds of this application are contained in the accompanying affidavit.

DATED this .... day of .... 20...

Signed

Address for service

Form 8: Notice of Hearing of Application

IN THE COURT OF FACULTIES

In the matter of [AB] a notary and

In the matter of the Notaries (Conduct and Discipline) Rules 2011

To the above named respondent [AB] of [address] and to the complainant [CD] of [address]

TAKE NOTICE that the complainant's application that the respondent be suspended from practice as a notary or that the practice of the respondent be restricted or limited or that conditions be imposed on the practice of the respondent will be heard by the Court on .... day the .... day of .... at [time of day] at .... when you are required to attend.

The Court may also give directions for the hearing of the substantive complaint.

If you do not attend the hearing may proceed in your absence.

DATED this .... day of .... 20...

Signed

Registrar

Form 9: Application under Rule 11

IN THE COURT OF FACULTIES

In the matter of [AB] a notary and

In the matter of the Notaries (Conduct and Discipline) Rules 2011

To the Registrar

I [AB] of [address for service] apply to the Court as follows:-

1.   By an Order of the Court made on [date] it was ordered that [set out the terms of the Order other than terms as to costs]

2.   I now apply that the said Order be reviewed pursuant to rule 11 of the said rules.

3.   The grounds of this application and the evidence in support of it are fully set out in the accompanying affidavit[s]

DATED this .... day of .... 20...

Signed

Petitioner

Form 10: Notice of Hearing of Petition under Rule 11

IN THE COURT OF FACULTIES

In the matter of [AB] a notary and

In the matter of the Notaries (Conduct and Discipline) Rules 2011

To the above named applicant [AB] of [address] and to [CD] of [address] appointed to act as respondent to this application.

TAKE NOTICE that this application will be heard by the Court on .... day the .... day of .... 20... at [time of day] at

.... when you are required to attend. If you do not attend the hearing may proceed in your absence.
DATED this .... day of .... 20...
Signed
Registrar

....
MASTER

NOTARIES (CONTINUING PROFESSIONAL EDUCATION) REGULATIONS 2010

WE CHARLES RICHARD GEORGE One of Her Majesty's Counsel Commissary or Master of the Faculties of the Most Reverend Father in God Rowan Douglas by Divine Providence Lord Archbishop of Canterbury Primate of All England and Metropolitan do make the following Regulations pursuant to Rule 19 of Our Notaries Practice Rules 2009:

PART I: PRELIMINARY

1.   Citation and Commencement

1.1.   These regulations are made under Rule 19 of the Notaries Practice Rules 2009.

1.2.   These regulations may be cited as the Notaries (Continuing Professional Education) Regulations 2010.

1.3.   These regulations shall come into force on 1st May 2010.

2.   Interpretation

In these regulations:-

the "continuing professional education period" is a recurring period which commences on 1st November in each year and ends on 31st October a year later except as otherwise provided by these regulations.

"continuing professional education" is participation in such programmes, courses or seminars accredited by the Master as may be necessary to acquire the number of credit points determined by the Master, and "continuing professional education activity" shall be construed accordingly.

"the Master" means the Master of the Faculties, or where the Master has delegated his functions under these regulations, the delegated person or persons.

"the Registrar" means the Registrar of the Court of Faculties.

"notary" means a public notary admitted by the Master of the Faculties to practice in England and Wales or any other person authorised to act as a notary in accordance with Directive 98/5/EC but does not include a notary serving a period of supervision under rule 3 of the Notaries (Post-Admission) Rules 2009 nor an ecclesiastical notary appointed under rule 4 of the Notaries (Qualification) Rules 1998.

"notarial activities" means those activities customarily carried on by virtue of enrolment as a notary in accordance with section 1 of the Public Notaries Act 1801 (c. 79), but not including probate activities or conveyancing.

"probate activities" means preparing any probate papers for the purposes of the law of England and Wales or in relation to any proceedings in England and Wales, on which to found or oppose-

(a)   a grant of probate, or

(b)   a grant of letters of administration.

"conveyancing" means:-

(a)   preparing any instrument of transfer or charge for the purposes of the Land Registration Act 2002 (c. 9);

(b)   making an application or lodging a document for registration under that Act;

(c)   preparing any other instrument to real property for the purposes of the law of England and Wales including a contract for the sale or other disposition of land (except a contract to grant a short lease), but does not include an agreement not intended to be executed as a deed, other than a contract that is included by virtue of the preceding provisions of this sub-paragraph,

In this paragraph a "short lease" means a lease such as is referred to in section 54(2) of the Law of Property Act 1925 (c. 20) (short leases).

For the avoidance of doubt the Interpretation Act 1978 applies to these regulations as it applies to an Act of Parliament.

PART II: THE REQUIREMENT

3.   Basic Requirement in Notarial Practice

3.1   A notary who practises during the continuing professional education period is required to obtain six credit points of continuing professional education in Notarial Practice during the same continuing professional education period.

3.2   At least 3 credits of this requirement must be obtained by participation in an accredited activity.

4.   Special Requirement in Conveyancing

4.1   A notary who carries out Conveyancing in his capacity as a notary during the continuing professional education period is required to obtain six credit points of continuing professional education in Conveyancing during the same continuing professional education period.

4.2   At least 3 credits of this requirement must be obtained by participation in an accredited activity.

5.   Special Requirement in Probate Activities

5.1   A notary carries out Probate Activities in his capacity as a notary during the continuing professional education period is required to obtain six credit points of continuing professional education in

Probate Activities during the same continuing professional education period.

5.2   At least 3 credits of this requirement must be obtained by participation in an accredited activity.

6.   Requirement to keep Records
A notary is required to keep a record of the continuing professional education that he has completed during the continuing professional education period in the form set out in Schedule 2 of these regulations a copy of which he must submit to the Registrar on applying for a notarial practising certificate and on request.

7.   Investigation by Registrar
The Registrar may call upon the notary to produce such evidence as may reasonably be required in order to ascertain that the information in the continuing professional education record is faithful and accurate.

PART III: CREDIT POINTS AND ACCREDITED COURSES

8.   Credit Points
8.1   One credit point represents one hour of continuing professional education.

8.2   Credit points may not be carried over from one continuing professional education period to another except as provided by these regulations.

9.   Credit Points Claimed Otherwise Than by Accredited Activities
9.1   A notary may claim credit points for activities which have not been accredited under these regulations by completing activities listed in Schedule 1 of these regulations.

9.2   Such activities that are listed in Schedule 1 must be completed at an appropriate level and contribute to a notary's professional skill and knowledge in the basic and special continuing professional education requirements, and not merely advance a particular fee-earning matter.

10.   Credit Points Claimed by Completing Accredited Activities
A notary may claim the number of credit points which are awardable by completing an accredited activity.

11.   Application for Accreditation to Award Credit Points
11.1   A person who provides a continuing professional education activity may apply to the Master in order that the activity provided be accredited for the purpose of awarding credit points in one or more of the basic or special continuing professional education requirements.

11.2 A person may apply to the Master in order that a continuing professional education activity provided by another person be accredited for the purpose of awarding credit points in one or more of the basic or special continuing professional education requirements.

11.3 On receiving an application for accreditation the Master will inform the applicant whether or not the application has been successful and specify a number of credit points which will be awarded to any notary who completes that activity.

11.4 The Master may in specific cases award credit points to notaries who participated on an accredited course before it became accredited provided that the application for accreditation is made no later than six months after the event.

12. Content of Accredited Courses

12.1 An accredited course must be relevant to the subject matter of the basic or special continuing professional education requirement.

12.2 An accredited course must have written learning objectives relevant to the basic or special continuing professional education requirement and a form of written assessment to evaluate the notary's achievement of those objectives.

12.3 A written assessment may take the form of a structured self-evaluation such as the completion of a questionnaire.

12.4 An accredited course should take one or more of the following forms:-
   (a)   physical attendance at a lecture or seminar;
   (b)   a course provided wholly or partly at a distance that involves assessment by dissertation or written assessment.

13. Completion of Accredited Activities

13.1 A notary completes an accredited activity and is awarded the number of credit points which belong to that activity if he completes the activity.

13.2 Completion of the accredited activity occurs if the following are satisfied:-
   (a)   the notary participates in an accredited activity which includes delivering or attending the activity; and
   (b)   attendance is attendance at the complete course. Partial attendance does not constitute completion.

13.3 The person providing an accredited activity shall give a certificate to any notary who completes the activity and such a certificate shall contain the following particulars:

(a)   the name of the person who provided the accredited activity;

(b)   the name of the notary who completed the activity;

(c)   the date on which the activity was completed;

(d)   a brief description of the activity;

(e)   that the activity is accredited by the Master for the purpose of these regulations;

(f)   the basic or special requirement in which the activity is accredited;

(g)   the number of credit points which have been awarded.

14.   Removal of Accreditation

The Master may at any time remove the accreditation of an activity by notice to the provider in writing, which will specify whether the revocation will have immediate effect or will take place at a specified future date.

PART IV: MISCELLANEOUS PROVISIONS

15.   Master's Waiver

The Master may in writing waive the requirements of these regulations in whole or in part or revoke such a waiver and any such waiver may be general or specific to one or more individual notaries.

16.   Master's Delegation

The Master may in writing delegate his functions under these regulations in whole or in part to another person or persons and revoke in writing such a delegation at any time.

17.   Transitional Provisions

17.1   The first continuing professional education period commences on 1st November after the commencement of these regulations and ends on 31st October two years later.

17.2   In the first continuing educational period the notary must complete 12 credit points in each of the basic and special requirements which apply to him.

17.3   After the date of the commencement of these regulations a notary may obtain credit points which shall then be carried into the first continuing professional education period and providers of activities may apply to the Master to become accredited.

SCHEDULE 1: CREDIT POINTS AWARDED OTHERWISE THAN BY ACCREDITED COURSES

Activity	Explanation/comments
Lectures and seminars	• Preparing and delivering or attending a lecture or seminar relevant to the subject matter of the basic or special CPE requirement • Actual time may be claimed
Coaching and mentoring sessions	• Structured coaching sessions and structured mentoring sessions relevant to the subject matter of the basic or special CPE requirement, delivered face to face, of a duration of thirty minutes or more • Includes acting as a supervisor for the purpose of the Notaries (Post-Admission Rules) 2009 • Actual time may be claimed up to one hour per basic or CPE requirement
Coaching and mentoring sessions delivered at a distance	• Structured coaching sessions and structured mentoring sessions relevant to the subject matter of the basic or special CPE requirement, delivered at a distance (eg by telephone, email or fax), of a duration of thirty minutes or more • Actual time may be claimed up to one hour per basic or CPE requirement
Writing on law or practice	• Legal writing on a subject matter relevant to the basic or special CPE requirement intended for publication either in hard copy form or on the Internet • Actual time may be claimed

Research on law or practice	• Legal research on a subject matter relevant to the basic or special CPE requirement which results in a form or written document including precedents, memorandums, questionnaires/surveys • Actual time may be claimed
Watching, reading or listening to material which is produced by a legal education provider.	• Watching, reading or listening to material which is produced by a legal education provider on a subject matter relevant to the basic or special CPE requirement • Actual time may be claimed
Work shadowing	• Participation in structured work shadowing schemes with clear aims and objectives on a subject matter relevant to the basic or special CPE requirement and requiring feedback or reflection on the shadowing activity • Actual time may be claimed
Participation in the development of specialist areas of law and practice	• Participation in the development of specialist areas of law and practice on a subject matter relevant to the basic or special CPE requirement by attending specialist committees and/or working parties of relevant professional or other competent bodies charged with such work • Actual time may be claimed
Study towards professional qualifications	• Study towards professional qualifications relevant to the basic or special CPE requirement • Actual time spent in study may be claimed
Setting, marking or moderation of examinations in professional qualifications	• Setting, marking or moderation in professional qualifications relevant to the basic or special CPE requirement • Actual time may be claimed

Schedule 2

Notaries (Continuing Professional Education) Regulations 2010
CPE Training Record

A copy of this form is to be submitted with your application for a practicing certificate
The original is to be retained for a period of at least six years

Name:...

CPE year: ....

Declaration (to be completed when submitting a copy of this form to the Registrar)
I practise in the following areas *as a notary*: probate activity / conveyancing (delete as inapplicable)
The information in this CPE record is faithful and accurate to the best of my knowledge and belief

Signature of notary: Date:

Date attended	Name of CPE activity and provider	Please indicate whether activity was accredited or non-accredited	Number of credit points awarded	Comments
Notarial Practice				

98

	Date attended	Name of CPE activity and provider	Please indicate whether activity was accredited or non-accredited	Number of credit points awarded	Comments
Probate Activity					
Conveyancing					

NB. You may continue on separate sheets in necessary, affixing the loose papers to this form

CHARLES GEORGE

MASTER
21st April 2010

NOTARIES (SUPERVISION FEES) REGULATIONS 2010

FACULTY OFFICE

We, CHARLES RICHARD GEORGE, One of Her Majesty's Counsel Commissary or Master of the Faculties of the Lord Archbishop of Canterbury so far as We lawfully can or may do hereby make the following regulation pursuant to the powers contained in Rule 8 of the Notaries (Post-Admission) Rules 2009:-

1.   This Regulation may be cited as the Notaries (Supervision Fees) Regulation 2010 and shall come into operation forthwith.

2.   The Notaries (Supervision Fees) Regulation 2009 dated 29th June 2009 is hereby revoked.

3.   The fee to be charged by a notary agreeing to act as a supervisor under Rule 8 of the Notaries (Post-Admission) Rules 2009, in respect of all visits made under Rule 5 (2) and (3), shall not exceed Two Hundred and Fifty Pounds (£250.00) together with reasonable expenses of travel, subsistence and (where necessary) accommodation together with the amount of any Value Added Tax due thereon

AS witness our hand this 27th day of January 2010

CHARLES GEORGE

MASTER

NOTARIES (CONDUCT AND DISCIPLINE) RULES 2009

WE SHEILA MORAG CLARK CAMERON One of Her Majesty's Counsel Commissary or Master of the Faculties of the Most Reverend Father in God Rowan Douglas by Divine Providence Lord Archbishop of Canterbury Primate of All England and Metropolitan in exercise of the powers conferred by section 4 of the Public Notaries Act 1843 and section 57 of the Courts and Legal Services Act 1990 and of all other powers Us enabling hereby make the following Rules:

PART I: PRELIMINARY

1. **Citation and Commencement**

1.1 These rules may be cited as the Notaries (Conduct and Discipline) Rules 2009

1.2 The rules come into force on the 20th day of March 2009

2. **Interpretation**

2.1 In these rules:-

'1993 Rules' means the Public Notaries (Conduct and Discipline) Rules 1993

'Approved Procedure' means a complaints resolution procedure approved under rule 3 of these rules or rule 3 of the 1993 Rules.

'Commissary' and **Deputy Commissary'** have the meanings assigned by the Notarial Appeals and Hearings Rules 2000.

'Competent Complainant' means:-

(i) A Nominated Notary.

(ii) The Incorporated Company of Scriveners or a member of that Company nominated by it, or:

(iii) Any person who has been a client of the notary in question where the complaint relates to Notarial Misconduct arising from notarial acts or other professional services performed by the notary for that client.

'The Court' means the Court of Faculties.

'The Contingency Fund' means the fund referred to in the Notarial Contingency Fund Rules 1981.

'Designated Society' means the Incorporated Company of Scriveners, the Notaries Society, the Society of Scrivener Notaries and such other bodies as the Master may from time to time designate for the purposes of these rules.

'The Master' means the Master of the Faculties.

'Nominated Notary' means a notary appointed by the Registrar under rule 4 of these rules.

'Notarial Misconduct' means:-
(i)   Fraudulent conduct,
(ii)   Practising as a notary public without a valid Practising Certificate or in breach of a condition or limitation imposed on a Practising Certificate, or
(iii)   Other serious conduct which may include falling seriously below the standard of service reasonably to be expected of a public notary.

'Panel' means not less than four notaries each of whom either holds or has held a Notarial Practising Certificate for a minimum of ten years.

'The Registrar' means the Registrar of the Court of Faculties.

'Scrivener Notary' means a notary who holds the qualifications to practise as a scrivener notary from time to time prescribed by the Incorporated Company of Scriveners of London or who did hold such qualifications before being struck off the Roll of Notaries or suspended from practice by an order of the Court.

'Specified Profession' and **'Relevant Body'** have the meanings specified in rule 10.

'The First Schedule', **'the Second Schedule'** and **'the Appendix'** mean respectively the First Schedule, the Second Schedule and the Appendix to these rules.

2.2   References in these rules to a "notary" are references to a notary enrolled on the Roll of Notaries maintained by the Court.

2.3   The Interpretation Act 1978 applies to these rules as it applies to an Act of Parliament.

PART II: COMPLAINTS

3.   Complaints Resolution Procedures
3.1   The Master may from time to time approve by written notice a complaints resolution procedure produced by a Designated Society and may at any time by written notice withdraw approval of any procedure.

3.2   An Approved Procedure may include provision:-
3.2.1   for the informal resolution of disputes between members of the public and notaries concerning notarial acts done by a notary or the conduct of a notary's practice,

3.2.2　for the informal resolution of disputes between members of the public and notaries concerning the charges made by notaries for notarial services,

3.2.3　for dealing with complaints about the conduct or practice of a notary referred to a Designated Society by the Registrar or the Law Society and for such other matters as the Master may from time to time specify.

3.3　Where a dispute with or complaint against a notary is referred by the Registrar to a Designated Society to be dealt with in accordance with an Approved Procedure it shall be a duty of the notary to cooperate with the Designated Society in the operation of the procedure.

3.4　An Approved Procedure shall not include provision for the resolution of complaints of Notarial Misconduct made against a notary.

4.　Nominated Notaries
A Nominated Notary appointed by the Registrar under these rules shall be a notary (but not a Scrivener Notary) who holds a Notarial Practising Certificate and has held such a Certificate for not less than five years.

5.　Functions of Nominated Notaries
5.1　A Nominated Notary may be appointed by the Registrar to investigate an allegation of Notarial Misconduct referred to him by the Registrar and, if he thinks fit, to prepare and prosecute disciplinary proceedings against a notary in the Court in accordance with the provisions of these rules and to carry out such other functions as may be provided in these rules.

5.2　A Nominated Notary appointed under this rule shall be independent of and not personally acquainted with the notary who is the subject of the allegations of Notarial Misconduct to be investigated.

5.3　If the Registrar is unable to identify a Nominated Notary who fulfils the requirements in Rule 5.2 the Master shall appoint an independent person, who may or may not be a notary, to act in place of a Nominated Notary for the purposes of Rule 5.1, and that person shall carry out all functions conferred on a Nominated Notary by these rules.

5.4　Where a Nominated Notary investigates an allegation of Notarial Misconduct referred to him by the Registrar but such investigation does not lead to the issue of disciplinary proceedings in the Court the Nominated Notary shall be entitled to be paid such fixed fee as may have been previously authorised by the Registrar or such fee as the Registrar may determine should be paid for work properly done after considering a bill and other representations submitted by the Nominated Notary and such fee shall be paid by the Registrar out of the Contingency Fund.

6. **Referral of Allegations by Registrar**

6.1 Where the Registrar receives an allegation concerning the conduct or practice of a notary which in his opinion does not amount to an allegation of Notarial Misconduct or where the precise nature of the allegation is unclear he shall refer the matter to a Designated Society to be dealt with in accordance with an Approved Procedure.

6.2 Where the Registrar receives an allegation concerning the conduct or practice of a notary (other than a Scrivener Notary) which appears to him to amount to an allegation of Notarial Misconduct he shall appoint a Nominated Notary to investigate the allegation pursuant to rule 5 of these rules.

6.3 Where the Registrar receives an allegation concerning the conduct or practice of a Scrivener Notary which appears to him to amount to an allegation of Notarial Misconduct he shall refer the allegation to the Incorporated Company of Scriveners.

6.4 Upon the referral of such an allegation to the Incorporated Company of Scriveners it shall be investigated by the Incorporated Company under arrangements made by it and approved by the Master and if it thinks fit the Incorporated Company or a member of the Company nominated by it shall prepare and prosecute disciplinary proceedings in the Court against the Scrivener Notary in question in accordance with the provisions of these rules and the Incorporated Company or the member so nominated shall be regarded as a Nominated Notary for the purposes of rule 9.5 of these rules.

6.5 Where the Registrar received an allegation concerning the conduct or practice of a notary which in his opinion does not amount to an allegation of Notarial Misconduct or where the precise nature of the allegation is unclear and the notary concerned is not a member of a Designated Society the Registrar shall refer the matter to two members drawn from the Panel to deal with the matter in accordance with an Approved Procedure.

7. **Referral of Allegations by Designated Societies**

Where an allegation against a notary comes to the attention of a Designated Society (whether or not in the course of the operation of an Approved Procedure) and it appears that such allegation amounts to an allegation of Notarial Misconduct the Designated Society shall refer the allegation to the Registrar for consideration in accordance with rule 6 of these rules.

PART III: DISCIPLINARY PROCEDURE

8. Disciplinary Proceedings in the Court of Faculties

8.1 A complaint of Notarial Misconduct may be made to the Court by any Competent Complainant.

8.2 Where:

8.2.1 An allegation concerning the conduct or practice of a notary has been received by the Registrar and he has not appointed a Nominated Notary to investigate the allegation or referred the allegation to the Incorporated Company of Scriveners (as the case may be) under rule 6.2 or rule 6.3 of these rules within 28 days of receiving the allegation, or

8.2.2 The Registrar has appointed a Nominated Notary or referred the allegation to the Incorporated Company of Scriveners and the Nominated Notary or the Incorporated Company has determined not to make a complaint of Notarial Misconduct to the Court in respect of the allegation or has not so made a complaint within 112 days of his appointment or the referral of the allegation (as the case may be);

then a complaint of Notarial Misconduct in respect of that allegation may be made to the Court by any notary who holds a Notarial Practising Certificate and such notary shall be deemed to be a Competent Complainant for the purposes of these rules.

8.3 Where a complaint against a notary has been made to the Court under rule 8.1 and the notary has been struck off or suspended from legal practice by a Relevant Body following a finding of misconduct the Court may of its own volition, or on the application of the complainant, suspend the notary from practice or make an order restricting or limiting or imposing conditions on the notary's practice pending the determination of the complaint, provided that the Court first considers any representations which the notary wishes to make about any such suspension or order.

8.4 The procedure set out in Part II of the First Schedule shall apply to all complaints of Notarial Misconduct made to the Court.

8.5 The forms set out in the Appendix with such variations or additions thereto as the Master may from time to time approve shall be used in all proceedings before the Court to which these rules relate.

9. Disciplinary Sanctions

9.1 Where the Court after hearing a complaint of Notarial Misconduct against a notary finds that it has been proved it may:

9.1.1 Order that the notary be struck off the Roll of Notaries,

9.1.2 Order that the notary be suspended from practice as a notary for a specified period or until certain conditions have been met or indefinitely,

9.1.3   Impose conditions as to the future scope or conduct of the notarial practice of the notary or conditions relating to the monitoring or supervision of his practice and direct that his Practising Certificate be endorsed or the endorsement on his Solicitor's Practising Certificate be marked accordingly,

9.1.4   Impose conditions as to the training that the notary must complete or further examination or examinations that he must pass before he may continue or resume practice as a notary, or

9.1.5   Order that the notary be admonished.

9.2   In addition to imposing any of the penalties listed in sub-rule 9.1 above the Court may order that unless the notary:-

9.2.1   Indemnifies any client of the notary whom the Court finds to have suffered actual loss as a result of the Notarial Misconduct in questions and;

9.2.2   Pays a monetary sum not exceeding £1,500 (or such higher sum as the Master may from time to time specify for the purpose of these rules) such sum to be paid to whomsoever the Court may direct the notary shall be struck off the Roll of Notaries.

9.3   Subject to rule 9.5 it shall be within the discretion of the Court to order:

9.3.1   That the costs of either party to the complaint be paid by the other party,

9.3.2   That the costs of the Court be paid by either party or by both parties (whether in equal or unequal shares),

9.3.3   That the costs of either party or of the court shall be paid from the Contingency Fund, and;

9.3.4   That a party against whom an order for Costs is made shall, instead of paying those costs to the other party or the Court, pay them into the Contingency Fund.

9.4   Any order for costs may be in a fixed sum assessed by the Court as representing or being a contribution towards the reasonable costs of the party concerned or may be for costs to be taxed.

9.5   The Court shall not make any order for costs against a Nominated Notary who shall in all cases be entitled to an order for costs in his favour such costs to be paid from the Contingency Fund.

9.6   Where an order is made for costs to be taxed the costs shall be taxed by the Registrar on such basis and in accordance with such scale applicable in the High Court or the County Court as the Court may direct.

10. Specified Professions and Relevant Bodies

10.1 For the purposes of these rules a 'Specified Profession' means a profession specified in the Second Schedule and in respect of a Specified Profession 'Relevant Body' means the disciplinary body named for that profession in the Second Schedule.

10.2 The Master may by order add to or amend the Second Schedule.

10.3 It shall be the duty of any notary who is also a member of a Specified Profession against whom a complaint has been made to the Relevant Body and found by that body to be substantiated to report such finding forthwith to the Registrar (whatever penalty is imposed by the Relevant Body).

10.4 Where it comes to the attention of the Registrar that a Relevant Body or the members of the Panel under rule 6.5 have found a complaint against a notary (other than a Scrivener Notary) to be substantiated, the Registrar shall appoint a Nominated Notary to investigate the matter and if he thinks fit to prepare and prosecute disciplinary proceedings as if he were acting under rule 5.

10.5 Where it comes to the attention of the Registrar that a Relevant Body has found a complaint against a Scrivener Notary to be substantiated, the Registrar shall refer the matter to the Incorporated Company of Scriveners for investigation in accordance with rule 6.4.

10.6 In proceedings under these rules the written decision of a Relevant Body shall be evidence of the facts stated in that decision.

11. Application for Review

11.1 Where as a result of an Order made under these rules or the 1993 Rules a notary:

    11.1.1 Has been struck off the Roll of Notaries other than pursuant to proceedings under rule 10 of the 1993 Rules and a period of not less than twelve months has elapsed since the date of striking off,

    11.1.2 has been suspended from practice for a period exceeding twelve months or for an indefinite period and a period of not less than twelve months has elapsed since the date of the suspension,

    11.1.3 has had conditions imposed as to the future scope or conduct of his notarial practice, or conditions relating to the monitoring or supervision of his practice, or

    11.1.4 has been struck off the Roll of Notaries pursuant to proceedings under rule 10 of the 1993 Rules and has since been restored to the Roll of Solicitors;

    the notary may apply to the Court to review the Order.

11.2 In the case of an application under rule 11.1.1, rule 11.1.2 or rule 11.1.4 above it shall be for the notary to prove to the satisfaction of the Court that circumstances have changed since the Order was made and that it is not contrary to the public interest or the interest of the notarial profession that the order be reviewed and, in the case of a petition under rule 11.1.3, it shall be for the notary to prove to the satisfaction of the Court that as a result of a change in circumstances the conditions imposed are no longer necessary or desirable in the public interest.

11.3 The procedure set out in Part III of the First Schedule shall apply to an application brought under this rule.

11.4 On receiving an application brought under this rule by a notary other than a Scrivener Notary the Registrar shall appoint a Nominated Notary to act as respondent to the application and on receiving an application brought under this rule by a Scrivener Notary the Registrar shall appoint the Incorporated Company of Scriveners to act as respondent to the application.

11.5 Except in exceptional circumstances the costs of the respondent to an application brought under this rule and of the Court shall be paid by the applicant in any event; but in all other respects the provisions of rule 9.3 shall apply mutatis mutandis.

11.6 Upon hearing an application brought under this rule the Court may:
11.6.1 In the case of an application under rule 11.1.1 or 11.1.4 order that the notary be restored to the Roll of Notaries either immediately or on some specified future date;
11.6.2 In the case of an application under rule 11.1.2 order that the suspension be lifted either immediately or on some specified future date;
11.6.3 In the case of an application under rule 11.1.3 order that the conditions imposed be lifted or that different conditions be imposed;
11.6.4 Impose such conditions upon any order or require such undertakings to be given by the petitioner as it thinks fit, or
11.6.5 dismiss the application.

12. First Schedule and Appendix
12.1 The provisions of Part I of the First Schedule shall apply to all proceedings under these rules.

12.2 It shall be within the discretion of the Registrar to grant to a party to proceedings before the Court such extension to any of the time limits contained in the First Schedule as appears to him to be reasonable.

12.3 Forms 3, 5, 6, and 8 set out in the Appendix shall be issued by the Registrar under the seal of the Court but any omission to affix the seal of the Court shall not invalidate a form or any proceedings to which it relates.

13. Revocation, Savings and Consequential Amendments

13.1 Subject to rule 13.2 the 1993 Rules are hereby revoked.

13.2 Where any proceedings before the Court had been commenced under the 1993 Rules prior to the coming into force of these rules the 1993 Rules shall continue to have effect in respect of those proceedings.

13.3 In rule 3.3 of the Notaries (Prevention of Money Laundering) Rules 2007 "Public Notaries (Conduct and Discipline) Rules 1993" is omitted and "Notaries (Conduct and Discipline) Rules 2009" substituted therefor.

THE FIRST SCHEDULE

PART I: PRELIMINARY

1. References in this Schedule to forms are to the forms set out in the Appendix, references in Part II to the complainant and the respondent are to the person bringing a complaint and the notary against whom a complaint is brought respectively and references in Part III to the applicant and the respondent are to the notary applying for review and the person or body appointed to act as respondent to the application respectively.

2. Any notice or document required by this Schedule to be delivered to the Registrar shall be delivered to him at the Court of Faculties, 1 The Sanctuary, Westminster, London SW1P 3JT and shall be deemed to be delivered on the day on which it is actually received by the Registrar.

3. Any notice or document required by this Schedule to be served by the Registrar may be served by sending it by ordinary first class post or document exchange to such address as may have been specified by the party concerned as his address for service or if no such address has been specified for a notary to the address appearing for him on the Roll of Notaries, and any notice or document so sent shall be deemed to have been served on the second working day after dispatch by post or document exchange.

4. The hearing of a complaint or application under these rules shall take place at such venue as the Commissary may direct and each party shall be entitled to be present and to be represented by a notary, a solicitor or counsel.

PART II: PROCEEDINGS UNDER RULE 8

1.   A complaint of Notarial Misconduct shall be made by a written complaint in form 1 and shall be supported by an affidavit in form 2.

2.   The written complaint and affidavit in support shall be delivered to the Registrar.

3.   On receiving a written complaint and affidavit in support the Registrar shall issue the complaint and serve a copy of each document together with notice of proceedings in form 3 on the respondent.

4.   Within twenty-one days of service of the notice of proceedings on him the respondent shall deliver to the Registrar an answer to the complaint in form 4 and on receipt of an answer the Registrar shall serve a copy on the complainant.

5.   Within forty-two days of service of the notice of proceedings on him the respondent shall, if he intends to contest the proceedings, deliver to the Registrar an affidavit in reply to the complaint and on receipt of such affidavit the Registrar shall send a copy to the complainant.

6.   If the respondent fails to deliver an answer within the time prescribed by paragraph 4 the Registrar shall appoint a date for the hearing of the complaint and give notice to both parties in form 5.

7.   If the respondent delivers an answer within the time prescribed the Registrar shall refer the papers to the Commissary who shall make such directions for the future conduct of the complaint as he thinks fit including directions:-

7.1   For the filing and service of further evidence including the affidavit evidence of witnesses.
7.2   For the preparation and disclosure of lists of documents and for the inspection of such documents.
7.3   For a preliminary hearing to consider any point of law or procedure which may be raised by the proceedings or to consider the making of further directions.
7.4   For the hearing of the complaint and the attendance of witnesses at the hearing and the Registrar shall serve a copy of the Commissary's directions and notice of any hearing (which shall be in form 5) on each party.

8.1   If a party to the complaint requires the deponent to any affidavit filed to attend at the hearing of the complaint he shall give notice to the Registrar and to the other party not less than fourteen days before the date appointed for the hearing.
8.2   If a deponent who has been so required to attend the hearing does not attend the onus shall be on the party seeking to rely on the affidavit

110

evidence of that witness to show why the affidavit should be accepted in evidence.

9.1 The procedure adopted at the hearing shall take such form as the Court thinks fit in all the circumstances of the case but shall ensure that both parties are given an opportunity to state their case to the Court and to cross-examine any witnesses giving evidence in person at the hearing.

9.2 Subject to the provisions of paragraph 8 the complaint shall be decided on the basis of the affidavits filed.

9.3 At any time prior to the conclusion of a hearing the Court may, if it thinks it expedient to do so, adjourn the hearing and give such further directions as it thinks fit.

10. After hearing the complaint the Court may give its decision at the hearing or reserve judgment and the Registrar shall give notice to the parties of the Court's Order in form 6.

11.1 If the complainant wishes to apply to the Court for an order suspending the respondent from practice or restricting or limiting or imposing conditions on the respondent's practice pending the determination of the complaint he shall make the application in form 7, and shall lodge an affidavit in support of the application.

11.2 Subject to paragraph 11.8, on receiving an application in form 7 and affidavit in support the Registrar shall serve a copy of each document on the respondent and appoint a date for the hearing of the application (which shall be not less than ten days after the date on which the documents are served on the respondent) and shall give notice to the parties in form 8.

11.3 If the respondent wishes to oppose the application he shall, within fourteen days of its service upon him, deliver to the Registrar an affidavit in response and the Registrar shall serve a copy of the response on the complainant.

11.4 When the application has been determined by the Court the Registrar shall give notice to the parties of the Court's order in form 6.

11.5 Unless the Court orders otherwise the costs of the parties to the application shall be reserved to the hearing of the substantive complaint.

11.6 An application under this paragraph shall be heard by the Commissary or a Deputy Commissary alone and when the application has been heard by the Commissary or a Deputy Commissary the Commissary or (as the case may be) the Deputy Commissary in question shall not sit on the hearing of the substantive complaint.

11.7 At the hearing of an application under this paragraph the Court may, if it considers it appropriate to do so, give directions under paragraph 7 for the hearing of the substantive complaint.

11.8 Where it appears to him to be necessary for the protection of the public the Commissary or Deputy Commissary to whom an application under this paragraph is referred may direct such modifications to the procedure as he thinks fit including the making of an interim order to suspend the respondent from practice or restrict or limit or impose conditions on the respondent's practice pending the hearing of the application pursuant to paragraph 11.2.

PART III: APPLICATION FOR REVIEW UNDER RULE 11

1.   An application under rule 11 of these rules shall be made in form 9 and shall be accompanied by an affidavit or affidavits setting out in full the grounds of the application and the evidence in support.

2.   Upon receiving an application and affidavits in support the Registrar shall issue the application and serve a copy of each document on the Nominated Notary (or, as the case may be, the Incorporated Company of Scriveners) appointed as respondent under rule 11.4 and the Registrar shall also serve on both parties notice of hearing of the application in form 10.

3.   Where the Order which the applicant is seeking to review was made as a result of a complaint brought by a person who was a Competent Complainant as a person who had been a client of the notary the Registrar shall also send copies of the above documents and notice and any affidavit delivered under paragraph 4 to the complainant who shall be entitled to attend the hearing and (if the Court so permits) to address the Court.

4.   The function of the respondent shall be to ensure that the applicant is put to proof of his case and to bring to the attention of the Court all such facts and matters as the respondent thinks should be before the Court and if the respondent wishes to present to the court an affidavit or affidavits in reply to the application he shall deliver the same to the Registrar not less than twenty-eight days before the date of the hearing and the Registrar shall forthwith serve copies on the applicant.

5.   At the hearing the Court shall consider all documents and evidence which were before the Court before making the order which the applicant is seeking to review and shall consider the affidavits filed in support of and any affidavits filed in answer to the application and the applicant may give evidence in person. The Court shall also consider representations made to it by the parties.

6.   After hearing the petition the Court may give its decision at the hearing or reserve judgment and the Registrar shall give notice to the parties of the Court's Order in form 6.

THE SECOND SCHEDULE

Specified Profession	Relevant Body
Solicitor of the Supreme Court of England and Wales	The Solicitors' Disciplinary Tribunal
Barrister in England and Wales	A Panel or Disciplinary Tribunal operated by the Bar Standards Board
Legal Executive	The Investigating Committee or the Disciplinary Tribunal of the Institute of Legal Executives
Licensed Conveyancer	The Investigating Committee established under section 24 of the Administration of Justice Act 1985 or the Discipline and Appeals Committee established under section 25(1) of that Act
Avocat or other legal practitioner in a country outside England and Wales	The body responsible for exercising disciplinary regulation over the avocat or other legal practitioner in the country in question

APPENDIX

Form 1: Written Complaint
IN THE COURT OF FACULTIES
In the Matter of [AB] a notary and
In the matter of the Notaries (Conduct and Discipline) Rules 2009
To the Registrar
I, the undersigned [CD] of [address] do hereby make complaint that the said [AB] of [address] has been guilty of Notarial Misconduct within the meaning of the said rules in that he/she has …(insert summary of allegation(s) of misconduct).
Details of my complaint are contained in the affidavit which accompanies this written complaint.
DATED this …………. day of ………….. 200..
Signed
Address for service

Form 2: Affidavit in support of Written Complaint
IN THE COURT OF FACULTIES
In the matter of [AB] a notary and
In the matter of the Notaries (Conduct and Discipline) Rules 2009
I [CD] of [address] make oath and say as follows:-
1. I am a Competent Complainant within the meaning of the said rules as [specify how the deponent is a Competent Complainant].
2. I make this affidavit in support of my written complaint against the above named [AB] a notary of [address]
3. [Here state the facts concisely in numbered paragraphs and show the complainant's means of knowledge.]

Form 3: Notice of Proceedings

IN THE COURT OF FACULTIES
In the matter of [AB] a notary and
In the matter of the Notaries (Conduct and Discipline) Rules 2009
TO: [AB] a notary of [address]
TAKE NOTICE that a written complaint has been received by the Court alleging that you have been guilty of Notarial Misconduct. A copy of the complaint and the affidavit supporting it are attached to this notice.
You are required:-
1. Within twenty-one days of service of this notice upon you to deliver to me an answer to the complaint in the form prescribed by the above rules, and
2. If you intend to contest these proceedings, to deliver to me within forty-two days of service of this notice upon you an affidavit in reply to the complaint.
If you fail to comply with these requirements I will proceed to appoint a date for the hearing of the complaint.
All communications should be addressed to "The Registrar, The Court of Faculties, 1 The Sanctuary, Westminster, London SW1P 3JT".
DATED this ……… day of ……………… 200..

Form 4: Answer to Complaint

IN THE COURT OF FACULTIES

In the matter of [AB] a notary and

In the matter of the Notaries (Conduct and Discipline) Rules 2009

To the Registrar

I, [AB] in answer to the complaint of [CD], say that:-

1.   I intend to contest the complaint OR I do not intend to contest the complaint [and I consent to being struck off the Roll of Notaries] [delete as applicable]

2.   My address for service is

DATED this .... day of .... 200..

Form 5: Notice of Hearing

IN THE COURT OF FACULTIES

In the matter of [AB] a notary and

In the matter of the Notaries (Conduct and Discipline) Rules 2009

To the above named respondent [AB] of [address] and to the complainant [CD] of [address]

TAKE NOTICE that this complaint will be heard by the Court on ....

day   the   .... day of .... at [time of day] at .... when you are required to attend.

If you do not attend the hearing may proceed in your absence.

DATED this .... day of .... 200..

Signed

Registrar

Form 6: Order

IN THE COURT OF FACULTIES

In the matter of [AB] a notary and

In the matter of the Notaries (Conduct and Discipline) Rules 2009

To the above named [respondent/petitioner] [AB] of [address] and to the [complainant/respondent] [CD] of [address]

The Court having heard this [complaint] [application] on the .... day of .... 200..

THE COURT ORDERS as follows:-

DATED this .... day of .... 200..

Signed

Registrar

Form 7: Application for Suspension etc pending determination of Complaint

IN THE COURT OF FACULTIES

In the Matter of [AB] a notary and

In the matter of the Notaries (Conduct and Discipline) Rules 2009

To the Registrar

I, the undersigned complainant [CD] of [address] apply to the Court for an order that pending the determination of this complaint [the said respondent [AB] of [address] be suspended from practice as a notary] *OR* [the practice of the said respondent [AB] of [address] be restricted or limited as follows: *[specify restrictions or limitations*] *OR* [the following conditions be imposed on the practice of the said respondent [AB] of [address]: [*specify conditions*]]

The grounds of this application are contained in the accompanying affidavit.

DATED this .... day of .... 200..

Signed

Address for service

Form 8: Notice of Hearing of Application

IN THE COURT OF FACULTIES

In the matter of [AB] a notary and

In the matter of the Notaries (Conduct and Discipline) Rules 2009

To the above named respondent [AB] of [address] and to the complainant [CD] of [address]

TAKE NOTICE that the complainant's application that the respondent be suspended from practice as a notary or that the practice of the respondent be restricted or limited or that conditions be imposed on the practice of the respondent will be heard by the Court on .... day the .... day of .... at [time of day] at .... when you are required to attend.

The Court may also give directions for the hearing of the substantive complaint.

If you do not attend the hearing may proceed in your absence.

DATED this .... day of .... 200..

Signed

Registrar

Form 9: Application under Rule 11

IN THE COURT OF FACULTIES

In the matter of [AB] a notary and

In the matter of the Notaries (Conduct and Discipline) Rules 2009

To the Registrar

I [AB] of [address for service] apply to the Court as follows:-

1.   By an Order of the Court made on [date] it was ordered that [set out the terms of the Order other than terms as to costs]

2.   I now apply that the said Order be reviewed pursuant to rule 11 of the said rules.

3.   The grounds of this application and the evidence in support of it are fully set out in the accompanying affidavit[s]

DATED this .... day of .... 200..

Signed

Petitioner

Form 10: Notice of Hearing of Petition under Rule 11

IN THE COURT OF FACULTIES

In the matter of [AB] a notary and

In the matter of the Notaries (Conduct and Discipline) Rules 2009

To the above named applicant [AB] of [address] and to [CD] of [address] appointed to act as respondent to this application.

TAKE NOTICE that this application will be heard by the Court on .... day the .... day of .... 200.. at [time of day] at

.... when you are required to attend. If you do not attend the hearing may proceed in your absence.
DATED this .... day of .... 200..
Signed
Registrar

MASTER

NOTARIES (POST-ADMISSION) RULES 2009
(As amended by Order of the Master dated the second day of February 2012

We, CHARLES RICHARD GEORGE One of Her Majesty's Counsel, Commissary or Master of the Faculties of the Most Reverend Father in God Rowan Douglas by Divine Providence Lord Archbishop of Canterbury Primate of All England and Metropolitan in exercise of the powers conferred by section 57 of the Courts and Legal Services Act 1990 and of all other powers Us enabling hereby make the following rules:

Citation and Commencement
1.   These rules may be cited as the Notaries (Post-Admission) Rules 2009, and shall come into force on the 20th day of March 2009.

1A.   Paragraphs 3A, 3B, 3C, 3D and 3E of Rule 3 paragraphs 1A, 1B, 1C 1D and 1E of Rule 4 and paragraphs 2(c) and 3(c) of Rule 5 shall come into force on the second day of February 2012.

Interpretation
2.   In these Rules
        '1991 Rules' means the Notaries (Post-Admission) Rules 1991 as amended by the Notaries (Qualification) Rules 1998;

        'The Faculty Office' means the Registry of the Court of Faculties;

        'The Master' means the Master of the Faculties;

        'The Registrar' means the Registrar of the Court of Faculties.

Period of practice under supervision
3.   (1)   This Rule shall apply to all notaries admitted to practise in England and Wales (other than notaries for ecclesiastical purposes only) on or after 13th day of June 1990

        (2)   A notary to whom this Rule applies shall be required to complete a period of practice under supervision in accordance with these Rules which shall commence
                (a)   in the case of a notary admitted after the date on which this Rule comes into effect, or of a notary admitted before that date but not in practice on that date, on the date on which he commences or resumes practice as a notary; or
                (b)   in any other case, as soon as arrangements for supervision can practicably be made, but not in any event later than two months after this Rule comes into effect.

        (3)   Subject to paragraph (4) of this Rule, the duration of the period of practice under supervision shall be two years, less either of the following:
                (a)   any period of apprenticeship served pursuant to section 2 of

the Public Notaries Act 1801 or pursuant to requirements of the Incorporated Company of Scriveners of London imposed under Section 57(11)(b) of the Courts and Legal Services Act 1990;

(b) any period spent in actual practice as a notary, prior to the coming into effect of these Rules, by a district notary appointed pursuant to the Public Notaries Act 1833.

(3A) A notary admitted to practise after 2 February 2012 who carries out conveyancing in his capacity as a notary shall be required to complete a period of practice under supervision of three years commencing no later than the first date that instructions for conveyancing are accepted by the notary in his capacity as a notary.

(3B) A notary admitted to practise after 2 February 2012 who carries out probate in his capacity as a notary shall be required to complete a period of practice under supervision of three years commencing no later than the first date that instructions for probate are accepted by the notary in his capacity as a notary.

(3C) Paragraph 3A of this Rule shall not apply to a notary who is a member of a professional partnership as defined in Rule 2 of the Notaries Practice Rules 2009 or who is an employee of that partnership where at least one other member of that professional practice also carries out conveyancing whether as a notary or by otherwise being entitled.

(3D) Paragraph 3B of this Rule shall not apply to a notary who is a member of a professional partnership as defined in Rule 2 of the Notaries Practice Rules 2009 or who is an employee of that partnership where at least one other member of that professional practice also carries out probate whether as a notary or by otherwise being entitled.

(3E) If a notary has already completed a period of supervision under this Rule but that supervision did not comply with Rules 3A-3D (additional supervision for notaries carrying out conveyancing and probate) and wishes to accept instructions to carry out conveyancing or probate in his capacity as a notary he shall apply to the Master to set a period of supervision of three years or less relating solely to conveyancing or probate or both.

(4) The Master may direct that the period of practice under supervision be extended in any particular case, either

(a) as a condition of approving a change of supervisor under paragraph (5) of Rule 4, or

(b)   following his consideration of a report submitted pursuant to paragraph (3) of Rule 7, or

(c)   following disciplinary proceedings.

Selection of supervisor

4.   (1)   During the period of practice under supervision the notary to whom this Rule applies ("the supervised notary") shall practise as a notary only under the supervision (as defined in Rule 5) of another notary ("the supervisor") who holds a current practising certificate entered in or issued from the Court of Faculties, and who has been engaged in actual practice as a notary for a minimum period of five years from the date of admission as a notary.

(1A)   A notary acting as a supervisor for a notary to which paragraph 3A of Rule 3 applies shall have carried out conveyancing as a substantial part of his practice for the previous five years whether as a notary or by otherwise being entitled.

(1B)   A notary acting as a supervisor for a notary to which paragraph 3B of Rule 3 applies shall have carried out probate as a substantial part of his practice for the previous five years whether as a notary or by otherwise being entitled.

(1C)   For the purposes of paragraphs 1A and 1B of this Rule a notary may have more than one supervisor.

(1D)   A notary requiring supervision to whom either or both paragraphs 3A and 3B of Rule 3 applies may obtain supervision from a solicitor or (in the case of paragraph 3A of Rule 3 only) a licensed conveyancer who has been in practice as such for a minimum period of five years.

(1E)   If for the purposes of paragraphs 1A and 1B of this Rule a notary has more than one supervisor each of those supervisors shall carry out the full extent of supervision required by these rules save that an additional supervisor may restrict his supervision to supervising the conveyancing or probate practice of the notary (or both) for which reason he has been appointed.

(2)   A notary (or solicitor or licensed conveyancer where paragraph 1D of this Rule applies) acting as a supervisor shall be located within a reasonable distance from the office at which the supervised notary proposes to practice so as to enable the supervisor to visit that office from time to time as required by Rule 5(2).

(3)   It shall be the duty of a supervised notary to notify the Faculty Office upon request of the name and address of his supervisor; and it shall be the duty of any notary to notify the Faculty Office upon request of the names and addresses of all notaries of whom he is the supervisor.

(4)   A supervised notary shall, upon the death or retirement from practice of his supervisor, forthwith make arrangements for another notary qualified under this Rule to supervise his practice for the remainder of the required period; and any time between the death or retirement of the former supervisor and the coming into effect of such arrangements shall not count towards the period of supervised practice.

(5)   If for any reason other than the death or retirement of the supervisor, either party wishes the appointment of a particular supervisor to be terminated before the expiry of the required period of supervised practice, application shall be made for that purpose to the Master, who may terminate the supervision upon such conditions as he shall think fit.

Extent of supervision
5.   (1)   The following aspects of a notary's practice shall be excluded from the general requirement of supervision (but not from the obligation to produce records and accounts under paragraph (2) of this Rule):
        (a)   conveyancing and probate, in the case of a notary who is also a solicitor and who would be entitled to carry out conveyancing and probate as a solicitor without supervision, or who does in fact receive such supervision in relation to his practice as a solicitor as is required by the Solicitors Act 1974 and rules made thereunder;
        (b)   conveyancing, in the case of a notary who is also a licensed conveyancer and who would be entitled to carry out conveyancing as such without supervision, or who does in fact receive such supervision in relation to his practice as a licensed conveyancer as is required by the statutes and rules governing that profession.

        (2)   The supervisor shall visit the office of the supervised notary
        (c)   within one month after the supervised notary has been admitted as a notary and has been issued with a practising certificate from the Court of Faculties, and
        (d)   for a second time within twelve months from the date of the visit under subparagraph (a) of this Rule, and
        (e)   in respect of a supervised notary to whom rule 3(A) and/or Rule 3(B) applies for a third time within twelve months from the date of the visit under sub paragraph (b) of this Rule

and shall on each visit inspect the records and accounts of the supervised notary which the supervised notary shall (subject to paragraph (4) of this Rule) produce to the supervisor on request.

(3)   The supervised notary shall visit the office of the supervisor
        (a)   no later than six months after the supervisor's visit required by paragraph (2)(a) of this Rule, and
        (b)   for a second time no later than six months after the supervisor's visit required by paragraph (2)(b) of this Rule, and
        (c)   in respect of a supervised notary to whom rule 3(A) and/or Rule 3(B) applies for a third time no later than six months after the supervisor's visit required by paragraph (2)(c) of this Rule,

and shall (subject to paragraph (4) of this Rule) produce to the supervisor for inspection the records and accounts of the supervised notary relating to the period since the supervisor's last visit to the supervised notary's office.

(4)   If it appears to a supervised notary that papers relating to the business of a particular client cannot be shown to his supervisor without causing a breach of the duty of confidentiality owed to that client (whether on account of a relationship between the client and the supervisor, or because the supervisor is known to act for a person in competition with the client, or for any other reason), he shall inform the supervisor of that fact. The supervisor may nominate another notary (qualified to be a supervisor under Rule 4(1) but not subject to the same objections of confidentiality as respects the client concerned) and the notary nominated shall, if willing to act, have the supervisor's rights and duties in relation to those papers.

(5)   The supervisor shall make himself available at all reasonable times to offer advice and guidance to the supervised notary on matters covered by the supervision and shall make enquiries of the supervised notary at least once in every three months period by e-mail or other means of communication as to the notary's progress and any matter of concern to the supervised notary, and the supervised notary shall within one week of receipt of the supervisor's communication provide the supervisor by e-mail or other means of communication a short report about the notary's progress and shall include any request for advice and guidance as necessary, and both the supervisor and the supervised notary shall keep a record of these communications.

(6)   The supervisor shall take particular care to ensure (so far as he is able) that the supervised notary is aware of, and complies with, all Rules and Orders made by the Master under section 57 of the Courts and Legal Services Act 1990, and conducts himself in a

manner calculated to maintain the reputation of the office and profession of a public notary.

Post-Admission Education

6. Every supervised notary shall, during each year of his period of practice under supervision, attend
    (a) one full day course or seminar approved by the Master covering the topics of Bills of Exchange, Notarial Practice and Professional Conduct;
    (b) if desiring to carry out conveyancing as part of his notarial practice, one full day continuing education course or seminar in conveyancing approved by the Master; and
    (c) if desiring to carry out probate work as part of his notarial practice, one full day continuing education course or seminar in probate approved by the Master;
    and shall make a report to his Supervisor on the course or seminar attended.

Records and reporting

7. (1) A report of every visit and inspection made pursuant to paragraphs (2) and (3) of Rule 5 shall be made by the supervisor, and shall be inserted in the Register or other permanent record kept by each notary pursuant to the Notaries (Records) Rules 1991.

    (2) The supervisor shall enter in the Register or other permanent record kept by him pursuant to the Notaries (Records) Rules 1991 a note of any advice or guidance given to a supervised notary pursuant to paragraph (4) of Rule 5.

    (3) Upon the completion of a period of practice under supervision (or upon the retirement from practice of a supervisor during such a period), the supervisor shall report the fact of such completion to the Master in writing and shall indicate the courses or seminars attended by the supervised notary pursuant to Rule 6, and whether in his opinion the supervised notary shall thereafter be permitted to practise without supervision. The supervisor and the supervised notary shall respond in writing to any questions put by the Master in relation to the period of supervision, and produce to the Faculty Office such documents as the Master may require.

Fees

8. A notary agreeing to act as a supervisor shall be entitled to charge the supervised notary a fee not exceeding the level prescribed from time to time in Regulations made by the Master (which may include provision for expenses), together with the amount of any Value Added Tax due thereon. If for any reason the appointment of the supervisor ceases before the end of the period of supervision, the fee shall be apportioned pro rata or as the Master may direct.

Dispensations

9.   The Master may, upon such application made to him as he deems sufficient, for good cause dispense any notary from the requirement of supervision under these Rules or permit such lesser supervision as he considers practicable in the circumstances of any particular case.

10.   The provisions of these Rules shall not apply to any Notary who, immediately prior to his admission, was recognised by the Master as qualified for admission under the provision of Rule 9 of the Notaries (Qualification) Rules 1998.

Revocation and Savings

11.   (1)   Subject to Rule 11(2) the 1991 Rules are hereby revoked.

       (2)   Where a notary has commenced a period of practice under supervision prior to the coming into force of these Rules the 1991 Rules, as amended, shall continue to have effect in respect of that period of practice under supervision.

DATED this second day of February 2012.

CHARLES GEORGE

MASTER

NOTARIES PRACTICE RULES 2009
(as amended by the Order of the Master of the Faculties
dated 8th April 2011)

WE CHARLES RICHARD GEORGE One of Her Majesty's Counsel Commissary or Master of the Faculties of the Most Reverend Father in God Rowan Douglas by Divine Providence Lord Archbishop of Canterbury Primate of All England and Metropolitan in exercise of the powers conferred by section 4 of the Public Notaries Act 1843 and section 57 of the Courts and Legal Services Act 1990 and of all other powers Us enabling hereby make the following Rules:

PART I: PRELIMINARY

1. **Citation and Commencement**
   1.1 These rules may be cited as the Notaries Practice Rules 2009.

   1.2 These rules shall come into force on 1st December 2009.

   1.2A Rule 5A shall come into force on 1st May 2011.

2. **Interpretation**
   In these rules:-
   "approved regulator" has the meaning given to it in section 20 of the Legal Services Act 2007;

   "arrangement" means any express or tacit agreement between a notary and another person, whether contractually binding or not;

   "client" includes any person who has instructed a notary to carry out a reserved legal activity within the meaning of section 12 of the Legal Services Act 2007 and any person who has placed legitimate reliance on a Notarial Act;

   "firm" includes a sole practitioner and a professional partnership;

   "holding company" and "subsidiary company" have the meanings assigned to them by the Companies Act 2006, and two companies are "associated" where they are subsidiary companies of the same holding company;

   "the Master" means the Master of the Faculties;

   "notarial act" means any act that has validity by virtue only of its preparation, performance, authentication, attestation or verification by a notary, and includes any such act carried out by electronic means;

   "notary" includes a firm of notaries;

   "performance" includes execution, completion and carrying out;

125

"person" includes a body corporate or unincorporated association or group of persons;

"professional partnership" includes a limited liability partnership and any other body corporate, the members of which are authorised to conduct legal practice as such;

"qualified legal practitioner" means
(i)   a person qualified to provide legal services to the public in England and Wales, or
(ii)   a person qualified to provide legal services to the public under the laws of any other jurisdiction who practises as such in England and Wales;

"the Registrar" means the Registrar of the Court of Faculties;

for the purposes of these rules a notary's practice includes the preparation and performance of notarial acts and any other service undertaken as a notary whether or not such service may only be undertaken by a notary; and for the avoidance of doubt the Interpretation Act 1978 applies to these rules as it applies to an Act of Parliament.

PART II: PRACTICE AS A NOTARY

3.   **Oath of Office**
A notary shall exercise the office of public notary in accordance with the Oath or Declaration made by him at the time of the grant of his Notarial Faculty, as set out in section 7 of the Public Notaries Act 1843 and shall offer appropriate notarial services to any person lawfully and reasonably requiring the same.

4.   **Bankruptcy**
A notary who is bankrupt may not, until he is discharged from bankruptcy, practise as a notary on his own behalf or as the sole member of a professional partnership, but may practise as the employee of another notary.

5.   **Obtaining Instructions**
A notary shall not directly or indirectly obtain or attempt to obtain instructions for professional work or permit another person to do so on his behalf, or do anything in the course of practising as a notary, in any manner which compromises or impairs or is likely to compromise or impair any of the following:
5.1   the notary's independence or integrity;
5.2   a person's freedom to instruct a notary of his choice;
5.3   the notary's ability to act in the best interests of the client;
5.4   the good repute of the notary or of the notarial profession;
5.5   the notary's proper standard of work;

5.6   the notary's duty of care to persons in all jurisdictions who may place legitimate reliance on his notarial acts.

5A.   Duty to inform instructing person of right to complain

5A.1   When a notary accepts instructions for professional work or changes the terms on which he is acting he must provide the instructing person with a copy of a form of words prescribed by the Master from time to time which explains that the instructing person has a right to make a complaint under the Conduct and Discipline Rules 2011 and the Legal Services Act 2007 and how to make such a complaint.

5A.2   The form of words prescribed under 5A.1 above (the "prescribed form of words") may be provided to the instructing person electronically.

5A.3   If at the time of this rule coming into force a notary is acting under pre-existing instructions for professional work he must provide the person who instructed him with the prescribed form of words at the next available opportunity.

6.   Conflicts of Interest

6.1   Conflicts of Interest (General)
        In the conduct of his practice a notary shall not favour the interests of one client over those of another and shall not favour his own interests or those of any other person over those of his clients.

6.2   Conflicts of Interest (Conveyancing Transactions)
        6.2.1   A notary conducting a conveyancing transaction in the capacity of a solicitor, or a licensed conveyancer, or member of another professional body with an approved regulator, is subject to the rules and any guidance relating to (a) conflicts of interest and (b) relations with third parties laid down by the approved regulator of that professional body, and should comply with such rules and have regard to any such guidance accordingly.
        6.2.2   A notary conducting a conveyancing transaction in the capacity of a notary must not act for both seller and buyer in a transaction relating to property situated in England and Wales unless:-
                (a)   The notary, whether or not the transaction is between parties at arm's length, is satisfied that no conflict of interest exists or is likely to arise during the course of the transaction; and
                (b)   Both parties are established clients in that they have instructed the notary on previous occasions; or
                (c)   The consideration does not exceed £10,000 in an individual transaction; and

(d)   Both clients are informed of the advantages of separate representation before they give their written consent to the notary acting for both of them; and

(e)   Both parties consent in writing.

6.3   Relations with third parties

6.3.1 A notary shall not communicate directly by any means whatsoever with any other party to a conveyancing transaction where that party is represented by a lawyer except:-

(a)   to obtain information about the name and address (including e-mail address) of that lawyer; or

(b)   with the consent of that lawyer; or

(c)   after notifying the lawyer of the intention to contact the party direct because the other party's lawyer has refused or without good reason failed to pass on messages or to reply to communications, or

(d)   in exceptional circumstances where it is impracticable to contact that party's lawyer provided that any communication under (a) to (d) of this rule shall be in writing.

6.3.2 A notary who is dealing with any unrepresented party to a conveyancing transaction must not take unfair advantage of that party, and where it is necessary for practical reasons to communicate orally with an unrepresented party the notary should immediately thereafter make a written note of the communication and should as soon as possible confirm the substance of it in writing to the unrepresented party.

6.4   Conflicts of Interest (notarial activities other than conveyancing transactions)

6.4.1 In respect of notarial activities other than conveyancing transactions, a notary may act for both parties to a transaction but only if:

(a)   each party has consented in writing to the notary so acting, and

(b)   the notary is satisfied that there is no conflict of interest between the parties.

6.4.2 For the avoidance of doubt a notary does not act for both parties to a transaction merely by preparing or authenticating a notarial act in his capacity as a public certifying officer even though that act may concern two or more parties.

7.   Duty to Act Impartially in respect of Notarial Acts

A notary must act impartially and in particular must not perform any notarial act which involves or may affect:

7.1   his own affairs, including matters in which he is personally interested jointly with another person;

7.2   the affairs of his spouse or partner or a person to whom the notary is engaged to be married (for the purpose of this sub-rule, "partner" means a person with whom the notary cohabits or with whom he has a sexual relationship and includes a partner of the same sex);

7.3   the affairs of a person to whom he is directly and closely related;

7.4   the affairs of a person with whom he is in a professional partnership or by whom he is employed or from whom he receives a benefit by being provided with office accommodation or other facilities for his notarial practice;

7.5   the affairs of a person who has appointed the notary to be his attorney which concern a matter within the scope of the power of attorney granted;

7.6   the affairs of a trust of which he is a trustee or of an estate where he is a personal representative of the deceased;

7.7   the affairs of a body corporate of whose board of directors or governing body he is a member;

7.8   the affairs of an employee of the notary;

7.9   the affairs of a partnership of which he is a member or of a company in which the notary holds shares either exceeding five percent of the issued share capital or having a market value exceeding such figure as the Master may from time to time specify.

8. Employed Notaries

8.1   Save as permitted by rule 8.2 a notary who is the employee of a non-notary shall not perform any notarial act as part of his employment or do or perform any notarial act for his employer or his employer's holding, associated or subsidiary company.

8.2   A notary may act for a person who is also the client of the qualified legal practitioner or firm of qualified legal practitioners by which he is employed but he shall take all proper and reasonable steps in the exercise of his notarial practice to maintain his independence of his employer and in particular he shall:

8.2.1   ensure that his independence as a notary is fully recognised in writing in any contract of employment entered into by him,

8.2.2   annually send to his employer a written statement of professional independence in a form approved by the Master from time to time, and shall declare in his application for a notarial practising certificate that he has complied with this rule.

9. **Language**

9.1 Notarial acts shall normally be drawn up in the English language.

9.2 A notary may upon request or in appropriate circumstances prepare a notarial act in a language other than English if he has sufficient knowledge of the language concerned.

9.3 A notary may not authenticate by means of a notarial act a document drawn up in a language other than English unless he has satisfied himself as to its meaning but this does not prevent a notary from authenticating the execution or signature of a document in any language.

9.4 A notary may not certify the accuracy of a translation that has been made by someone other than himself unless he has knowledge of the language sufficient to satisfy himself as to the accuracy of the translation but this does not prevent a notary from attesting a translator's affidavit or authenticating a verification.

10. **Undertakings**

10.1 Any notary giving an undertaking, whether oral or in writing, shall be personally liable for that undertaking, and the implementation of any such undertaking is required as a matter of conduct. Save in exceptional cases a failure by a notary to honour an undertaking will constitute notarial misconduct for the purposes of the Public Notaries (Conduct and Discipline) Rules 2011.

10.2 An undertaking given by a notary shall be in writing or confirmed in writing and signed by the notary giving it.

11. **Publicity**

A notary may advertise his practice and seek to obtain directly or indirectly clients and business in any manner and through any medium whether informative or promotional with the exception of unsolicited telephone calls or unsolicited visits to persons or organisations, as long as:

11.1 the client's freedom to instruct a qualified person of the client's choice is not thereby unduly restricted;

11.2 the notary's good reputation for integrity and professional standards of work is not thereby damaged;

11.3 he complies with the UK Code of Non-Broadcast Advertising, Sales Promotion and Direct Marketing, the Independent Broadcasting Authority Code of Advertising Standards and Practice and the Direct Marketing Code of Practice in force from time to time,

but nothing in this Rule shall be construed as authorising the use of the word "notaries" or any word designating or indicating notarial services in any publicity for activities which are not of a notarial nature.

12. **Scrivener Notaries**

No notary shall describe himself professionally as a Scrivener or a Scrivener notary unless he holds the qualifications to practise as a Scrivener notary from time to time prescribed by the Incorporated Company of Scriveners.

13. Introductions and Referrals

When a notary enters into an arrangement with another person for the introduction of clients to the notary or by the notary to the other person he must ensure:

13.1 that the client is informed in writing of the arrangement and of any commission or other benefit the notary may be receiving or pay;

13.2 that he either obtains the client's written agreement as to the destination of the commission or accounts to the client for the commission;

13.3 that he remains able to advise the client independently in accordance with these rules and continues to do so regardless of his own interests.

14. Offering Services other than as a Notary

14.1 Where a notary by himself or with any other person operates, actively participates in or controls any business, other than a notary's practice, the notary shall ensure:

14.1.1 that the name of that business has no substantial element in common with the name of any practice of the notary;

14.1.2 that the words "notary", "notaries," "attorney(s)" or "lawyer(s)" or any words designating or indicating a notarial or legal practice are not used in connection with the notary's involvement with that business;

14.1.3 that any client referred by any practice of the notary to the business is informed in writing that, as a customer of that business, he does not enjoy any protection attaching to the client of a notary, and that where that business shares premises or reception staff with any practice of the notary, every customer of the business is informed in writing that, as a customer of that business, he does not enjoy the protection attaching to the client of a notary.

14.2 Rule 14.1 does not apply to the practice of a qualified legal practitioner.

15. Fees

15.1 A notary may charge a professional fee for all notarial work undertaken by him, and the basis upon which that fee will be calculated or the fee to be charged for the work done, shall be made known in advance to any new instructing person.

15.2 Subject to rule 15.3, a notary shall not share or agree to share his professional fees with any person not entitled to act as a notary; provided that this rule shall not prohibit the payment of any allowance or allowances, sum or sums of money, that are or shall be agreed to be made or paid to the widows or children of any deceased notary or notaries, by any surviving partner or partners of such deceased notary or notaries.

15.3 A notary who also practises as a qualified legal practitioner either in a professional partnership or as an employee may share professional fees with his professional partners or employer who are also so qualified provided that a notary who shares fees by virtue of this paragraph shall keep accounts which enable the income and expenditure arising from his practice as a notary to be distinguished from the income and expenditure arising from his practice or employment as a qualified legal practitioner and shall furnish the Faculty Office with such additional information as to his professional partnership and accounting arrangements or his employment as the case may be as may be prescribed in rules or orders of the Master.

16. Name of a Firm of Notaries

16.1 The name of a firm of notaries shall consist only of:

16.1.1 the name or names of one or more present or former principals together with, if desired, conventional references to the firm and to such persons;

16.1.2 a firm name in use on 1st January 1989;

16.1.3 the name of a firm of qualified legal practitioners of which a notary is a partner; or

16.1.4 one approved in writing by the Master.

16.2 Any notary starting to use an internet domain as a name after the date of commencement of these Rules shall comply with one or more of the requirements in 16.1.1 to 16.1.4 of this rule.

17. Investment Business

17.1 A notary shall not in connection with any regulated activity have any arrangement with another person under which the notary could be constrained to recommend to clients or effect for them (or refrain from so doing) transactions in some investments but not others, with some persons but not others, or through the agency of some persons but not others; or to introduce or refer clients or other persons with whom he deals to some persons but not others, nor shall a notary be an appointed representative.

17.2 Notwithstanding any provision in rule 14 a notary shall not by himself or with any other person set up, operate, actively participate in or control any separate business which is an appointed representative.

17.3 This rule shall have effect in relation to the conduct of regulated activity within or into any part of the United Kingdom.

17.4 In this rule "appointed representative" and "regulated activity" have the meanings assigned to them by the Financial Services and Markets Act 2000.

18. Supervision of a Notary's Office

18.1 A notary shall take reasonable steps to ensure that every office where he practises is and can be seen to be;

    18.1.1 open, save exceptionally and for a good reason, during normal office hours for the provision of appropriate notarial services to members of the public, and

    18.1.2 properly supervised.

In particular a notary shall ensure that he or another notary holding a Practising Certificate shall spend sufficient time at such office to ensure adequate control of the staff employed there and afford requisite facilities for consultation with clients. Such notary may be a principal, employee or consultant of the firm or a locum tenens.

18.2 In determining whether or not there has been compliance with the requirement as to supervision in rule 18.1, account shall be taken of, inter alia, the arrangements for the principals to see or be apprised of incoming communications,

18.3 Where the operation or supervision of a notary's office in accordance with this rule is prevented by illness, accident or other sufficient or unforeseen cause for a prolonged period, suitable alternative arrangements shall be made without delay to ensure compliance.

18.4 In cases where a notary is not in attendance on days when his office is normally open to the public, he shall make adequate arrangements to ensure the provision of notarial services to persons requiring the same.

19. Continuing Professional Education

19.1 After commencing practice and having satisfactorily completed the required period of supervision, a notary shall, within every such successive period as shall be determined by the Master, participate in such programmes, courses or seminars approved by the Master as may be necessary to acquire the number of credit points determined by the Master.

19.2 Upon determination by the Master of the periods and number of credit points, they shall be specified in Guidance published by the Registrar, which shall incorporate such revised determinations as the Master may make from time to time.

20. Duty to Keep Records

20.1 A notary shall keep proper records of his notarial acts in accordance with this rule.

20.2 The records so kept shall be sufficient to identify:

    20.2.1 the date of the act;

20.2.2   the person at whose request the act was performed;

20.2.3   the person or persons, if any, intervening in the act and, in the case of a person who intervened in a representative capacity, the name of his principal;

20.2.4   the method of identification of the party or parties intervening in the notarial act, and in the case of a party intervening in a representative capacity, any evidence produced to the notary of that party's entitlement so to intervene;

20.2.5   the nature of the act;

20.2.6   the fee charged.

20.3   In the case of a notarial act in the public form, the notary shall place an original of the act or a complete photographic copy of the same in a protocol which shall be preserved permanently by the notary.

20.4   Records of acts not in public form kept in accordance with rule 19.2 shall be preserved for a minimum period of twelve years and, for the avoidance of doubt, such preservation may be by means of a suitable digital or other electronic system providing for the storage of documents in an indelible and unalterable format.

20.5   A copy of a notarial act or of the record of a notarial act preserved in accordance with rules 20.3 and 20.4 shall, upon payment of a reasonable fee, be issued upon the application of any person or authority having a proper interest in the act unless prevented by order of a competent court.

20.6   Any question as to whether a person has a proper interest in an act for the purposes of rule 20.5 shall be determined by the Master.

21.   Inspection of Records

Records kept pursuant to rule 20 shall be open at any time to inspection by the Master or a person authorised by him.

22.   Notaries Ceasing to Practise

22.1   When a notary ceases to practise as such, then he, or failing him his continuing notarial partners or the person having possession or custody of the records maintained by him pursuant to rule 20, shall arrange for such records to be transferred:

22.1.1   to another notary in practice appointed by him or by his continuing notarial partners,

22.1.2   to another notary in practice appointed, with the approval of the Master, by the persons having possession or custody of the records, or

22.1.3   to an archive designated for the purpose under regulations made by the Master from time to time,

and the persons making such transfer shall give written particulars to the Registrar of the date of transfer and the person or archive to which the records were transferred.

22.2   The provisions of rules 20 and 21 shall apply to a notary or archive to which the records of any notary are transferred pursuant to this rule as they apply to the notary himself.

23. Application to Ecclesiastical Notaries

The provisions of this Part shall apply to notaries appointed for ecclesiastical purposes only subject to the following modifications:

23.1   The requirement of rule 20 to keep a record of notarial acts shall apply only to such ecclesiastical acts as law or custom requires to be performed in the presence of a public notary and recorded in writing.

23.2   Any act or transaction properly recorded in the Act Book of any Archbishop or Bishop, or in the Minute Book of any Cathedral Chapter, shall be deemed to have been properly recorded in accordance with rule 20.

23.3   Rule 22 shall not apply to ecclesiastical notaries, but upon a person ceasing for any reason to hold the office in respect of which he was appointed an ecclesiastical notary, any records kept by him pursuant to this Part shall be transferred to the succeeding holder of that office (being an ecclesiastical notary) upon his appointment.

PART IV: MISCELLANEOUS

24. Waivers

The Master shall have power to waive any of the provisions of these rules in any particular case or classes of case for the purpose expressed in such waiver, and to revoke such waiver.

25. Repeals and Savings

25.1   Subject to rule 25.2 the Notaries Practice Rules 2001 are hereby revoked.

25.2   Rule 25.1 does not absolve any notary from the duty to comply with the Notaries Practice Rules 2001 prior to the coming into force of these rules and records maintained by a notary in accordance with Rules 20-23 of the Notaries Practice Rules 2001 prior to the coming into force of these rules shall continue to be so maintained by him and rules 20.5, 20.6, 21, 22 and 23 of these rules shall apply to such records.

The Right Worshipful Charles R George, Q.C.
Master

Amended 8th April 2011

NOTARIES PRACTICE RULES 2009
Statement of Professional Independence pursuant to Rule 8.2.2

Explanatory Note

Under Rule 8.2 of the Notaries Practice Rules 2009, a notary may act for a person who is also a client of the qualified legal practitioner or firm of qualified legal practitioners by whom he is employed. In the exercise of his notarial practice he must maintain independence from his employer and he is required, amongst other things, to send annually to his employer a written statement of professional independence in a form approved by the Master from time to time. This applies to assistant solicitors, consultants and those who are employed as "in house" solicitors.

The Master has approved the following form:

<u>Approved Form</u>

Statement of Professional Independence

To [*name of employer*]

My practice as a notary public is regulated by the Notaries Practice Rules 2009. As a notary employed by a qualified legal practitioner, I am able to act as a notary for a person who is also a client of my employer, but I am required under Rule 8.2.2 to send annually to my employer a written statement of professional independence.

This statement is therefore to remind you that in the exercise of my notarial practice I am bound to observe the professional standards and requirements of a notary public, and that in so acting I must maintain my independence of you as my employer and give precedence to my professional duties over my duties to you as your employee.

Signed [*notary*]

Dated

NOTARIES (ADVISORY BOARD) RULES 2008

We, SHEILA MORAG CLARK CAMERON One of Her Majesty's Counsel, Commissary or Master of the Faculties of the Most Reverend Father in God ROWAN DOUGLAS by Divine Providence Lord Archbishop of Canterbury Primate of all England and Metropolitan in exercise of the powers conferred by section 4 of the Public Notaries Act 1843 and section 57 of the Courts and Legal Services Act 1990 and of all other powers Us enabling hereby make the following Rules

1.   Citation and Commencement
         These rules may be cited as the Notaries (Advisory Board) Rules 2008.

1.2   These Rules shall come into force on the 6th day of April 2008.

2.   Interpretation
         In these rules:

         'Public Notaries' includes General and Scrivener Notaries;

         'the Board' means the Advisory Board established under rule 3;

         'the Faculty Office' means the Registry of the Court of Faculties;

         'the Master' means the Master of the Faculties; and

         'the Registrar' means the Registrar of the Court of Faculties.

3.   3.1   There shall be established an Advisory Board constituted in accordance with the Schedule hereto.

         3.2   the functions of the Board shall be to advise the Master and the Registrar on any matter pertaining to the notarial profession in England and Wales and its regulation that may be referred to it
                 (a)   by the Master or the Registrar;
                 (b)   by or on behalf of a body representing notaries in practice in England or Wales; or
                 (c)   by any other body or person provided that the Board considers that the matter to be referred to it is of sufficient general interest to or in connection with the notarial profession to justify its consideration.

         3.3   The Board may consider any matter pertaining to the notarial profession in England and Wales and its regulation notwithstanding that it has not been referred to the Board under rule 3.2.

         3.4   The expenses of the Board and of its members shall be paid from the general notarial income of the Faculty Office.

4.   Rules 3 and 4 of the Notaries (Miscellaneous Provisions) Rules 2002 are hereby revoked.

SCHEDULE

1.   The Board shall consist of six persons appointed by the Master comprising:

    (a)   two Public Notaries in practice and holding a valid practising certificate;

    (b)   the Secretaries of the Notaries Society and of the Society of Scrivener Notaries of London; and

    (c)   two independent persons, not being notaries, one of whom shall be the Chair of the Board

2.   Members of the Board, including the Chair, appointed under paragraph 1 (a) and (c) of this Schedule shall hold office for a period of three years but any member may be removed from office at any time if the Master has reasonable grounds for doing so.

3.   A Member appointed under paragraph 1 (a) or (c) of this Schedule will be eligible for re-appointment for one further period of three years only.

4.   Any member of the Board wishing to resign from office shall do so in writing to the Registrar giving not less than two months notice of the intention to resign.

5.   Where a vacancy arises in the membership of the Board within one of the categories in paragraph 1 (a) or (c) of this Schedule the Master shall as soon as practicable appoint a new member within that category who shall hold office for a period of three years and be eligible for re-appointment as under paragraph 3 of this Schedule.

6.   The Registrar shall act as Clerk to the Board or may appoint or nominate another person to act as Clerk in his place.

7.   The Board shall meet as often as may be necessary and in any event not less than once each year.

DATED this 12th day of March 2008

SHEILA CAMERON

MASTER

NOTARIES (QUALIFICATION) (AMENDMENT) RULES 2008

We, SHEILA MORAG CLARK CAMERON One of Her Majesty's Counsel, Commissary or Master of the Faculties of the Most Reverend Father in God ROWAN DOUGLAS by Divine Providence Lord Archbishop of Canterbury Primate of all England and Metropolitan in exercise of the powers conferred by section 4 of the Public Notaries Act 1843 and section 57 of the Courts and Legal Services Act 1990 and of all other powers Us enabling hereby make the following Rules:

1. **Citation and Commencement**
    These rules may be cited as the Notaries (Qualification) (Amendment) Rules 2008 and shall come into force on the 1st day of June 2008.

2. **Interpretation**
    In these rules:

    'The 1998 Rules' means the Notaries (Qualification) Rules 1998

3. **Amendment to 1998 Rules**
    Schedule 2 "Prescribed Subjects" shall be amended as follows

    "5. **Roman Law as Introduction to Civil-Law Systems**
    The law of obligations: contract – including quasi contractual obligations; the development of agency ; delict and its development

    The law of property: classifications; the concept of ownership; rights attached to property

    The law of persons: issues of personal status; *Patria potestas*; marriage and divorce

    The law of succession: wills and intestacy; the position of heirs; legacies and *fideicommissa*

    Issues of Procedure and Evidence where modern parallels apply."

    "7. **Private International Law**
    Structure of conflict of laws; jurisdiction; choice of law; recognition and enforcement; proof of foreign law

    Classification (characterization) and the distinction between rules of substance and rules of procedure

    Domicile and residence

    Introduction to choice of law: contractual obligations; tortious obligations; moveable and immoveable property; husband and wife and civil partnerships; succession

Introduction to the jurisdiction of the English courts

Recognition and enforcement of foreign judgments; arbitration awards and authentic instruments."

4.   Paragraphs 5 and 7 of Schedule 2 of the 1998 Rules are hereby revoked.

DATED this 30th day of May 2008

SHEILA CAMERON

MASTER

NOTARIES (MISCELLANEOUS PROVISIONS) RULES 2002

PART I: PRELIMINARY

1.   Citation and Commencement

1.1   These rules may be cited as the Notaries (Miscellaneous Provisions) Rules 2002.

1.2.   These rules shall come into force on the 1st day of May 2002

2.   Interpretation

In these rules:
'1998 Rules' means the Notaries (Qualification) Rules 1998;

'2000 Rules' means the Notarial Appeals and Hearings Rules 2000;

'Board' means the Notarial Advisory Board established by rule 3;

'Master' means the Master of the Faculties;

'Qualifications Board' means the Board established by rule 7.1 of the 1998 Rules; and

'Registrar' means the Registrar of the Court.

PART II: NOTARIAL ADVISORY BOARD

3.   Establishment of Board

3.1   There shall be established a Notarial Advisory Board.

3.2   The Board shall comprise the members from time to time of the Qualifications Board and the chairman of the Qualifications Board shall also be chairman of the Board.

3.3   The Board shall meet as necessary and may meet immediately before or immediately after a meeting of the Qualifications Board.

4.   Functions of the Board

The functions of the Board shall be to advise the Master and the Registrar on any matter pertaining to the notarial profession in England and Wales and its regulation that may be referred to it by the Master or the Registrar or that it may of its own motion wish to consider.

PART III: MISCELLANEOUS AMENDMENTS

5. **Amendments to the 2000 Rules**

5.1 In rule 4.2 of the 2000 Rules '4.1' shall be substituted for '5.1'.

5.2 In rule 6 of the 2000 Rules after 'Rule 8' there shall be inserted '(except Rules 8(1) and 8(3)(c)(ii))' and after 'Part III' there shall be inserted '(except Rules 8(d) and 9(b)(ii))'.

NOTARIES PRACTICE RULES 2001

PART I: PRELIMINARY

1.   **Citation and Commencement**

1.1.   These rules may be cited as the Notaries Practice Rules 2001.

1.2.   These rules shall come into force on the 1st day of November 2001.

2.   **Interpretation**

In these rules:

'arrangement' means any express or tacit agreement between a notary and another person, whether contractually binding or not;

'firm' includes a sole practitioner;

'holding company' and 'subsidiary company' have the meanings assigned to them by the Companies Acts 1985 and 1989, and two companies are 'associated' where they are subsidiary companies of the same holding company

'the Master' means the Master of the Faculties;

'notarial act' means any act that has validity by virtue only of its preparation, performance, authentication, attestation or verification by a notary;

'notary' includes a firm of notaries;

'performance' includes execution, completion and carrying out;

'person' includes a body corporate or unincorporated association or group of persons;

'qualified legal practitioner' means
(i)   a person qualified to provide legal services to the public in England and Wales, or
(ii)   a person qualified to provide legal services to the public under the laws of any other jurisdiction who practises as such in England and Wales;

'the Registrar' means the Registrar of the Court of Faculties;
for the purposes of these rules a notary's practice includes the preparation and performance of notarial acts and any other service undertaken as a notary whether or not such service may only be undertaken by a notary;

and for the avoidance of doubt the Interpretation Act 1978 applies to these rules as it applies to an Act of Parliament.

PART II: PRACTICE AS A NOTARY

3.   **Oath of Office**
A notary shall exercise his office in accordance with the Oath or Declaration made by him at the time of the grant of his Notarial Faculty, as set out in section 7 of the Public Notaries Act 1843.

4.   **Bankruptcy**
A notary who is bankrupt may not, until he is discharged from bankruptcy, practise as a notary on his own behalf, but may practise as the employee of another notary.

5.   **Obtaining Instructions**
A notary shall not directly or indirectly obtain or attempt to obtain instructions for professional work or permit another person to do so on his behalf, or do anything in the course of practising as a notary in any manner which compromises or impairs or is likely to compromise or impair any of the following:
5.1   the notary's independence or integrity;
5.2   a person's freedom to instruct a notary of his choice;
5.3   the notary's ability to act in the best interests of the client;
5.4   the good repute of the notary or of the notarial profession;
5.5   the notary's proper standard of work;
5.6   the notary's duty of care to persons in all jurisdictions who may place legitimate reliance on his notarial acts.

6.   **Conflicts of Interest**
6.1   In the conduct of his practice a notary shall not favour the interests of one client over those of another and shall not favour his own interests or those of any other person over those of his clients.

6.2   A notary must not act for both parties to a transaction unless:
6.2.1   both have consented in writing; and
6.2.2   he is satisfied that there is no conflict of interest between the parties but where a conflict of interests exists or arises a notary may act or continue to act for both parties for the sole purpose of resolving or attempting to resolve that conflict of interest.

7.   **Duty to Act Impartially in respect of Notarial Acts**
A notary must act impartially and in particular must not perform any notarial act which involves or may affect:
7.1   his own affairs, including matters in which he is personally interested jointly with another person;

7.2   the affairs of his spouse or partner or a person to whom the notary is engaged to be married. For the purpose of this sub-rule, "partner" means a person with whom the notary cohabits or with whom he has a sexual relationship and includes a partner of the same sex;

7.3   the affairs of a person to whom he is directly and closely related;

7.4   the affairs of a person with whom he shares a practice or with whom he shares offices;

7.5   the affairs of a person who has appointed the notary to be his attorney which concern a matter within the scope of the power of attorney granted;

7.6   the affairs of a trust of which he is a trustee or of an estate where he is a personal representative of the deceased;

7.7   the affairs of a body corporate of whose board of directors or governing body he is a member;

7.8   the affairs of an employee of the notary;

7.9   the affairs of a partnership of which he is a member or of a company in which the notary holds shares either exceeding five percent of the issued share capital or having a market value exceeding such figure as the Master may from time to time specify.

8.   **Employed Notaries**
8.1   Save as permitted by rule 8.2 a notary who is the employee of a non-notary shall not perform any notarial act as part of his employment or do or perform any notarial act for his employer or his employer's holding, associated or subsidiary company.

8.2   A notary may act for a person who is also the client of the qualified legal practitioner or firm of qualified legal practitioners by which he is employed but he shall take all proper and reasonable steps in the exercise of his notarial practice to maintain his independence of his employer and in particular he shall:

8.2.1   ensure that his independence as a notary is fully recognised in writing in any contract of employment entered into by him,

8.2.2   annually send to his employer a written statement of professional independence in a form approved by the Master from time to time, and shall declare in his application for a notarial practising certificate that he has complied with this rule.

9. Language

9.1 Notarial acts shall normally be drawn up in the English language.

9.2 A notary may upon request or in appropriate circumstances prepare a notarial act in a language other than English if he has sufficient knowledge of the language concerned.

9.3 A notary may not authenticate by means of a notarial act a document drawn up in a language other than English unless he has satisfied himself as to its meaning but this does not prevent a notary from authenticating the execution or signature of a document in any language.

9.4 A notary may not certify the accuracy of a translation that has been made by someone other than himself unless he has knowledge of the language sufficient to satisfy himself as to the accuracy of the translation but this does not prevent a notary from attesting a translator's affidavit or authenticating a verification.

10. Undertakings

10.1 Any notary giving an undertaking, whether oral or in writing, shall be personally liable for that undertaking, and the implementation of any such undertaking is required as a matter of conduct. Save in exceptional cases a failure by a notary to honour an undertaking will constitute notarial misconduct for the purposes of the Public Notaries (Conduct and Discipline) Rules 1993.

10.2 An undertaking given by a notary shall be in writing or confirmed in writing and signed by the notary giving it.

11. Publicity

A notary may advertise his practice and seek to obtain directly or indirectly clients and business in any manner and through any medium whether informative or promotional with the exception of unsolicited telephone calls or unsolicited visits to persons or organisations, as long as:

11.1 the client's freedom to instruct a qualified person of the client's choice is not thereby unduly restricted;

11.2 the notary's good reputation for integrity and professional standards of work is not thereby damaged;

11.3 he complies with the British Code of Advertising Practice, the Independent Broadcasting Authority Code of Advertising Standards and Practice and the Direct Mail Regulations in force from time to time.

but nothing in this Rule shall be construed as authorising the use of the word "notaries" or any word designating or indicating notarial services in any publicity for activities which are not of a notarial nature.

12. **Scrivener Notaries**

No notary shall describe himself professionally as a Scrivener or a Scrivener notary unless he holds the qualifications to practise as a Scrivener notary from time to time prescribed by the Incorporated Company of Scriveners of London.

13. **Introductions and Referrals**

When a notary enters into an arrangement with another person for the introduction of clients to the notary or by the notary to the other person he must ensure:

13.1　that the client is informed in writing of the arrangement and of any commission or other benefit the notary may be receiving or pay;

13.2　that he either obtains the client's written agreement as to the destination of the commission or accounts to the client for the commission;

13.3　that he remains able to advise the client independently in accordance with these rules and continues to do so regardless of his own interests.

14. **Offering Services other than as a Notary**

14.1　Where a notary by himself or with any other person operates, actively participates in or controls any business, other than a notary's practice, the notary shall ensure:

14.1.1　that the name of that business has no substantial element in common with the name of any practice of the notary;

14.1.2　that the words "notaries," "attorney(s)" or "lawyer(s)" or any words designating or indicating a notarial or legal practice are not used in connection with the notary's involvement with that business;

14.1.3　that any client referred by any practice of the notary to the business is informed in writing that, as a customer of that business, he does not enjoy any protection attaching to the client of a notary, and that where that business shares premises or reception staff with any practice of the notary, every customer of the business is informed in writing that, as a customer of that business, he does not enjoy the protection attaching to the client of a notary.

14.2　Rule 14.1 does not apply to the practice of a qualified legal practitioner.

15. Fees

15.1 A notary may charge a professional fee for all notarial work undertaken by him, and the basis upon which that fee will be calculated or the fee to be charged for the work done, shall be made known in advance to any new client.

15.2 Subject to rule 15.3, a notary shall not share or agree to share his professional fees with any person not entitled to act as a notary; provided that this rule shall not prohibit the payment of any allowance or allowances, sum or sums of money, that are or shall be agreed to be made or paid to the widows or children of any deceased notary or notaries, by any surviving partner or partners of such deceased notary or notaries.

15.3 A notary who also practises in partnership as a qualified legal practitioner may share professional fees with his professional partners who are also so qualified, provided that a notary who shares fees by virtue of this paragraph shall keep accounts which enable the income and expenditure arising from his practice as a notary to be distinguished from the income and expenditure arising from his practice as a qualified legal practitioner, and shall furnish the Faculty Office with such additional information as to his partnership and accounting arrangements as may be prescribed in rules or orders of the Master.

16. Name of a Firm of Notaries

The name of a firm of notaries shall consist only of:

16.1 the name or names of one or more present or former principals together with, if desired, conventional references to the firm and to such persons;

16.2 a firm name in use on 1st January 1989;

16.3 the name of a firm of qualified legal practitioners of which a notary is a partner; or

16.4 one approved in writing by the Master.

17. Investment Business

17.1 A notary shall not in connection with investment business have any arrangement with another person under which the notary could be constrained to recommend to clients or effect for them (or refrain from so doing) transactions in some investments but not others, with some persons but not others, or through the agency of some persons but not others; or to introduce or refer clients or other persons with whom he deals to some persons but not others; nor shall a notary be an appointed representative.

17.2 Notwithstanding any provision in rule 14 a notary shall not by himself or with any other person set up, operate, actively participate in or control any separate business which is an appointed representative.

17.3 This rule shall have effect in relation to the conduct of investment business within or into any part of the United Kingdom.

17.4 In this rule "appointed representative," "investment" and "investment business" have the meanings assigned to them by the Financial Services Act 1986.

18. Supervision of a Notary's Office

18.1 A notary shall ensure that every office where he practises is and can reasonably be seen to be properly supervised. Such supervision shall be exercised by a notary holding a Practising Certificate who shall spend sufficient time at such office to ensure adequate control of the staff employed there and afford requisite facilities for consultation with clients. Such notary may be a principal, employee or consultant of the firm or a locum tenens.

18.2 In determining whether or not there has been compliance with the requirement as to supervision in rule 18.1, account shall be taken of, inter alia, the arrangements for the principals to see or be apprised of incoming communications.

18.3 Where supervision in accordance with this rule is prevented by illness, accident or other sufficient or unforeseen cause for a prolonged period, suitable alternative arrangements shall be made without delay to ensure compliance.

18.4 In cases where a notary is not in attendance on days when his office is normally open to the public, he shall make adequate arrangements to ensure the provision of notarial services to persons requiring the same.

PART III: RECORDS

19. Duty to Keep Records

19.1 A notary shall keep proper records of his notarial acts in accordance with this rule.

19.2 The records so kept shall be sufficient to identify:
19.2.1 the date of the act;
19.2.2 the person at whose request the act was performed;
19.2.3 the person or persons, if any, intervening in the act and, in the case of a person who intervened in a representative capacity, the name of his principal;

19.2.4 the method of identification of the party or parties intervening in the notarial act, and in the case of a party intervening in a representative capacity, any evidence produced to the notary of that party's entitlement so to intervene;

19.2.5 the nature of the act;

19.2.6 the fee charged.

19.3 In the case of a notarial act in the public form, the notary shall place an original of the act or a complete photographic copy of the same in a protocol which shall be preserved permanently by the notary.

19.4 Records of acts not in public form kept in accordance with rule 19.2 shall be preserved for a minimum period of twelve years and, for the avoidance of doubt, such preservation may be by means of a suitable digital or other electronic system providing for the storage of documents in an indelible and unalterable format.

19.5 A copy of a notarial act or of the record of a notarial act preserved in accordance with rules 19.3 and 19.4 shall, upon payment of a reasonable fee, be issued upon the application of any person or authority having a proper interest in the act unless prevented by order of a competent court.

19.6 Any question as to whether a person has a proper interest in an act for the purposes of rule 19.5 shall be determined by the Master.

20. Inspection of Records
Records kept pursuant to rule 19 shall be open at any time to inspection by the Master or a person authorised by him.

21. Notaries Ceasing to Practise
21.1 When a notary ceases to practise as such, then he, or failing him his continuing notarial partners or the person having possession or custody of the records maintained by him pursuant to rule 19, shall arrange for such records to be transferred:

21.1.1 to another notary in practice appointed by him or by his continuing notarial partners,

21.1.2 to another notary in practice appointed, with the approval of the Master, by the persons having possession or custody of the records, or

21.1.3 to an archive designated for the purpose under regulations made by the Master from time to time,

and the persons making such transfer shall give written particulars to the Registrar of the date of transfer and the person or archive to which the records were transferred.

21.2 The provisions of rules 19.5 and 20 shall apply to a notary or archive to which the records of any notary are transferred pursuant to this rule as they apply to the notary himself.

22. Application to Ecclesiastical Notaries

The provisions of this Part shall apply to notaries appointed for ecclesiastical purposes only subject to the following modifications:

22.1 The requirement of rule 19 to keep a record of notarial acts shall apply only to such ecclesiastical acts as law or custom requires to be performed in the presence of a public notary and recorded in writing.

22.2 Any act or transaction properly recorded in the Act Book of any Archbishop or Bishop, or in the Minute Book of any Cathedral Chapter, shall be deemed to have been properly recorded in accordance with rule 19.

22.3 Rule 21 shall not apply to ecclesiastical notaries, but upon a person ceasing for any reason to hold the office in respect of which he was appointed an ecclesiastical notary, any records kept by him pursuant to this Part shall be transferred to the succeeding holder of that office (being an ecclesiastical notary) upon his appointment.

PART IV: MISCELLANEOUS

23. Waivers

The Master shall have power to waive any of the provisions of these rules in any particular case or classes of case for the purpose expressed in such waiver, and to revoke such waiver.

24. Repeals and Savings

24.1 Subject to rule 24.2 the Notaries' Practice Rules 1989 and the Notaries (Records) Rules 1991 are hereby revoked.

24.2 Rule 24.1 does not absolve any notary from the duty to comply with the Notaries' Practice Rules 1989 and the Notaries (Records) Rules 1991 prior to the coming into force of these rules and records maintained by a notary in accordance with Rule 3 or Rule 6 of the Notaries (Records) Rules 1991 prior to the coming into force of these rules shall continue to be so maintained by him and rules 19.5, 19.6, 20, 21 and 22 of these rules shall apply to such records.

NOTARIAL APPEALS AND HEARINGS RULES 2000
As amended by the Notaries (Miscellaneous Provisions) Rules 2002

Citation and Commencement
These rules may be cited as the Notarial Appeals and Hearings Rules 2000
These rules shall come into force on the 21st day of November 2000

Interpretation
In these rules:
'1991 Rules' means the Public Notaries (Practising Certificates) Rules 1991;

'1993 Rules' means the Public Notaries (Conduct and Discipline) Rules 1993;

'Assessor' means a member of the Panel;

'Commissary' means the Commissary appointed by the Archbishop of Canterbury under section 3 of the Ecclesiastical Licences Act 1533 to be the Commissary for the purposes of these rules;

'Deputy Commissary' means a Commissary appointed by the Archbishop of Canterbury under section 3 of the Ecclesiastical Licences Act 1533 to be a Deputy Commissary for the purposes of these rules;

'Lay Assessor' means an Assessor who is not a notary public;

'Master' means the Master of the Faculties;

'Notary Assessor' means an Assessor who is a notary public;

'Panel' means the Panel of Assessors established under rule 3;

'Registrar' means the Registrar of the Court of Faculties

Assessors
There shall be established a panel of assessors comprising at least six persons of whom one half shall be notaries public who have held a practising certificate for not less than ten consecutive years at the date of their appointment and one half shall be persons of good standing who are not notaries public.

The members of the Panel shall be appointed by the Master for a term of five years (which may be renewed for further terms of five years on expiry) but an Assessor who is involved in an appeal or hearing shall continue in office until the conclusion of that appeal or hearing notwithstanding the expiry of his term of office.

An Assessor's appointment may be terminated by the Master with the consent of the Commissary for gross misconduct.

Appeals and Hearings
These rules apply to:
An appeal under rule 8(2) of the 1991 Rules; and
The hearing of a complaint or petition under Part III of the 1993 Rules.
The Master may by Order add to the list in rule 4.1.

Conduct of Appeals and Hearings
In respect of an appeal or hearing to which these rules apply interlocutory issues shall be deal with by the Commissary but the matter will be heard by the Commissary sitting with two Assessors chosen by him, one being a Notary Assessor and the other being a Lay Assessor

Where the Commissary is sitting with Assessors questions of law shall be determined by the Commissary alone but all other issues shall be determined by a majority decision

Interpretation of the 1991 and 1993 Rules
References in Rule 8 (except Rules 8(1) and 8(3)(c)(ii)) of the 1991 Rules and Part III (except Rules 8(d) and 9(b)(ii)) of and the Schedule and Appendix to the 1993 Rules to the Master shall be read as if they were references to the Commissary or the Commissary and two Assessors as the case may be.

Reference of other matters to Commissary

Where the Master is required to hear any application appeal or other matter not provided for in rule 4 whether under rules made by him or under his inherent jurisdiction he may direct that the matter should be heard by the Commissary.

Where the Master has made a direction under rule 7.1 the Commissary shall determine whether to hear the matter alone or with Assessors and rule 5 shall apply to a hearing with Assessors.

Deputy Commissary
If for any reason the Commissary is unable or unwilling to perform his functions under these rules in relation to any matter, that matter shall be assigned by the Registrar to a Deputy Commissary.
Where a matter has been assigned under rule 8.1 to a Deputy Commissary that Deputy Commissary shall perform all of the functions in relation to that matter which would have been performed by the Commissary.

Transitional Provisions
Nothing in these rules shall affect any appeal where notice under rule 8(3)(a) of the 1991 Rules has been given or any hearing where proceedings have been commenced under the 1993 Rules before the date on which these rules come into force.

NOTARIES (ACCESS TO JUSTICE ACT) (CONSEQUENTIAL PROVISIONS) RULES 1999

1. Citation and Commencement

1.1 These rules may be cited as the Notaries (Access to Justice Act) (Consequential Provisions) Rules 1999.

1.2 This rule and rule 11 shall come into force on the date hereof and the remainder of these rules shall come into force on the day on which Section 53 of the Access to Justice Act 1999 comes into force which shall be "the Operative Date" for the purposes of these rules.

2. Notarial Faculties

2.1 For the avoidance of doubt any provision in the faculty of a notary public which would operate so as to prevent him from practising in, or within three miles of, the City of London, shall automatically cease to have effect on the Operative Date and it shall not be necessary for a further or amended faculty to be issued.

2.2 Any notary whose faculty contains a restriction of the type described in rule 2.1 may, on application to the Registrar and on payment of such a fee as the Master may from time to time prescribe, be issued with a revised faculty omitting such restriction.

2.3 In this rule "the Master" means the Master of the Faculties and "the Registrar" means the Registrar of the Court of Faculties.

3. Practising Certificates

For the avoidance of doubt, from the Operative Date, any notarial practising certificate limited by the words "outside the jurisdiction of the Scriveners Company" shall automatically have effect as if such limitation were omitted.

4. Amendment to Public Notaries (Practising Certificates) Rules 1982

The Schedule to the Public Notaries (Practising Certificates) Rules 1982 is amended as follows:-

4.1 In the form of application for entry or issue of a practising certificate the question "Does your Faculty exclude the area of the Scriveners' Company jurisdiction?" is omitted.

4.2 In the form of practising certificate the words "outside the jurisdiction of the Scriveners Company" are omitted.

5. Amendments to the Notaries' Practice Rules 1989

The Notaries' Practice (Rules) 1989 are amended as follows:-

5.1 The following new rule is added after Rule 2:
"Rule 2A (Scrivener Notaries)
No notary shall describe himself as a Scrivener or a Scrivener

notary unless he holds the qualifications to practise as a Scrivener notary from time to time prescribed by the Incorporated Company of Scriveners of London".

5.2   Rule 7(3) is omitted

6.   Amendment to Notaries' Accounts (Deposit Interest) Rules 1989
In rule 5 of the Notaries' Accounts (Deposit Interest) Rules 1989 the words "Scrivener notary" are omitted and the words "notary who is a member of that Society" are substituted therefor.

7.   Amendments to the Public Notaries (Qualification) Rules 1991
In rule 7 of the Public Notaries (Qualification) Rules 1991 the words "outside the jurisdiction of the Company" are omitted.

8.   Amendments to the Order of the Master made pursuant to the Notaries (Records) Rules 1991
In the Order of the Master made pursuant to the Notaries (Records) Rules 1991 on 4 March 1992 the words "outside the jurisdiction of the Incorporated Company of Scriveners of London" are omitted in paragraph 2.

9.   Amendments to the Public Notaries (Conduct and Discipline) Rules 1993
In the Public Notaries (Conduct and Discipline) Rules 1993 paragraph (j) of rule 2 is omitted and the following substituted therefor:-

"'Scrivener notary' means a public notary who holds the qualifications to practise as a Scrivener notary from time to time prescribed by the Incorporated Company of Scriveners of or who did hold such qualifications before being struck off the Roll of Notaries or suspended from practice by an order of the Court."

10.   Amendments to the Notaries (Qualification) Rules 1998
The Notaries (Qualification) Rules 1998 are amended as follows:-
10.1   Rule 5 is omitted and the following new rule substituted therefor:-
"5 General Notaries
Any person who satisfies the requirements of rule 3 and who has obtained the qualifications required under Part III of these rules may apply for admission as a general notary to practise in England and Wales."

10.2   Rule 6 is omitted.

10.3   In rule 8.1 the words "or to obtain a certificate of eligibility for admission" are omitted.

10.4   In rule 9.2 the words "other than within the exclusive jurisdiction of the Company" are omitted.

10.5 Rule 12.3 is omitted and the following substituted therefor:-
"Any person who had, before the Operative Date, entered an apprenticeship agreement in accordance with Rule 5 of the Scriveners (Qualification) Rules 1991 may within five years of the Operative Date apply for admission under Rule 5 upon producing a certificate of freedom of the Incorporated Company of Scriveners of London and a certificate from the Clerk of that Company that he has passed Parts I and II of the examinations and completed the period of apprenticeship prescribed under the Scriveners (Qualification) Rules 1991".

11. The Society of Scrivener Notaries
Where in any rule or order made by the Master prior to the date hereof reference is made to The Society of Public Notaries of London, that reference shall be deemed to be a reference to the body corporate called "The Society of Scrivener Notaries".

NOTARIES (QUALIFICATION) RULES 1998 as amended by the Notaries (Access to Justice Act) (Consequential Provisions) Rules 1999

PART I : PRELIMINARY

1.   Citation and Commencement

1.1   These rules may be cited as the Notaries (Qualification) Rules 1998.

1.2   Part I of these rules and rules 7 and 8 with the exception of rule 8.1 shall come into force on the date these rules are made and the remaining rules shall come into force on the 1st day of February 1999.

2.   Interpretation

In these rules:

'the Board' means the Qualifications Board established under rule 7;

'the Company' means the Incorporated Company of Scriveners of London;

'Degree' means a qualification awarded following a post secondary course of at least three years' duration (or of an equivalent duration part time) at a university or an establishment of higher education or an establishment of similar level;

'the Directive' means the Council Directive of 21st December 1988 (89/48/EEC);

'the Examination Regulations' means the Regulations made by the Master on 8th July 1991 pursuant to his Order dated 1st July 1991;

'the Faculty Office' means the Registry of the Court of Faculties;

'the Master' means the Master of the Faculties;

'the Operative Date' means the 1st day of February 1999; and

'the Registrar' means the Registrar of the Court of Faculties.

PART II : GENERAL PROVISIONS AS TO ADMISSION

3.   Qualification for Admission as a Notary Public

No person shall be admitted as a notary public to practise in England and Wales unless such person:

3.1   Is at least 21 years of age and has satisfied the requirements of these rules,

3.2   Has taken the oath of allegiance and the oath required by Section 7 of the Public Notaries Act 1843 and;

3.3 Is, except where such application is made under rule 4 (ecclesiastical notaries) or rule 9 (European Economic Area notaries) either a solicitor of the Supreme Court, or a barrister at law or holds a Degree.

4. Ecclesiastical Notaries
Any person appointed as registrar of either of the provinces of Canterbury or York, as registrar to the Archbishop of Wales, as legal adviser to the General Synod to the Church of England, as legal secretary to the Governing Body of the Church in Wales, as registrar of any diocese in England or Wales, as an officer of the ecclesiastical court in Jersey or Guernsey or (being a solicitor) as chapter clerk in any cathedral church in England and Wales, or as the deputy to any such officer, may apply for admission as a notary public for ecclesiastical purposes only, upon satisfying the Master of the fact of such an appointment.

5. General Notaries
Any person who satisfies the requirements of rule 3 and who has obtained the qualifications required under Part III of these rules may apply for admission as a general notary to practise in England and Wales.

6. [Revoked]

PART III: QUALIFICATIONS

7. Qualifications Board and Fees for Applications
7.1 There shall be established a Qualifications Board constituted in accordance with schedule 1.

7.2 The functions of the Board shall be:
7.2.1 To advise the Master whether a degree or other qualification should be approved by him for the purpose of these rules.
7.2.2 To advise the Master on the standard of the qualifications of any person applying for admission as a general notary under these rules.
7.2.3 To advise the Master on the qualifications and experience of persons applying for recognition that they are eligible for admission as a general notary under rule 9.
7.2.4 To advise any other body concerned with the administration or regulation of the notarial profession in England and Wales or any part of it on matters relating to qualifications and experience.

7.3 The Master may by Order delegate to the Board any of his functions under these rules relating to the approval or recognition of degrees, qualifications and experience.
7.4 The Master may from time to time by Order prescribe fees or the maximum fees which may be charged in respect of any application to the Master under these rules and such fees may be applied by the

Faculty Office towards meeting the expenses of the Board but subject thereto the expenses of the Board and of its members shall be paid from and such fees shall form part of the general notarial income of the Faculty Office.

8.   Practical Qualifications

8.1   Any person wishing to be admitted as a general notary under rule 5 shall have followed and attained a satisfactory standard in a course or courses of studies covering all of the subjects listed in schedule 2.

8.2   Whether a particular course of studies satisfies the requirements of these rules and whether a person has obtained a satisfactory standard in that course shall be determined by the Master after seeking the advice of the Board.

8.3   The Master after seeking the advice of the Board may by order direct that the award of a particular qualification meets the requirements of these rules as to some or all of the subjects listed in schedule 2.

8.4   The Master may as a condition of making a direction under rule 8.3 require the body by which the qualification is awarded to issue those pursuing a course of studies leading to that qualification with such information about the notarial profession, these rules and other rules made by the Master and the Company as the Master may specify.

8.5   The Master may by Order add any subjects to the list in schedule 2 or remove any subjects from that list or alter any of the provisions of that schedule but before doing so he shall consult the Board.

9.   European Economic Area Notaries

9.1   This rule applies to a person who:
(a)   holds the office of notary public in a member state of the European Economic Area other then the United Kingdom,
(b)   holds all the qualifications and has completed all the practical training necessary for appointment or admission to that office in such a member state but has not yet been so appointed or admitted, or
(c)   holds the office of notary public in Scotland or Northern Ireland.

9.2   Any person to whom this rule applies may apply to the Master for recognition that he is qualified for the purposes of rule 10.1 for admission as a general notary to practise anywhere in England and Wales and such application shall be made to the Faculty Office in such form and accompanied by such information as the Master may from time to time by Order prescribe.

9.3 The Master shall after consultation with the Board examine any application made under rule 9.2 in accordance with the procedures set out in articles 3 and 4 of the Directive. If compensatory measures are required, the applicant may be required to pass an aptitude test in accordance with the derogation in the final sub-paragraph of article 4.

9.4 Where an application is made to the Master under rule 9.2 he shall determine the application as soon as possible and communicate the outcome to the applicant in a reasoned decision within four months of the production of all the certificates and documents relating to the applicant referred to in article 8.1 of the Directive.

9.5 If the Master refuses an application under rule 9.2 or has not determined the application within the time prescribed by rule 9.4 the Master shall be deemed to have refused an application for a faculty and the applicant may pursue the remedy provided for in the Ecclesiastical Licences Act 1533 and mentioned in section 5 of the Public Notaries Act 1843.

PART III : PROCEDURE FOR ADMISSION

10. Application for Admission
10.1 A person qualified for admission as a notary under these rules shall apply in writing to the Faculty Office on such form as the Master may from time to time specify.

10.2 The application shall be accompanied by:
(a) A certificate of fitness in such form as the Master may from time to time prescribe to be given by a notary public to the effect that the applicant is known to him and that having made due enquiry to the best of his knowledge and belief the applicant is a fit and proper person to be created a notary public, and;
(b) A certificate of good character in such form as the Master may from time to time prescribe to be given by a person who is qualified under paragraph 10.3 testifying to the good character, honesty, reliability, diligence and trustworthiness of the applicant and stating that the person giving the certificate knows of no reason why the applicant should not be created a notary public.

10.3 A person is qualified to give the certificate of good character required by paragraph 10.2(b) of this rule if he is a person of good standing and character, he has known the applicant for a period of not less than five years, he is not related to the applicant by blood, marriage or adoption, and he is not a professional partner, employer or employee of the applicant.

10.4 In the case of a person qualified under rule 4 the certificate of fitness shall further state that the applicant is conformable to the doctrine and discipline of the Church of England as by law established (or, in the case of a person qualified only by reason of holding an ecclesiastical appointment in Wales, the doctrine, discipline and constitution of the Church in Wales).

10.5 The application shall be accompanied by such fee as the Master may from time to time prescribe.

11. Publicity, Refusal of Applications and Admissions

11.1 The Master may give, or require an applicant to give, such publicity to an application made under rule 10 as in the circumstances appear to the Master to be necessary.

11.2 Any representations made to the Master following such publicity shall be notified to the applicant, and the Master shall consider any response thereto made by the applicant before deciding whether a faculty shall be granted.

11.3 Any decision by the Master to refuse an application under rule 10 shall be notified to the applicant by the Registrar in writing to enable the applicant to pursue (if so advised) the remedy provided for in The Ecclesiastical Licences Act 1533 and mentioned in Section 5 of the Public Notaries Act 1843.

11.4 Upon the Master deciding to grant an application under rule 10, the Registrar shall cause a faculty to pass the seal in accustomed form. The applicant shall appear personally before the Registrar to make the oaths mentioned in rule 3.2 and the Registrar shall then admit him by delivering the faculty to him and causing his name to be entered upon the roll of notaries. The Master may appoint a Commissioner to act in place of the Registrar for this purpose.

PART V : TRANSITIONAL PROVISIONS REPEALS AND AMENDMENTS

12. Transitional Provisions

12.1 Subject to rules 12.2 and 12.3 these rules shall not apply to any person who on the Operative Date has given notice under regulation 4 of the Examination Regulations and such person may if qualified make application under rule 9(2) of the Public Notaries (Qualification) Rules 1991 within two years of the Operative Date.

12.2 These rules shall apply to any person to whom rule 12.1 applies if he so requests in writing to the Faculty Office.

12.3 Any person who had, before the Operative Date, entered an apprenticeship agreement in accordance with Rule 5 of the

Scriveners (Qualification) Rules 1991 may within five years of the Operative Date apply for admission under Rule 5 upon producing a certificate of freedom of the Incorporated Company of Scriveners of London and a certificate from the Clerk of that Company that he has passed Parts I and II of the examinations and completed the period of apprenticeship prescribed under the Scriveners (Qualification) Rules 1991.

13. Repeals and Savings

13.1 Save as provided in rule 12 the Public Notaries (Qualification) Rules 1991 and the Examination Regulations are hereby revoked.

13.2 Subject to the further Order of the Master the certificates of fitness and good character prescribed by the Master's Orders of 27th August 1992 and 13th September 1993 respectively shall be the certificates prescribed for the purposes of rule 10.2.1 of these rules

14. Notaries (Post-Admission) Rules 1991

The Notaries (Post-Admission) Rules 1991 shall be amended as follows:

14.1 In Rule 3(1) after the words "other than" there shall be inserted "Notaries to whom Rule 10 applies and".

14.2 The following additional rule shall be added:
"European Economic Area Notaries 10. The provisions of these Rules shall not apply to any Notary who, immediately prior to his admission, was recognised by the Master as qualified for admission under the provisions of rule 9 of the Notaries (Qualification) Rules 1998."

SCHEDULE 1

QUALIFICATIONS BOARD

1   The Board shall comprise not more than 10 persons appointed by the Master after consultation with the Company, the Society of Public Notaries of London, the Notaries' Society and the Association of Solicitor Notaries in Greater London and such other persons or bodies as the Master may consider appropriate.

2   The Master shall appoint one member of the Board to be Chairman for such period as the Master may determine.

3   Members of the Board, including the Chairman, shall hold office for such period as the Master may determine and may be removed from office by the Master at any time.

4   The Registrar shall act as Clerk to the Board or may appoint or nominate another person to act as Clerk in his place.

5   The Board shall meet as often as may be necessary and in any event not less than once each year.

6   The Board may delegate any of its functions under these rules to a subcommittee comprising not fewer than three of its members.

SCHEDULE 2

PRESCRIBED SUBJECTS

1.   **Public/Constitutional Law**
     Characteristics and sources of the constitution
     The legislature
     Introduction to the objectives and structure of the European Union
     Implications of membership of the European Union
     The citizen and the state
     Administrative Law: control of administrative powers, including non-judicial   forms of control; judicial review

2.   **The Law of Property**
     The nature of legal and equitable interests
     Principles relating to the transfer of legal estates and interest in land, and enforceable equitable contracts
     Capacity and incapacity of individuals, corporations, charities and infants
     Registered and unregistered land
     Estates and interest in land: freehold, leases, mortgages, easements, covenants relating to land, licences
     Trusts of land, the Trusts of Land and Appointment of Trustees Act, 1996, including, pre Act settled land, joint tenancies and tenancies in common

3. **The Law of Contract**
   Formation of a contract: offer, acceptance, consideration, etc.
   Contents of a contract: express and implied terms; rules on exemption clauses and unfair terms
   Viciating factors: duress, undue influence, non-disclosure, misrepresentation, mistake
   Discharge of contracts: performance, agreement, breach, frustration
   Remedies: damages, specific remedies, etc.

4. **The Law of the European Union**
   European institutional structures, functions and powers
   Constitutional structures of the European Union; its law and the law-making process; the role of the European Court of Justice
   Sources and hierarchy of law in the European Union
   Relation of the Law of the European Union to national laws, and associated constitutional issues
   Introduction to key aspects of the substantive law of the European Union, e.g. the internal market, competition law, free movement of labour, free movement of goods, etc.

5. **Roman Law**
   Sources of law: legal development through the grant of new remedies.
   Equity jurists in Roman Law
   Persons: family and marriage in Roman Law
   Property: category of thing in Roman Law
   Obligations: contracts, quasi-contracts and delicts
   Succession
   European legal history: the revival of Roman Law, Roman Law in England.
   Developments in France, Germany and elsewhere
   Unjustified enrichment
   or Civil Law
   The legal systems, institutions and principles of a modern Civil Law jurisdiction

6. **Equity and the Law of Trusts**
   What the trust does
   Creation of the trust: formalities, transfer to trustees, certainty
   Powers of appointment
   Discretionary trusts
   Secret trusts
   Constructive and resulting trusts
   Charitable trusts
   Appointment and removal of trustees
   Trustees duty to maintain equality between beneficiaries
   Maintenance and advancement
   Powers of investment
   Breach of Trust
   Tracing and proprietory remedies

Specific performance and injunctions

7. **Conflicts of Law**
Structure of Conflict of Laws
Proof of foreign law
Domicile and residence
Jurisdiction of English Courts at common law
Staying of actions and restraint of foreign proceedings
Recognition and enforcement of foreign judgments at common law
Jurisdiction and judgments under the Brussels Convention
Obligations: Contract and Tort
Property: immovables and movable
Husband and wife, other family partnerships (unmarried partners), children
Wills and Succession in civil law and other jurisdictions
Renvoi

8. **Conveyancing**
A typical conveyancing transaction
Conflict of interests - between clients/client-lender. Reporting to client
Contract: formation and enforceability
Particulars of sale - property rights and incumbrances
Conditions of sale: title, vacant possession, time, price and chattels (apportionment), deposit, Standard Conditions and other special conditions
Pre contract searches and enquiries before contract. National "Protocol" Scheme
Tax implications: Capital Gains Tax, Inheritance Tax, Stamp Duty
Financing. Charges and Mortgages
From contract to completion - exchange methods, Requisitions on Title
Pre completion searches - nature and effect
Investigation of Title - registered and unregistered
Registration, Land Registration Act 1987
Conveyancing remedies
Post completion - redemption of mortgage and account to client
Conveyancing practice and the drafting of standard conveyancing documents

9. **Business Law and Practice**
Partnerships - characteristics of a partnership; partnership management and finance; liability of partners; termination of and retirement from a partnership Companies - limited companies and their formation; Directors and secretary; shareholders; company finance; disposal of shares; company meetings and resolutions
The law relating to the sale of goods and international sales
The European Union - the right to establish, to provide services, and free movement of goods; Treaty of Rome Articles 85 and 86
Insolvency - bankruptcy; company insolvency proceedings

10. **Wills Probate and Administration**

Wills: nature and validity, mental element, formal requirements, revocation, alteration, re-publication, revival, incorporation

Testamentary gifts: principles of construction, legacies and devises

Intestate succession

Family provision

Principles of probate

Powers and duties of Personal Representatives

Administration, including grants of representation, dealing with the estate, oaths, Inland Revenue accounts, affidavit evidence, caveats, citations and other court proceedings, variation, disclosures and other post death changes

Distribution of the estate

Beneficiaries rights and remedies

Inheritance Tax, Capital Gains Tax, Income tax, taxation of trusts and settlements

The drafting of wills

11. **Notarial Practice (including Bills of Exchange)**

History, authority and organisation

Notarial equipment and records

Professional practice and records

Notarial statutes and rules

Notarial Acts - formalities, evidential status and executive force

Attestation of signatures

Execution of documents by individual and company documents

Powers of attorney

Registration of British ships and shipping protests

Bills of Exchange - definitions, time, acceptance, payment, dishonour

PUBLIC NOTARIES (CONDUCT AND DISCIPLINE) RULES 1993
as amended by the Notaries (Access to Justice Act) (Consequential Provisions) Rules 1999

REVOKED BY THE NOTARIES (CONDUCT AND DISCIPLINE) RULES 2009 SUBJECT TO THE SAVINGS IN RULE 13.2

PART I: PRELIMINARY

Citation and Commencement

1. These rules may be cited as the Public Notaries (Conduct and Discipline) Rules 1993 and shall come into operation on October 1, 1993.

Interpretation

2. In these rules:
    (a) "Approved Procedure" means a complaints conciliation procedure approved under Rule 3 of these rules;
    (b) "Competent Complainant" means:
        (i) a Nominated Notary,
        (ii) the Incorporated Company of Scriveners or a member of that Company nominated by it, or
        (iii) any person who has been a client of the public notary in question where the complaint relates to Notarial Misconduct arising from notarial acts or other professional services performed by the public notary for that client;
    (c) "the Court" means the Court of Faculties;
    (d) "the Contingency Fund" means the fund referred to in the Notarial Contingency Fund Rules 1981;
    (e) "Designated Society" means the Incorporated Company of Scriveners, the Notaries' Society, the Society of Public Notaries of London and such other bodies as the Master may from time to time designate for the purposes of these rules;
    (f) "the Master" means the Master of the Faculties;
    (g) "Nominated Notary" means a public notary appointed by the Registrar under Rule 4 of these Rules;
    (h) "Notarial Misconduct" means:
        (i) fraudulent conduct,
        (ii) practising as a notary public without a valid Practising Certificate or in breach of a condition or limitation imposed on a Practising Certificate, or
        (iii) other conduct unbefitting the office of a public notary;
    (i) "the Registrar" means the Registrar of the Court of Faculties;
    (j) "Scrivener Notary" means a public notary who holds the qualifications to practise as a Scrivener notary from time to time prescribed by the Incorporated Company of Scriveners of London or who did hold such qualifications before being struck off the Roll of Notaries or suspended from practice by an order of the Court;
    (k) "Solicitor Notary" means a public notary who is or was enrolled as a solicitor of the Supreme Court of England and Wales;

(l)   "the Schedule" and "the Appendix" mean respectively the Schedule and Appendix to these Rules;

(m)   references in these Rules to a "notary" or a "public notary" are references to a public notary enrolled on the Roll of Notaries maintained by the Court.

PART II: COMPLAINTS

Complaints Conciliation Procedures

3.   (a)   The Master may from time to time approve by written notice a complaints conciliation procedure produced by a Designated Society and may at any time by written notice withdraw his approval of any procedure.

(b)   An Approved Procedure may include provision:

      (i)   for the informal resolution of disputes between members of the public and public notaries concerning notarial acts done by a public notary or the conduct of a public notary's practice;

      (ii)   for the informal resolution of disputes between members of the public and public notaries concerning the charges made by public notaries for notarial services;

      (iii)   for dealing with complaints about the conduct or practice of a public notary referred to a Designated Society by the Registrar or the Law Society;

and for such other matters as the Master may from time to time specify.

(c)   An Approved Procedure shall not include provision for the resolution of complaints of Notarial Misconduct made against a public notary.

Nominated Notaries

4.   A Nominated Notary appointed by the Registrar under these Rules shall be a public notary (but not a Scrivener Notary) who holds a Notarial Practising Certificate and has held such a Certificate for not less than ten years.

Functions of Nominated Notaries

5.   (a)   A Nominated Notary may be appointed by the Registrar to investigate allegations of Notarial Misconduct referred to him by the Registrar and, if he thinks fit, to prepare and prosecute disciplinary proceedings against public notaries in the Court of Faculties in accordance with the provisions of these Rules and to carry out such other functions as may be provided in these Rules.

(b)   Where a Nominated Notary investigates an allegation of Notarial Misconduct referred to him by the Registrar but such investigation does not lead to the issue of disciplinary proceedings in the Court the Nominated Notary shall be entitled upon submitting an account to the Registrar for approval to be paid such fixed fee or to be paid at such rate for the work done as the Master may from time to time specify by Order and such fee shall be paid by the Registrar out of the Contingency Fund.

Referral of Allegations by Registrar

6.   (a)   Where the Registrar receives an allegation concerning the conduct or practice of a public notary which in his opinion does not amount to an allegation of Notarial Misconduct or where the precise nature of the allegation is unclear he shall refer the matter to a Designated Society to be dealt with in accordance with an Approved Procedure.

    (b)   Where the Registrar receives an allegation concerning the conduct or practice of a public notary (other than a Scrivener Notary) which appears to him to amount to an allegation of Notarial Misconduct he shall appoint a Nominated Notary to investigate the allegation pursuant to Rule 5 of these Rules.

    (c)   (i)   Where the Registrar receives an allegation concerning the conduct or practice of a Scrivener Notary which appears to him to amount to an allegation of Notarial Misconduct he shall refer the allegation to the Incorporated Company of Scriveners.

        (ii)   Upon the referral of such an allegation to the Incorporated Company of Scriveners it shall be investigated by the Incorporated Company under arrangements made by it and approved by the Master and if it thinks fit the Incorporated Company or a member of the Company nominated by it shall prepare and prosecute disciplinary proceedings in the Court of Faculties against the Scrivener Notary in question in accordance with the provisions of these Rules and the Incorporated Company or the member so nominated shall be regarded as a Nominated Notary for the purposes of Rule 9(c)(iii) of these Rules.

Referral of Allegations by Designated Societies

7.   Where an allegation against a public notary comes to the attention of a Designated Society (whether or not in the course of the operation of an Approved Procedure) and it appears that such allegation amounts to an allegation of Notarial Misconduct the Designated Society shall refer the allegation to the Registrar for consideration in accordance with Rule 6 of these Rules.

PART III: DISCIPLINARY PROCEDURE

Disciplinary Proceedings in the Court of Faculties

8.   (a)   A complaint of Notarial Misconduct may be made to the Court by any Competent Complainant.

    (b)   Where:

        (i)   an allegation concerning the conduct or practice of a public notary has been received by the Registrar and he has not appointed a Nominated Notary to investigate the allegation or referred the allegation to the Incorporated Company of Scriveners (as the case may be) under Rule 6(b) or Rule 6(c)(i) of these Rules within 28 days of receiving the allegation, or

(ii) the Registrar has appointed a Nominated Notary or referred the allegation to the Incorporated Company of Scriveners and the Nominated Notary or the Incorporated Company has determined not to make a complaint of Notarial Misconduct to the Court in respect of the allegation or has not so made a complaint within 112 days of his appointment or the referral of the allegation (as the case may be),

then a complaint of Notarial Misconduct in respect of that allegation may be made to the Court by any public notary who holds a Notarial Practising Certificate and such public notary shall be deemed to be a Competent Complainant for the purposes of these Rules.

(c) The procedure set out in Part II of the Schedule shall apply to all complaints of Notarial Misconduct made to the Court.

(d) The forms set out in the Appendix with such variations or additions thereto as the Master may from time to time approve shall be used in all proceedings before the Court to which these Rules relate.

Disciplinary Sanctions

9. (a) Where the Master after hearing a complaint of Notarial Misconduct against a public notary finds that it has been proved he may:

(i) order that the notary be struck off the Roll of Notaries,

(ii) order that the notary be suspended from practice as a public notary for a specified period or until certain conditions have been met or indefinitely,

(iii) impose conditions as to the future scope or conduct of the notarial practice of the notary and direct that his practising certificate be endorsed or the endorsement on his solicitor's practising certificate be marked accordingly, or

(iv) order that the notary be admonished.

(b) In addition to imposing any of the penalties listed in paragraphs (ii), (iii) or (iv) of sub-rule (a) above the Master may order that unless the notary:

(i) indemnifies any client of the notary whom the Master finds to have suffered actual loss as a result of the Notarial Misconduct in question, and

(ii) pays a penalty not exceeding £250 (or such higher sum as the Master may from time to time specify for the purpose of these Rules) such penalty to be paid to whomsoever the Master may direct, the notary shall be struck off the Roll of Notaries.

(c) (i) Subject to paragraph (iii) of this sub-rule it shall be within the discretion of the Master to order:

a. that the costs of either party to the complaint be paid by the other party,

b.   that the costs of the Court be paid by either party or by both parties (whether in equal or unequal shares),

c.   that the costs of either party or of the Court shall be paid from the Contingency Fund, and

d.   that a party against whom an order for costs is made shall, instead of paying those costs to the other party or the Court, pay them into the Contingency Fund.

(ii)   Any order for costs may be in a fixed sum assessed by the Master as representing or being a contribution towards the reasonable costs of the party concerned or may be for costs to be taxed.

(iii)   The Master shall not make any order for costs against a Nominated Notary who shall in all cases be entitled to an order for costs in his favour such costs to be paid from the Contingency Fund.

(iv)   Where an order is made for costs to be taxed the costs shall be taxed by the Registrar on such basis and in accordance with such scale applicable in the High Court or the County Court as the Master may direct.

Special Provision for Solicitor Notaries

10.   (a)   (i)   Where a Solicitor Notary is ordered by the Solicitors' Disciplinary Tribunal to be struck off the roll of solicitors a complaint may be brought to the Court by a Competent Complainant for the notary to show cause why he should not be struck off the Roll of Notaries.

(ii)   Where it comes to the notice of the Registrar that a Solicitor Notary who is not a Scrivener Notary has so been struck off the roll of solicitors he shall appoint a Nominated Notary to bring such a petition.

(iii)   Where it comes to the notice of the Registrar that a Scrivener Notary has been so struck off the roll of solicitors he shall appoint the Incorporated Company of Scriveners to bring such a petition.

(b)   The provisions of Part III of the Schedule shall apply to a complaint brought under this rule.

(c)   On the hearing of a complaint brought under this rule the Master shall order that the notary be struck off the Roll of Notaries unless the notary satisfies the Master that there is good and sufficient cause why he should not be so struck off in which case the Master may impose one of the other penalties listed in Rule 9(a) of these Rules or no penalty.

(d)   Upon hearing a complaint brought under this rule the Master shall order that the costs of the complainant and of the Court be paid by the notary concerned but in all other respects the provisions of Rule 9(c) shall apply.

(e)   It shall be the duty of any Solicitor Notary against whom a complaint has been made to the Solicitors' Disciplinary Tribunal and found by that Tribunal to be substantiated to report such finding forthwith to the Registrar (whatever penalty is imposed by the said Tribunal).

Application for Review

11. (a) Where as a result of an Order made under these Rules a public notary:

(i) has been struck off the Roll of Notaries other than pursuant to proceedings under Rule 10 of these Rules and a period of not less than twelve months has elapsed since the date of striking off,

(ii) has been suspended from practice for a period exceeding twelve months or for an indefinite period and a period of not less than twelve months has elapsed since the date of the suspension,

(iii) has had conditions imposed as to the future scope or conduct of his notarial practice, or

(iv) has been struck off the Roll of Notaries pursuant to proceedings under Rule 10 of these Rules and has since been restored to the roll of solicitors,

the public notary may petition the Court to review the Order.

(b) In the case of a petition under paragraph (i), (ii) or (iv) of sub-rule (a) above it shall be for the public notary to prove to the satisfaction of the Court that circumstances have changed since the Order was made and that it is not contrary to the public interest or the interest of the notarial profession that the Order be reviewed and, in the case of a petition under paragraph (iii) of sub-rule (a), it shall be for the public notary to prove to the satisfaction of the Court that as a result of a change in circumstances the conditions imposed are no longer necessary or desirable in the public interest.

(c) (i) The procedure set out in Part IV of the Schedule shall apply to a petition brought under this rule.

(ii) On receiving a petition brought under this Rule by a notary other than a Scrivener Notary the Registrar shall appoint a Nominated Notary to act as respondent to the petition.

(iii) On receiving a petition brought under this Rule by a Scrivener Notary the Registrar shall appoint the Incorporated Company of Scriveners to act as respondent to the petition.

(iv) The costs of the respondent to a petition brought under this Rule and of the Court shall be paid by the petitioner in any event but in all other respects the provisions of Rule 9(c) shall apply mutatis mutandis.

(d) Upon hearing a petition brought under this Rule the Master may:

(i) in the case of a petition under paragraphs (i) or (iv) of sub-rule (a) above order that the notary be restored to the Roll of Notaries either immediately or on some specified future date,

	(ii)	in the case of a petition under paragraph (ii) of sub-rule (a) order that the suspension be lifted either immediately or on some specified future date,
	(iii)	in the case of a petition under paragraph (iii) of sub-rule (a) order that the conditions imposed be lifted or that different conditions be imposed,
	(iv)	impose such conditions upon any Order or require such undertakings to be given by the petitioner as he thinks fit, or
	(v)	dismiss the petition.

Schedule and Appendix

12.	(a)	The provisions of Part I of the Schedule shall apply to all proceedings under these Rules
	(b)	It shall be within the discretion of the Registrar to grant to a party to proceedings before the Court such extension to any of the time limits contained in the Schedule as appears to him to be reasonable.
	(c)	Forms 3,5,6,8 and 11 set out in the Appendix shall be issued by the Registrar under the seal of the Court but any omission to affix the seal of the Court shall not invalidate a form or any proceedings to which it relates.

THE SCHEDULE

PART I: PRELIMINARY

1. References in this Schedule to forms are to the forms set out in the Appendix, references in Parts II and III to the complainant and the respondent are to the person bringing a complaint and the public notary against whom a complaint is brought respectively and references in Part IV to the petitioner and the respondent are to the public notary petitioning for review and the person or body appointed to act as respondent to the petition respectively.

2. (1) Any notice or document required by this schedule to be delivered to the Registrar shall be delivered to him at the Court of Faculties, 1 The Sanctuary, Westminster, London SW1P 3JT and shall be deemed to be delivered on the day on which it is actually received by the Registrar.

   (2) Any notice or document required by this Schedule to be served by the Registrar may be served by sending it by ordinary first class post to such address as may have been specified by the party concerned as his address for service or if no such address has been specified for a public notary to the address appearing for him on the Roll of Notaries, and any notice or document so sent shall be deemed to have been served on the second working day after posting.

3. The hearing of a complaint or petition under these Rules shall take place at such venue as the Master may direct and each party shall be entitled to be present and to be represented by a public notary, a solicitor or counsel.

PART II: PROCEEDINGS UNDER RULE 8

1. A complaint of Notarial Misconduct shall be made by memorial of complaint in form 1 and shall be supported by an affidavit in form 2.

2. The memorial of complaint and affidavit in support shall be delivered to the Registrar.

3. On receiving a memorial of complaint and affidavit in support the Registrar shall issue the complaint and serve a copy of each document together with notice of proceedings in form 3 on the respondent.

4. Within twenty-one days of service of the notice of proceedings on him the respondent shall deliver to the Registrar an answer to the complaint in form 4 and on receipt of an answer the Registrar shall serve a copy on the complainant.

5. Within forty-two days of service of the notice of proceedings on him the respondent shall, if he intends to contest the proceedings, deliver to the Registrar an affidavit in reply to the complaint and on receipt of such affidavit the Registrar shall send a copy to the complainant.

6. If the respondent fails to deliver an answer within the time prescribed by paragraph 4 or an affidavit within the time prescribed by paragraphs the Registrar shall appoint a date for the hearing of the complaint and give notice to both parties in form 5.

7. If the respondent serves an answer to the complaint and an affidavit in reply within the times prescribed the Registrar shall refer the papers to the Master who shall make such directions for the future conduct of the complaint as he thinks fit including directions:-
    (i) for the filing and service of further evidence;
    (ii) for the preparation and disclosure of lists of documents and for the inspection of such documents;
    (iii) for a preliminary hearing to consider any point of law or procedure which may be raised by the proceedings or to consider the making of further directions;
    (iv) for the hearing of the complaint and the attendance of witnesses at the hearing. And the Registrar shall serve a copy of the Master's directions and notice of any hearing (which shall be in form 5) on each party.

8. (1) If a party to the complaint requires the deponent to any affidavit filed to attend at the hearing of the complaint he shall give notice to

174

the Registrar and to the other party not less than fourteen days before the date appointed for the hearing.

(2)   If a deponent who has been so required to attend the hearing does not attend the onus shall be on the party seeking to rely on the affidavit evidence of that witness to show why the affidavit should be accepted in evidence.

9.   (1)   The procedure adopted at the hearing shall take such form as the Master thinks fit in all the circumstances of the case but shall ensure that both parties are given an opportunity to state their case to the Master and to cross-examine any witnesses giving evidence in person at the hearing.

(2)   Subject to the provisions of paragraph 8 the complaint shall be decided on the basis of the affidavits filed.

(3)   At any time prior to the conclusion of a hearing the Master may, if he thinks it expedient to do so, adjourn the hearing and give such further directions as he thinks fit.

10.   After hearing the complaint the Master may give his decision at the hearing or reserve judgment and the Registrar shall give notice to the parties of the Master's Order in form 6.

PART III: PROCEEDINGS UNDER RULE 10

1.   A complaint under Rule 10 of these Rules should be made by memorial of complaint in form 7 and shall be accompanied by a copy of the order of the Solicitors' Disciplinary Tribunal ordering the respondent to be struck off the roll of solicitors certified as being a true copy by the clerk of the said Tribunal (which certificate shall be conclusive for the purposes of the proceedings).

2.   The memorial of complaint shall be delivered to the Registrar who shall issue the complaint and appoint a date for the hearing of the complaint and shall serve a copy of the complaint and notice of hearing in form 8 on the respondent.

3.   Within twenty-eight days of service of the notice of hearing upon him the respondent shall deliver to the Registrar an acknowledgement of the complaint in form 9 and affidavits of any evidence which he wishes to bring before the Master and the Registrar shall serve copies of the same on the complainant.

4.   At the hearing of the complaint:
     (i)   the complainant shall not be required to attend or take part in the hearing but may do so if he wishes;
     (ii)   the respondent shall be entitled to address the Master and to give

evidence in person and to place before the Master such affidavits as he has delivered to the Registrar in accordance with paragraph 3 and if the complainant attends the hearing he shall take such part in it as the Master may permit.

5. After hearing the complaint the Master may give his decision at the hearing or reserve judgment and the Registrar shall give notice to the parties of the Master's Order in form 6.

PART IV: APPLICATION FOR REVIEW UNDER RULE 11

1. A petition under rule 11 of these Rules shall be made in form 10 and shall be accompanied by an affidavit or affidavits setting out in full the grounds of the petition and the evidence in support of the petition.

2. (1) Upon receiving a petition and affidavit the Registrar shall issue the petition and serve a copy of each document on the Nominated Notary (or, as the case may be, the Incorporated Company of Scriveners) appointed as respondent under Rule 11(c) (ii) or (iii) and the Registrar shall also serve on both parties notice of hearing of the petition in form 11.

    (2) Where the order which the petitioner is seeking to review was made as a result of a complaint brought by a person who was Competent Complainant qualified under Rule 2(b) (iii) the Registrar shall also send copies of the above documents and notice and any affidavit delivered under paragraph 3 to the complainant who shall be entitled to attend the hearing and (if the Master so permits) to address the Court.

3. The function of the respondent shall be to ensure that the petitioner is put to proof of his case and to bring to the attention of the Court all such facts and matters as the respondent thinks should be before the Court and if the respondent wishes to present to the Court an affidavit or affidavits in reply to the petition he shall deliver the same to the Registrar not less than twenty-eight days before the date of the hearing and the Registrar shall forthwith serve copies on the petitioner.

4. At the hearing the Master shall consider all documents and evidence which was before the Court before making the Order which the petitioner is seeking to review and shall consider the affidavits filed in support of and any affidavits filed in answer to the petition and the petitioner may give evidence in person. The Master shall also consider representations made to him by the parties.

5. After hearing the petition the Master may give his decision at the hearing or reserve judgment and the Registrar shall give notice to the parties of the Master's Order in form 6.

APPENDIX

Form 1: Memorial of Complaint
IN THE COURT OF FACULTIES
in the matter of [AB] a public notary and
in the matter of the Public Notaries (Conduct and Discipline) Rules 1993
To the Registrar
I, the undersigned [CD], of [address] do hereby make complaint that the said [AB] of [address] has been guilty of Notarial Misconduct within the meaning of the said Rules.
The grounds of this complaint are contained in the affidavit which accompanies this memorial.
DATED this day of   19
Signed
Address for service

Form 2: Affidavit in Support of Memorial of Complaint
IN THE COURT OF FACULTIES
in the matter of [AB] a public notary and
in the matter of the Public Notaries (Conduct and Discipline) Rules 1993 I [CD]
of [address] make oath and say as follows:-
1.   I am a Competent Complainant within the meaning of the said Rules as [specify how the deponent is a Competent Complainant].
2.   I make this affidavit in support of my memorial of complaint against the above named [AB], a public notary of [address].
3.   [Here state the facts concisely in numbered paragraphs, and show the deponent's means of knowledge].

Form 3: Notice of Proceedings
IN THE COURT OF FACULTIES
in the matter of [AB] a public notary and
in the matter of the Public Notaries (Conduct and Discipline) Rules 1993
TO: [AB] a public notary of [address]
TAKE NOTICE that a memorial of complaint has been received by the Court alleging that you have been guilty of Notarial Misconduct. A copy of the memorial and the affidavit supporting it are attached to this notice.
You are required:-
1.   Within twenty-one days of service of this notice upon you to deliver to me an answer to the complaint in the form prescribed by the above Rules, and
2.   If you intend to contest these proceedings, to deliver to me within forty-two days of service of this notice upon you an affidavit in reply to the complaint.
If you fail to comply with these requirements I will proceed to appoint a date for the hearing of the complaint.
All communications should be addressed to "The Registrar, The Court of Faculties, 1 The Sanctuary, Westminster, London SW1P 3JT".
DATED this day of   19
Signed
Registrar

Form 4: Answer to Complaint
IN THE COURT OF FACULTIES
in the matter of [AB] a public notary and
in the matter of the Public Notaries (Conduct and Discipline) Rules 1993
To the Registrar
I, [AB] in answer to the complaint of [CD], say that:-
1.   I intend to contest the complaint
or I do not intend to contest the complaint [delete as applicable]
2.   My address for service is
DATED this day of
Signed

Form 5: Notice of Hearing
IN THE COURT OF FACULTIES
in the matter of [AB] a public notary and
in the matter of the Public Notaries (Conduct and Discipline) Rules 1993
To the above named respondent [AB] of [address] and to the complainant [CD] of
[address]
TAKE NOTICE that this complaint will be heard by the Master of the Faculties
on   day the   day of   19   at   o'clock in the noon
at   when you are required to attend.
If you do not attend the hearing may proceed in your absence.
DATED this day of 19
Signed Registrar

Form 6: Order
IN THE COURT OF FACULTIES
in the matter of [AB] a public notary and
in the matter of the Public Notaries (Conduct and Discipline) Rules 1993
To the above named [respondent/petitioner] [AB] of [address] and to the
[complainant/respondent] [CD] of [address]
The Master of the Faculties having heard this [complaint] [petition] on the
 day of   19 THE COURT DOTH ORDER as follows:-
DATED this day of   19
Signed
Registrar

Form 7: Memorial of Complaint under Rule 10
IN THE COURT OF FACULTIES
in the matter of [AB] a public notary and
in the matter of the Public Notaries (Conduct and Discipline) Rules 1993 To the
Registrar
I, the undersigned [CD] of [address] being a Competent Complainant within the
meaning of the said Rules do hereby make complaint that the said [AB] of
[address] being a Solicitor Notary within the meaning of the said Rules was, by
an order of the Solicitors' Disciplinary Tribunal made on the   day of
 19 ,ordered to be struck off the roll of solicitors of the Supreme Court and that
he should now be required to show cause why he should not be struck off the Roll
of Notaries.

A certified copy of the order of the said Tribunal accompanies this memorial.
DATED this day of 19
Signed
Address for service

Form 8: Notice of Hearing under Rule 10
IN THE COURT OF FACULTIES
in the matter of [AB] a public notary and
in the matter of the Public Notaries (Conduct and Discipline) Rules 1993
To the above named respondent [AB], a public notary of [address] and to the complainant [CD] of [address]
TAKE NOTICE that a memorial of complaint has been received by the Court against you [AB] under Rule 10 of the said Rules and it appears to the Court that you, being a Solicitor Notary within the meaning of the said Rules, have been struck off the roll of solicitors by the Solicitors' Disciplinary Tribunal. A copy of the memorial and the order of the Solicitors' Disciplinary Tribunal is attached to this notice.
NOW YOU [AB] are required:-
1.   Within twenty-eight days of the service of this notice upon you to deliver to me an acknowledgement of the complaint in the form prescribed by the said Rules and affidavits of any evidence which you wish to bring before the Court.
2.   To attend before the Master of the Faculties on   day the   day of   19   at   o'clock in the   noon
at
to show cause why you should not be struck off the Roll of Notaries, and if you do not attend the hearing may proceed in your absence.
All communications should be addressed to "The Registrar, The Court of Faculties, 1 The Sanctuary, Westminster, London SW1P 3JT"
DATED this day of   19
Signed Registrar

Form 9: Acknowledgement to Complaint under Rule 10
IN THE COURT OF FACULTIES
in the matter of [AB] a public notary and
in the matter of the Public Notaries (Conduct and Discipline) Rules 1993 To the Registrar
I [AB] acknowledge service of the Notice of hearing of this complaint.
[Affidavits setting out the evidence which I wish to bring before the Master accompany this form]
or [I do not wish to bring any evidence before the Master] (delete as applicable)
My address for service is
DATED this   day of   19
Signed

Form 10: Petition under Rule 11
IN THE COURT OF FACULTIES
in the matter of [AB] a public notary and
in the matter of the Public Notaries (Conduct and Discipline) Rules 1993
To the Registrar

I [AB] of [address for service] petition the Court as follows:-

1. By an order of the Court made on [date] it was ordered that [set out the terms of the order other than terms as to costs]

2. I now ask that the said order be reviewed pursuant to Rule 11 of the said Rules

3. The grounds of this petition and the evidence in support of it are fully set out in the accompanying affidavit[s]

DATED this day of 19

Signed

Petitioner

Form 11: Notice of Hearing of Petition under Rule 11

IN THE COURT OF FACULTIES

in the matter of [AB] a public notary and

in the matter of the Public Notaries (Conduct and Discipline) Rules 1993

To the above named petitioner [AB] of [address] and to [CD] of [address] appointed to act as respondent to this petition

TAKE NOTICE that this petition will be heard by the Master of the

Faculties on   day the   day of   19   at   o'clock in the noon at

when you are required to attend. If you do not attend the hearing may proceed in your absence

DATED this day of 19

Signed

Registrar

ORDER OF THE MASTER MADE PURSUANT TO THE NOTARIES (RECORDS) RULES ON 4TH MARCH 1992 as amended by the Notaries (Access to Justice Act) (Consequential Provisions) Rules 1999

THE NOTARIES (RECORDS) RULES 2001 WERE REVOKED BY THE NOTARIES PRACTICE RULES 2001 SUBJECT TO THE SAVINGS IN RULE 24.2

We, JOHN ARTHUR DALZIEL OWEN, Knight, One of Her Majesty's Justices of the High Court, Commissary or Master of the Faculties of the Lord Archbishop of Canterbury do hereby make the following Order pursuant to Rule 3 (2) of The Notaries (Records) Rules 1991:

1.   The Rules adopted by the Society of Public Notaries of London on the 11th day of December 1990 are hereby approved for the Members of that Society. The said Rules are hereby annexed in Schedule A

2.   The Statement of Good Notarial Practice contained on Page 7 of The Provincial Notary (3rd Edition) 1991 shall apply to all other Notaries practising in England and Wales. The said Statement is hereby annexed in Schedule B

AS WITNESS Our hand this Fourth day of March 1992

John Owen

MASTER

SCHEDULE A

SOCIETY of PUBLIC NOTARIES of LONDON

NOTARIAL RECORDS

RULES adopted at the Committee Meeting held on 11 December 1990

The following Rules shall apply to the preservation of notarial records by Members of the Society:

1.   **Documents in notarial or authentic form:**
        Normal practice shall be for such documents to be executed in duplicate original and for the original not issued to the client to be kept on a notarial protocol. In exceptional cases, where a duplicate original cannot be retained by the notary, a complete photographic copy of the document should be kept in the protocol. Such protocol shall be preserved permanently either by the notary concerned or by his firm or, in the event of the notary ceasing to practise, by his successor practice, if any, failing which, by the Society.

2.   **Other documents:**
Documents which are not in notarial or authentic form and which are attested by a Scrivener notary need not be fully recorded by the attesting notary. It shall be sufficient for a record to be kept consisting of the name of the party or parties whose signatures are attested and the nature of the document attested. Such records shall be preserved as in 1. above for a minimum term of six years.

SCHEDULE B

Notaries should maintain a Register and Protocol which shall contain at least:

(i)   the date of the notarial act

(ii)   the full name and UK address of the person appearing before the Notary and a statement of the means by which that person is identified

(iii)   a description of the Act

(iv)   a description of any document produced to the Notary

(v)   In the case of any private document EITHER a description of any such document prepared by the Notary or executed signed or sworn before the Notary OR an extract of any such document (each description or extract must be sufficient to enable the parties to the document, its nature purpose and effect to be identified, to give particulars of any person to whom any power or authority is given, to identify any property which is affected and to identify the jurisdiction in which any transaction is to take effect) OR a complete copy of any such document OR a reference to the Protocol containing such document

(vi)   In the case of any document in the public or authentic form the original or a complete copy of such document OR a reference to the Protocol containing such document

(vii)   a statement of the fee charged.

NOTARIES (POST-ADMISSION) RULES 1991
Incorporating amendments made by the Notaries (Qualification) Rules 1998
with effect from 1 February 1999

REVOKED BY THE NOTARIES (POST-ADMISSION) RULES 2009
SUBJECT TO THE SAVINGS IN RULE 11(2)

Citation and Commencement
1.   These rules may be cited as the Notaries (Post-Admission) Rules 1991, and shall come into operation on the 8th day of July 1991.

Interpretation
2.   In these Rules:
"The Faculty Office" means the Registry of the Court of Faculties; "The Master" means the Master of the Faculties;

"The Registrar" means the Registrar of the Court of Faculties.

Period of Practice Under Supervision
3.   (1)   This Rule shall apply to all Notaries admitted to practise in England and Wales (other than Notaries to whom Rule 10 applies and Notaries for ecclesiastical purposes only) on or after the 13th day of June 1990

(2)   A notary to whom this Rule applies shall be required to complete a period of practice under supervision in accordance with this Rule which shall commence
(a)   in the case of a notary admitted after the date on which this Rule comes into effect, or of a notary admitted before that date but not in practice on that date, on the date on which he commences or resumes practice as a notary; or
(b)   in any other case, as soon as arrangements for supervision can practicably be made, but not in any event later than two months after this rule comes into effect.

(3)   Subject to paragraph (4) of this Rule, the duration of the period of practice under supervision shall be two years, less either of the following:
(a)   any period of apprenticeship served pursuant to section 2 of the Public Notaries Act 1801 or pursuant to requirements of the Incorporated Company of Scriveners of London imposed under section 57(11)(b) of the Courts and Legal Services Act 1990;
(b)   any period spent in actual practice as a notary, prior to the coming into effect of these Rules, by a district notary appointed pursuant to the Public Notaries Act 1833.

(4)   The Master may direct that the period of practice under supervision be extended in any particular case, either:

183

(a) as a condition of approving a change of supervision under paragraph (5) of rule 4, or

(b) following his consideration of a report submitted pursuant to paragraph (3) of rule 7, or

(c) following disciplinary proceedings.

Selection of Supervisor

4. (1) During the period of practice under supervision the notary to whom this Rule applies ("the supervised notary") shall practise as a notary only under the supervision (as defined in rule 5) of another notary ("the supervisor") who holds a current practising certificate entered in or issued from the Court of Faculties, and who has been engaged in actual practice as a notary for not less than five years immediately preceding the period of supervision.

(2) A person who has no usual place of business within 50 miles (or within a distance which he is able to travel in two hours in normal conditions, if shorter) of the office from which a supervised notary proposes to practise shall not act as supervisor of that notary unless his appointment as such is confirmed by the Master.

(3) It shall be the duty of a supervised notary to notify the Faculty Office upon request of the name and address of his supervisor; and it shall be the duty of any notary to notify the Faculty Office upon request of the names and addresses of all notaries of whom he is the supervisor.

(4) A supervised notary shall, upon the death or retirement from practice of his supervisor, forthwith make arrangements for another notary qualified under this Rule to supervise his practice for the remainder of the required period; and any time between the death or retirement of the former supervisor and the coming into effect of such arrangements shall not count towards the period of supervised practice.

(5) If for any reason other than the death or retirement of the supervisor, either party wishes the appointment of a particular supervisor to be terminated before the expiry of the required period of supervised practice, application shall be made for that purpose to the Master, who may terminate the supervision upon such conditions as he shall think fit.

Extent of Supervision

5. (1) The following aspects of a notary's practice shall be excluded from the general requirement of supervision (but not from the obligation to produce records and accounts under paragraph (2) of this Rule):

(a) conveyancing and probate, in the case of a notary who is also a solicitor and who would be entitled to carry out conveyance and probate as a solicitor without supervision, or who does in fact receive such supervision in relation to his practice as a solicitor as is required by the Solicitors Act 1974 and Rules made thereunder;

(b)   conveyancing, in the case of a notary who is also a licensed conveyancer and who would be entitled to carry out conveyancing as such without supervision, or who does in fact receive such supervision in relation to his practice as a licensed conveyancer as is required by the statutes and rules governing that profession.

(2)   The supervisor shall visit the office of the supervised notary at least once in every period of four months, and shall inspect the records and accounts of the supervised notary relating to that period, which the supervised notary shall (subject to paragraph (3) of this Rule) produce to the supervisor on request.

(3)   If it appears to a supervised notary that papers relating to the business of a particular client cannot be shown to his supervisor without causing a breach of the duty of confidentiality owed to that client (whether on account of a relationship between the client and the supervisor, or because the supervisor is known to act for a person in competition with the client, or for any other reason), he shall inform the supervisor of that fact. The supervisor may nominate another notary (qualified to be a supervisor under rule 4(1) but not subject to the same objections of confidentiality as respects the client concerned) and the notary nominated shall, if willing to act, have the supervisor's rights and duties in relation to those papers.

(4)   The supervisor shall make himself available at all reasonable times to offer advice and guidance to the supervised notary on matters covered by the supervision.

(5)   The supervisor shall take particular care to ensure (so far as he is able) that the supervised notary is aware of, and complies with, all Rules and Orders made by the Master under section 57 of the Courts and Legal Services Act 1990, and conducts himself in a manner calculated to maintain the reputation of the office and profession of a public notary.

Post-Admission Education
6.   Every supervised notary shall, during each year of his period of practice under supervision, attend

(a)   one full-day course or seminar approved by the Master covering the topics of Bills of Exchange, Notarial Practice and Professional Conduct;

(b)   if desiring to carry out conveyancing as part of his notarial practice, one full-day continuing education course or seminar in

185

conveyancing approved by the Master; and

(c)   if desiring to carry out probate work as part of his notarial practice, one full-day continuing education course or seminar in probate approved by the Master;

and shall make a report to his supervisor on the course or seminar attended.

Records and reporting

7.   (1)   A report of every visit and inspection made pursuant to paragraph (2) of rule 5 shall be made by the supervisor, and shall be inserted in the Register or other permanent record kept by each notary pursuant to the Notaries (Records) Rules 1991.

(2)   The supervisor shall enter in the Register or other permanent record kept by him pursuant to the Notaries (Records) Rules 1991 a note of any advice or guidance given to a supervised notary pursuant to paragraph 4 of rule 5.

(3)   Upon the completion of a period of practice under supervision (or upon the retirement from practice of a supervisor during such a period), the supervisor shall report the fact of such completion to the Master in writing and shall indicate the courses or seminars attended by the supervised notary pursuant to rule 6, and whether in his opinion the supervised notary should thereafter be permitted to practise without supervision. The supervisor and the supervised notary shall respond in writing to any questions put by the Master in relation to the period of supervision, and produce to the Faculty Office such documents as the Master may require.

Fees

8.   A notary agreeing to act as a supervisor shall be entitled to charge the supervised notary a fee not exceeding the level prescribed from time to time in Regulations made by the Master (which may include provision for expenses), together with the amount of any Value Added Tax due thereon. If for any reason the appointment of the supervisor ceases before the end of the period of supervision, the fee shall be apportioned pro rata or as the Master may direct.

Dispensations

9.   The Master may, upon such application made to him as he deems sufficient, for good cause dispense any notary from the requirement of supervision under these Rules or permit such lesser supervision as he considers practicable in the circumstances of any particular case.

European Economic Area Notaries

10.   The provisions of these Rules shall not apply to any Notary who, immediately prior to his admission, was recognised by the Master as qualified for admission under the provisions of rule 9 of the Notaries (Qualification) Rules 1998.

NOTARIES (RECORDS) RULES 1991

REVOKED BY THE NOTARIES PRACTICE RULES 2001 SUBJECT TO THE SAVINGS IN RULE 24.2

Citation and Commencement

1. These Rules may be cited as the Notaries (Records) Rules 1991, and shall come into operation on the 1st day of October 1991. These Rules shall not however apply to ecclesiastical notaries until such date as the Master shall, by a subsequent Order, appoint.

Interpretation

2. In these Rules "The Master" means the Master of the Faculties.

Duty to keep a record of notarial acts

3. (1) It shall be the duty of every public notary practising as such in England or Wales to maintain and keep in accordance with good notarial practice a permanent record of all notarial acts made and performed by him after the date on which these Rules come into effect.

   (2) For the purposes of this Rule "good notarial practice" as to the information required to be recorded in the Register in relation to any class of instrument, the classes of instrument of which copies or duplicates are required to be kept, the materials or stationery to be used in making any record, and the storage and security of records, may be conclusively defined in
      (a) regulations made by the Master from time to time, or
      (b) publications (or parts thereof) approved by the Master in writing as containing a statement of good notarial practice.

Inspection of Records

4. (1) Records kept pursuant to these Rules shall be open at any time to inspection by the Master or a person authorised by him for the purpose.

   (2) A notary having custody of any record kept pursuant to these Rules shall, on request by any person having a proper interest in the subject-matter of any instrument so recorded (or believed to be so recorded), cause a diligent search to be made for such instrument, and shall (if it is found) furnish to that person on request a notarially certified copy of the instrument (if he has a copy or duplicate in his custody), or an extract from the Register relating thereto, or both; provided that a proper fee shall be paid by the person making any such request.

   (3) Any question as to whether a person has a proper interest in the subject-matter of any instrument for the purposes of paragraph (2) of this Rule may be determined by the Master.

187

Notaries ceasing to practise

5. (1) Upon a notary ceasing for any reason to practise as such, arrangements shall be made by him, or failing him by his continuing notarial partners or failing them by the persons having for the time being possession or custody of the records kept by him pursuant to these Rules, for such records to be transferred

   (a) to another notary in practice appointed by him or by his continuing notarial partners, or

   (b) to another notary in practice appointed, with the approval of the Master, by the persons having possession or custody of the records, or

   (c) to an archive designated for the purpose under Regulations made by the Master from time to time.

   (2) The provisions of Rule 4 shall apply to a notary or archive to which the records of any notary are transferred pursuant to paragraph (1) of this Rule as they apply to the notary himself.

Application of Rules to Ecclesiastical Notaries

6. The provisions of these Rules shall apply to notaries appointed for ecclesiastical purposes only subject to the following modifications:

   (1) The requirement of Rule 3 to keep a record of notarial acts shall apply only to such ecclesiastical acts as law or custom requires to be performed in the presence of a public notary and recorded in writing.

   (2) Any act or transaction properly recorded in the Act Book of any Archbishop or Bishop, or in the Minute Book of any Cathedral Chapter, shall be deemed to have been properly recorded in accordance with good notarial practice.

   (3) The Master may make different Regulations, or approve different publications, under paragraph (2) of Rule 3 for the definition of "good notarial practice" in relation to ecclesiastical notaries from those made or approved in relation to other classes of notary.

   (4) Paragraphs (2) and (3) of Rule 4 shall not apply to ecclesiastical notaries.

   (5) Rule 5 shall not apply to ecclesiastical notaries, but upon a person ceasing for any reason to hold the office in respect of which he was appointed an ecclesiastical notary, any records kept by him pursuant to these Rules shall be transferred to the succeeding holder of that office (being an ecclesiastical notary) upon his appointment.

NOTARIAL RULES AND ORDERS (RATIFICATION & CITATION) RULES 1991

Citation and Commencement
1.   These rules may be cited as the Notarial Rules and Orders (Ratification and Citation) Rules 1991, and shall come into operation on the 8th day of July 1991.

Interpretation
2.   In these Rules "The Master" means the Master of the Faculties.

Revocation of Rules and Orders
3.   The following Orders of the Master are hereby revoked; Order dated 30th September 1981 concerning the level of contribution to the Contingency Fund and publication of accounts.

Order dated 30th September 1981 concerning examinations and insurance (so far as not already revoked).

Order dated 30th September 1981 concerning practising certificate registration fees and evidence of indemnity insurance (so far as not already revoked).

Order dated 26th February 1982 concerning fees.

Rules dated 15th October 1984 concerning advertising.

Order dated 25th October 1984 concerning fees.

Order dated 4th September 1986 concerning fees for the issue or registration of practising certificates.

Fee-sharing
4.   Rule 7 of the Notaries Practice Rules 1989 is hereby replaced by the following:

"7.   (1)   Subject to paragraph (2) of this Rule, a notary shall not share or agree to share his professional fees with any person not entitled to act as a notary; provided that this Rule shall not prohibit the payment of any allowance or allowances, sum or sums of money, that are or shall be agreed to be made or paid to the widows or children of any deceased notary or notaries, by any surviving partner or partners of such deceased notary or notaries.

(2)   A notary who also practises in partnership as a solicitor may share professional fees with his partners who are solicitors, provided that a notary who shares fees by virtue of this paragraph shall keep accounts which enable the income and

189

expenditure arising from his practice as a notary to be distinguished from the income and expenditure arising from his practice as a solicitor, and shall furnish the Faculty Office with such additional information as to his partnership and accounting arrange-ments as may be prescribed in Rules or Orders of the Master.

(3)   Paragraph (2) of this Rule shall not apply to a notary, any part of whose practice as a notary is within the jurisdiction of the Incorporated Company of Scriveners of London."

Ratification of remaining Orders and Rules
5.   For the avoidance of doubt the following Orders and Rules are hereby ratified and confirmed and shall have effect as though they were repeated herein:
(a)   Order dated 30th September 1981 establishing the Contingency Fund.
(b)   Order dated 16th June 1982 concerning notification of change of address by notaries.
(c)   Order dated 21st October 1985 concerning fees for the issue of notarial faculties (so far as it concerns faculties for practice within England and Wales).
(d)   Order dated 17th February 1989 concerning fees for the issue or registration of practising certificates.
(e)   The Notaries Practice Rules 1989 (subject to the variation therein effected by Rule 4).
(f)   The Notaries Accounts Rules 1989.
(g)   The Notaries Trust Accounts Rules 1989.
(h)   The Notaries Accounts (Deposit Interest) Rules 1989.

Citation of ratified Orders and Rules
6.   The Orders and Rules mentioned against the following paragraph letters in Rule 5 may be cited by the short titles given against those letters in this Rule:
(a)   The Notarial Contingency Fund Rules 1981.
(b)   The Notaries (Notification of Address) Rules 1982.
(c)   The Notarial Faculties (Fees) Order 1985.
(d)   The Notaries (Practising Certificate Fees) Order 1989.

Exclusion of Ecclesiastical Notaries from scope of Rules
7.   The following Rules shall not apply to ecclesiastical notaries in respect of their practice as such:
(a)   The Notarial Contingency Fund Rules 1981.
(b)   The Notaries Practice Rules 1989.

PUBLIC NOTARIES (PRACTISING CERTIFICATES) RULES 1991
as amended by the Public Notaries (Practising Certificates) (Amendment) Rules 1993, 1995 and 1999

Citation and Commencement
1.   These Rules may be cited as the Public Notaries (Practising Certificates) Rules 1991, and shall come into operation on the 1st day of October 1991 (with the exception of Rule 4 which shall come into operation on the 1st day of January 1992).

Interpretation
2.   In these Rules

"The Faculty Office" means the Registry of the Court of Faculties;

"The Master" means the Master of the Faculties;

"The Registrar" means the Registrar of the Court of Faculties;

"The 1982 Rules" means the Public Notaries (Practising Certificates). Rules 1982.

Ratification of 1982 Rules
3.   For the avoidance of doubt the 1982 Rules are hereby ratified and confirmed and shall have effect (save insofar as they are hereby varied) as though they were repeated herein.

Duty to hold Practising Certificate
4.   No person admitted as a public notary, whether before or after the coming into effect of these Rules, shall hold himself out as a public notary in practice, or perform any notarial act, in England or Wales unless he holds a current solicitor's practising certificate duly entered in the Court of Faculties, or a notarial practising certificate issued out of the Court of Faculties, pursuant to the 1982 Rules.

Insurance Requirements
5.   In the 1982 Rules
    (a)   for every reference to the Solicitors Indemnity Rules 1975 there shall be substituted a reference to the Solicitors Indemnity Rules 1987; and
    (b)   for every reference to insurance issued under The Law Society's Professional Indemnity Insurance Master Policy there shall be substituted a reference to solicitors' professional indemnity insurance provided by the Solicitors Indemnity Fund Limited.

Form of Application for Entry or Issue of Practising Certificate
6.   [revoked]

Power to Place Restrictions on Practising Certificates

7.   For the avoidance of doubt it is declared that the Master may direct the entry or issue of any practising certificate under the 1982 Rules to be restricted in such manner as he may think fit, as to the matters or fields in which, or the conditions under which, the holder is thereby entitled to practise as a notary; and the Registrar shall adapt the wording of the certificate or endorsement (as the case may be) prescribed by the 1982 Rules to give effect to the Master's directions in any such case.

8.   (1)   The Registrar may on the entry or issue of any practising certificate under the 1982 Rules having regard to the provisions of the 1982 Rules and of any general direction made by the Master restrict the certificate or endorsement as to the matters or fields in which the holder is thereby entitled to practise as a notary and the wording of the certificate or endorsement (as the case may be) prescribed by the 1982 Rules shall be adapted to give effect to such restriction.

     (2)   Any person aggrieved by

         (a)   the refusal of the Registrar to issue a practising certificate to him under the 1982 Rules, or

         (b)   the imposition by the Registrar pursuant to sub-rule (1) of this rule of a restriction on a practising certificate granted to him may appeal to the Master against such refusal or the imposition of such a restriction.

     (3)   (a)   An appeal under sub-rule (2) of this rule shall be made by delivering written notice to the Faculty Office within twenty-eight days of the date of notification of the Registrar's refusal to issue a practising certificate or the date on which a practising certificate is issued on which a restriction has been imposed (as the case may be).

         (b)   An appeal under sub-rule (2) of this rule shall be heard by the Master in chambers but may if the appellant so requests be disposed of by the Master on the basis of written representations.

         (c)   Upon hearing an appeal under sub-rule (2) of this rule the Master may:

            (i)   direct the Registrar to issue or enter a practising certificate to the appellant without condition or restriction,

            (ii)   direct the Registrar to issue or enter a practising certificate to the appellant containing restrictions or conditions imposed by the Master pursuant to rule 7 of these Rules,

            (iii)   dismiss the appeal.

9.   (1)   In this Rule "specified profession" means barrister-at-law, chartered or certified accountant, chartered surveyor, licensed conveyancer, licensed probate practitioner, solicitor of the supreme court and such other profession as the Master may specify by order.

   (2)   Where a Public Notary practises or is a member of a specified profession he shall be under a duty to inform the Registrar forthwith if he is struck off, dismissed or otherwise debarred or disqualified or suspended from practising that specified profession or is subject to any disciplinary sanction imposed by any body regulating that profession.

   (3)   The failure by a Public Notary to comply with the duty imposed by sub-rule (2) of this Rule shall be Notarial Misconduct within the meaning of Rule 2(h) of the Public Notaries (Conduct and Discipline) Rules 1993.

   (4)   If it comes to the attention of the Registrar that a Public Notary has been struck off, dismissed or otherwise debarred or disqualified or suspended from practising a specified profession or is subject to any disciplinary sanction imposed by any body regulating that profession, the Registrar may restrict or endorse the practising certificate of the notary in question and Rule 8 shall apply as if the practising certificate were being entered or issued but the Registrar shall notify the notary concerned in writing of the terms of the restriction or endorsement.

SCHEDULE

[revoked]

FACULTY OFFICE

We, CHARLES RICHARD GEORGE One of Her Majesty's Counsel, Commissary or Master of the Faculties of the Lord Archbishop of Canterbury so far as We lawfully can or may do hereby ORDER pursuant to the provisions of Rule 10 of the Public Notaries (Practising Certificate) Rules 1982 that the minimum figure of insurance against civil liability for professional negligence shall be One Million Pounds (£1,000,000) with effect from the date hereof until further Order

As witness Our hand this 17th day of April 2012

CHARLES GEORGE

MASTER

NOTARIES' ACCOUNTS (DEPOSIT INTEREST) RULES 1989
as amended by the Notaries (Access to Justice Act) (Consequential Provisions) Rules 1999

Citation and Commencement
1. These Rules may be cited as the Notaries' Accounts (Deposit Interest) Rules 1989 and shall come into operation on the First day of April 1990.

Interpretation
2. In these Rules the expression a separate designated account" shall mean a deposit account at a bank or building society in the name of the notary or his firm in the title of which the word "client" appears and which is designated by reference to the identity of the client or matter concerned; the expressions 'bank" and "building society" shall have the meanings assigned to them by the Notaries' Accounts Rules 1989.

Obligation to account for interest
3. Subject to Rule 6, when a notary holds money for a client, the notary shall account to the client for interest in the following circumstances:
    (a) Separate designated account Where the money is held in a separate designated account, the notary shall account for the interest earned on it.
    (b) Undesignated accounts

    Where the money is not held in a separate designated account, the following provisions shall apply:
        (i) Sums held for specified periods. The notary shall account to the client for interest at a rate calculated in accordance with Rule 4, if the money is held for as long as or longer than the number of weeks set out in the left hand column of the Table below and the minimum balance held during that period equals or exceeds the corresponding figure in the right hand column of the Table.

TABLE

No. of Weeks	Minimum Balance
8	£500
4	£1,000
2	£5,000
1	£10,000

        (ii) Sums held for less than one week. The notary shall account to the client for interest at a rate calculated in accordance with Rule 4 if he holds a sum of money exceeding £10,000 for less than one week and it is fair and reasonable to do so having regard to all the circumstances.

(iii)   Variable balances. Where money continuously held for a client varies significantly in amount over the period during which it is held, then having regard to any sum payable under sub-paragraph (i) the notary shall account to the client for such interest (or additional interest) at a rate calculated in accordance with Rule 4 as is fair and reasonable having regard to the varying amounts of money and the length of time for which these are held.

(iv)   Money held intermittently. Where a notary during the course of acting for a client holds sums of money for the client intermittently, the notary shall account to the client for interest at a rate calculated in accordance with Rule 4, if it is fair and reasonable to do so having regard to all the circumstances including the aggregate of the sums held and the periods for which they are held, notwithstanding that no individual sum would have attracted interest under paragraph (i).

(c)   Transfers between designated and undesignated accounts.

Where the money is held successively in designated and undesignated accounts, but as a result of the previous paragraphs, interest or a sum equivalent thereto is not payable on the money for the whole time it was held, then the notary shall account to the client for such interest (or fair and reasonable; for this purpose regard shall be had to the additional interest) at a rate calculated in accordance with Rule 4 as is provisions of paragraph (b) as if for the whole time the money was held, it was not held in a separate designated account.

Rate of Interest

4.   (1)   The rate of interest to be applied for the purposes of Rules 3(b) and (c) shall be the rate of interest which would have been earned by the money, or its gross equivalent if the rate would have been net of tax, if the money had been kept in a separate designated account earning interest at a rate not less than that from time to time posted publicly by the relevant bank or building society for small deposits subject to the minimum period of notice of withdrawals.

    (2)   for the purpose of paragraph (1), the relevant bank or building society shall mean:

(a)   the bank or building society where the money is held, or

(b)   where the money, or part of it, is held in successive and concurrent client accounts maintained at different banks or building societies, whichever of those banks or building societies was offering the highest rate for small deposits subject to the minimum period of notice of withdrawals on the day when interest payable under Rules 3(b) and (c) commenced to accrue, or

     (c)   where, contrary to the provisions of the Notaries' Accounts Rules 1989, the money is not held in a client account, any bank or building society nominated by the client.

Certification by The Notaries' Society or The Society of Public Notaries of London

5.   Without prejudice to any other remedy which may be available to him, any client of a notary who feels aggrieved that interest or a sum equivalent thereto has not been paid to him under these Rules shall be entitled to apply to The Society of Public Notaries of London, when he is the client of a notary who is a member of that Society, or to The Notaries' Society in any other case for a certificate as to whether or not interest ought to have been earned for him and, if so, the amount of such interest, and upon the issue of such a certificate the sum certified to be due shall be payable by the notary to the client.

Exception

6.   Nothing in these Rules shall:
     (a)   affect any arrangement in writing, whenever made, between a notary and his client as to the application of the client's money or interest thereon; or
     (b)   apply to money received by a notary being money subject to a trust of which the notary is a trustee.

NOTARIES ACCOUNTS RULES 1989
(As amended by Order of the Master dated the 21st day of February 2012)

We, CHARLES RICHARD GEORGE One of Her Majesty's Counsel, Commissary or Master of the Faculties of the Most Reverend Father in God Rowan Douglas by Divine Providence Lord Archbishop of Canterbury Primate of All England and Metropolitan in exercise of the powers conferred by section 57 of the Courts and Legal Services Act 1990 and of all other powers Us enabling hereby make the following rules:

Citation and Commencement
These Rules may be cited as the Notaries Accounts Rules 1989 and shall come into operation on the 1st day of April 1990.

1. These Rules shall be known as the Notaries Accounts Rules 1989.

1A. Rule 9(2)(d) and Rule 11A shall come into force on the first day of April 2012.

2. (1) In these Rules, unless the context otherwise requires:
      "Notary" shall mean a Notary Public and shall include a firm of notaries;

      "Client's Money" shall mean money held or received by a notary on account of a person for whom he is acting in relation to the holding or receipt of such money either as a notary or, in connection with his practice as a notary, as agent, bailee, stakeholder or in any other capacity; provided that the expression "client's money" shall not include-
      (a) money held or received on account of the trustees of a trust of which the notary is a notary-trustee; or
      (b) money to which the only person entitled is the notary himself or, in the case of a firm of notaries, one or more of the partners in the notaries firm;

      "Client" shall mean any person on whose account a notary holds or receives client's money;

      "Trust Money" shall mean money held or received by a notary which is not client's money and which is subject to a trust of which the notary is a trustee whether or not he is a notary-trustee of such trust;

      "Client Account" shall mean a current or deposit account at a bank or deposit account with a building society in the name of the notary and in the title of which account the word "client" appears;

"Bank" shall mean the branch, situated in England or Wales, of a Bank as defined by section 87(1) of the Solicitors Act 1974, as amended by paragraph 9 of Schedule 6 to the Banking Act 1979;

"Building Society" shall mean the branch, situated in England or Wales, of a building society as defined by paragraph 11(5) of Schedule 18 to the Building Societies Act 1986;

"Notary-Trustee" shall mean a notary who is a sole trustee or co-trustee only with one or more of his partners or employees.
"Public Officer" shall mean an officer whose remuneration is defrayed out of moneys provided by Parliament, the revenues of the Duchy of Cornwall or the Duchy of Lancaster, the general fund of the Church Commissioners, the Forestry Fund or the Development Fund;

"Statutory undertakers" shall mean any person authorised by or under an Act of Parliament to construct, work, or carry on any railway, canal, inland navigation, dock, harbour, tramway, gas, electricity, water or other public undertaking;

"Local Authority" shall have the same meaning as is given to this expression by the Local Government Act 1972;

"The Faculty Office" shall mean the Court of Faculties of the Lord Archbishop of Canterbury and the words "Master" and "Registrar" shall mean the Master and Registrar thereof respectively.

(2) The Interpretation Act 1889 shall apply to these Rules in the same manner as it applies to an Act of Parliament.

3. Subject to the provisions of Rule 9 hereof, every notary who holds or receives client's money, or money which under Rule 4 hereof he is permitted and elects to pay into a client account, shall without delay pay such money into a client account. Any notary may keep one client account or as many such accounts as he thinks fit.

4. There may be paid into a client account-
   (a) trust money;
   (b) such money belonging to the notary as may be necessary for the purpose of opening or maintaining the account;
   (c) money to replace any sum which for any reason may have been drawn from the account in contravention of paragraph (2) of Rule 8 of these Rules; and
   (d) a cheque or draft received by the notary which under paragraph (b) of Rule 5 of these Rules he is entitled to split but which he does not split.

5.   Where a notary holds or receives a cheque or draft which includes client's money or trust money of one or more trusts-
   (a)   he may where practicable split such cheque or draft and, if he does so, he shall deal with each part thereof as if he had received a separate cheque or draft in respect of that part; or
   (b)   if he does not split the cheque or draft, he shall, if any part thereof consist of client's money, and may, in any other case, pay the cheque or draft into a client account.

6.   No money other than money which under the foregoing Rules a notary is required or permitted to pay into a client account shall be paid into a client account, and it shall be the duty of a notary into whose client account any money has been paid in contravention of this Rule to withdraw the same without delay on discovery.

7.   There may be drawn from a client account-
   (a)   in the case of client's money-
      (i)   money properly required for a payment to or on behalf of the client;
      (ii)   money properly required for or towards payment of a debt due to the notary from the client or in reimbursement of money expended by the notary on behalf of the client;
      (iii) money drawn on the client's authority;
      (iv)   money properly required for or towards payment of the notary's costs where there has been delivered to the client a bill of costs or other written intimation of the amount of the costs incurred and it has thereby or otherwise in writing been made clear to the client that money held for him is being or will be applied towards or in satisfaction of such costs and
      (v)   money which is transferred into another client account;
   (b)   in the case of trust money-
      (i)   money properly required for a payment in the execution of the particular trust, and
      (ii)   money to be transferred to a separate bank or building society account kept solely for the money of the particular trust;
   (c)   such money, not being money to which either paragraph (a) or paragraph (b) of this Rule applies, as may have been paid into the account under paragraph (b) of Rule 4 or paragraph (b) of Rule 5 of these Rules; and
   (d)   money which for any reason may have been paid into the account in contravention of Rule 6 of these Rules; provided that in any case under paragraph (a) or paragraph (b) of this Rule the money so drawn shall not exceed the total of the money held for the time being in such account or account of such client or trust.

8. (1) No money drawn from a client account under sub-paragraph (ii) or sub-paragraph (iv) of paragraph (a) or under paragraph (c) or paragraph (d) of Rule 7 of these Rules shall be drawn except by-

        (a) a cheque drawn in favour of the notary, or

        (b) a transfer to a bank or building society account in the name of the notary not being a client account.

    (2) No money other than money permitted by Rule 7 to be drawn from a client account shall be so drawn unless the Master upon an application made to him by the notary specifically authorise in writing its withdrawal.

9. (1) Notwithstanding the provisions of these Rules, a notary shall not be under obligation to pay into a client account client's money held or received by him-

        (a) which is received by him in the form of cash and is without delay paid in cash in the ordinary course of business to the client or on his behalf to a third party; or

        (b) which he pays into a separate bank or building society account opened or to be opened in the name of the client or of some person designated by the client in writing or acknowledged by the notary to the client in writing.

    (2) Notwithstanding the provisions of these Rules, a notary shall not pay into a client account money held or received by him-

        (a) which the client for his own convenience requests the notary to withhold from such account, such request being either in writing from the client or acknowledged by the notary to the client in writing; or

        (b) which is received by him for or towards payment of a debt to the notary from the client or in reimbursement of money expended or to be expended by the notary on behalf of the client; or

        (c) which is expressly paid to him either:-

            (i) on account of costs incurred in respect of which a bill of costs or other written intimation of the amount of the costs incurred has been delivered for payment; or

            (ii) as an agreed fee (or on account of an agreed fee) for business undertaken or to be undertaken; or

        (d) which is expressly paid to him for a disbursement or disbursements which he has agreed with the client to incur and pay within two months of the receipt of the payment.

    (3) Where a cheque or draft includes client's money as well as money of the nature described in paragraph (2) of this Rule such cheque or draft shall be dealt with in accordance with Rule 5 of these Rules.

    (4) Notwithstanding the provisions of these Rules the Master may upon application made to him by a notary specifically authorise him in writing to withhold any client's money from a client account.

10.   No sum shall be transferred from the ledger account of one client to that of another except in circumstances in which it would have been permissible under these Rules to have withdrawn from client account the sum transferred from the first client and to have paid into client account the sum transferred from the first client and to have paid into client account the sum so transferred to the second client.

11.   (1)   Subject to the provisions of Rule 11A below, every notary shall at all times keep properly written up such accounts as may be necessary-

        (a)   to show all his dealings with-

            (i)   client's money received, held or paid by him; and

            (ii)   any other money dealt with by him through a client account; and

        (b)   (i)   to show separately in respect of each client all money of the categories specified in sub-paragraph (a) of this paragraph which is received, held or paid by him on account of that client; and

            (ii)   to distinguish all money of the said categories received, held or paid by him, from any other money received, held or paid by him.

    (2)   (a)   All dealings referred to in sub-paragraph (a) of paragraph (1) of this Rule shall be recorded as may be appropriate-

            (i)   either in a clients' cash book, or a clients' column of a cash book, or

            (ii)   in a record of sums transferred from the ledger account of one client to that of another, and in addition

            (iii)   in a clients' ledger or a clients' column of a ledger, and no other dealings shall be recorded in such clients' cash book and ledger or, as the case may be, in such clients' columns, and

        (b)   all dealings of the notary relating to his practice as a notary other than those referred to in sub-paragraph (a) of paragraph (1) of this Rule shall (subject to compliance with the Notaries Trust Accounts Rules 1989) be recorded in such other cash book and ledger or such other columns of a cash book and ledger as the notary may maintain.

    (3)   In addition to the books, ledgers and records referred to in paragraph (2) of this Rule, every notary shall keep a record of all bills of costs (distinguishing between profit costs and disbursements) and of all written intimations under Rule 7(a)(iv) and under Rule 9(2)(c) of these Rules delivered or made by the notary to his clients, which record shall be contained in a bills delivered book or a file of copies of such bills and intimations.

(4)   Every notary shall within three months of the coming into force of this sub-rule or of his commencing practice on his own account (either alone or in partnership) which shall be later and thereafter not less than once in every succeeding period of three months cause the balance of his clients' cash book (or clients' column of his cash book) to be agreed with his client bank and building society pass book or statements and shall keep in the cash book or other appropriate place a reconciliation statement showing this agreement.

(5)   In this Rule the expression "accounts," "books," "ledgers" and records" shall be deemed to include loose-leaf books and such cards or other permanent documents or records as are necessary for the operation of any system of book-keeping, mechanical or otherwise.

(6)   Every notary shall preserve for at least six years from the date of the last entry therein all accounts, books, ledgers and records kept by him under this Rule.

(7)   No money may be withdrawn from a bank or building society account, being or forming part of a client account, otherwise than under the signature of one at least of the following (either alone or in conjunction with other persons) namely;
        (a)   a notary who holds a current practising certificate, or
        (b)   an employee of such a notary being a notary, or
        (c)   a solicitor or other person holding a registered legal or accounting qualification.

11A   Every notary who in his capacity as a notary holds or receives client money which must be paid into client account under these Rules shall, in addition to the provisions of Rule 11 above:
        (1)   Procure the preparation by a Reporting Accountant of an Accountant's Report for the Accounting Period and to provide a copy to the Registrar when applying for a practising certificate in accordance with the Public Notaries (Practising Certificates) Rules 1982 and 1991 or such other Rules as may be in force from time to time.

        (2)   The Accountant's Report must be prepared and a copy provided to the Registrar within six months of the end of the Accounting Period

        (3)   In this Rule 11A:
                a.   "Reporting Accountant" means an accountant who is a member of the Association of Chartered Certified Accounts or the Institute of Chartered Accountants in England and Wales or the Chartered Institute of Public Finance and Accountancy and holds a current practising certificate issued by that body

203

b. Accountant's Report" means a report which contains the information and in such form and with such completed check list as may be determined by the Faculty office signed by a Reporting Accountant relating to client's money held or received by the notary

c. "Accounting Period" means the period for which accounts of the notary are ordinarily made up provided however that it must begin at the end of the previous Accounting Period and cover not more than twelve months

d. The Reporting Accountant may not be an accountant who:-
   i. either at any time between the beginning of the Accounting Period to which the Accountant's Report relates and the signing of the accountant's Report was a partner, employee, employer or officer of the Notary to whose business the Accountant's Report relates or
   ii. has been disqualified by the Faculty Office and has been given by the Faculty Office notice of disqualification which has not been withdrawn.

e. The Faculty Office may disqualify an accountant from giving an Accountant's Report if:
   i. he has been found guilty by the disciplinary tribunal of his professional body of professional misconduct or discreditable conduct; or
   ii. the Faculty Office is satisfied that the Reporting Accountant has failed in his Accountant's Report to properly identify and explain to the satisfaction of the Faculty Office any breaches of these Rules;
   iii. in coming to a decision the Faculty Office will take into account any representations made by the accountant and their professional body;
   iv. the Faculty Office shall notify the notary if he is likely to be affected by an accountant's disqualification,

f. The Notary must provide the Reporting Accountant with details of all accounts kept or operated by him in connection with the notary's business at any Bank or Building Society at any time during the Accounting Period to which the Accountant's Report relates, including Client Accounts, Office Accounts and

g. accounts which are not Client Accounts but which contain Client Money.

12. (1) In order to ascertain whether these Rules have been complied with the Master, acting either-
   (a) on his own motion; or
   (b) on a written statement and request transmitted to him by or on behalf of The Notaries Society or The Society of Scrivener Notaries; or

204

(c)   on a written complaint lodged with him or his Registrar by a third party, may require any notary to produce at a time and place to be fixed by the Master, his books of account, bank and building society pass books, loose-leaf bank and building society statements, statements of account, vouchers and any other necessary documents for the inspection of any person appointed by the Master and to supply to such person any necessary information and explanations and such person shall be directed to prepare for the information of the Master a report on the result of such inspection. Such report may be used as a basis for proceedings in the Faculty Office.

(2)   Upon being required so to do a notary shall produce such books of account, bank and building society pass-books, loose-leaf bank and building society statements, statements of accounts, vouchers and documents at the time and place fixed.

(3)   In any case in which The Notaries Society or The Society of Scrivener Notaries are of opinion that an inspection should be made under this Rule of the books of account, bank and building society pass books, loose-leaf bank and building society statements, statements of account, vouchers and any other necessary documents of a notary, it shall be the duty of such Society to transmit to the Master a statement containing all relevant information in their possession and a request that such an inspection be made.

(4)   Before instituting an inspection on a written complaint lodged with him by a third party, the master shall require prima facie evidence that a ground of complaint exists, and may require the payment by such party to the Master of a reasonable sum to be fixed by him to cover the costs of the inspection and the costs of the notary against whom the complaint is made. The Master may deal with any sum so paid in such manner as he thinks fit.

13.   Every requirement to be made by the Master of a notary under these Rules shall be made in writing, and sent by registered post or the recorded delivery service to the last address of the notary appearing in the Roll or in the Register kept by the Registrar and, when so made and sent, shall be deemed to have been received by the notary within 48 hours (excluding Saturdays, Sundays and Bank Holidays) of the time of posting.

14.   Nothing in these Rules shall deprive a Notary of any recourse or right, whether by way of lien, set off, counterclaim, charge or otherwise, against moneys standing to the credit of a client account.

15.   These Rules shall not apply to a notary acting in the course of his employment as (a) a public officer, or (b) an officer of statutory undertakers', or (c) an officer of a local authority.

16. In any particular case or cases the Master of the Faculties shall have power to waive in writing any of the provisions of these Rules for a particular purpose or purposes expressed in such waiver, and to revoke such waiver.

DATED this 21st day of February 2012.

C R GEORGE

MASTER

ACCOUNTANT'S REPORT

PART A: ACCOUNTANT'S REPORT FORM

Notes:
Every notary who, in his capacity as a notary, holds or receives client money paid into client account under the Notaries Accounts Rules 1989 ('the Notaries Accounts Rules') must procure a copy of a report relating to the client's money so held or received ('the Accountant's Report') in accordance with Rule 11A of the Notaries Accounts Rules.

The accountant preparing the Accountant's Report ('the Reporting Accountant') must be qualified in accordance with Rules 11A (3) a. and 11A (3) d. of the Notaries Accounts Rules.

The report must be provided to the Registrar in accordance with Rules 11A (1) and 11A (2) of the Notaries Accounts Rules.

Please complete in block capitals.

1. Details
Name of notary who is the subject of this report ('the Notary'):

Company number as registered at Companies House – please indicate if not applicable:

2. Trading Names and Addresses
All address(es) at which the Notary practises during the reporting period must be covered by the Accountant's Report. If an address is not covered the reason must be stated. Please list on a separate sheet all offices not covered by this report with a short written explanation as to why they are not covered by the report.

Please continue on a separate sheet if necessary.

3. Accounting Period
Accounting period complying with Rule 11A (3) c. of the Notaries Accounts Rules ('the Accounting Period'):

Beginning: Ending:

ACCOUNTANT'S REPORT

4. Declaration

I have conducted a review of the accounts provided to me in respect of the Notary to which the Accountant's Report relates. My review incorporated the examination of client account reconciliations at various times during the Accounting Period covered by this report and the testing of procedures and transactions on a sample basis to enable me to form an opinion as to whether the Notary has complied with the provisions of the Notaries Accounts Rules. I am satisfied that during the abovementioned Accounting Period the Notary has complied with the provisions of the Notaries Accounts Rules except so far as concerns:

A.   certain trivial breaches due to clerical errors or mistakes in book-keeping, all of which were rectified on discovery and none of which resulted in any loss to any client;

B.   the matters set out at 7. below;

C.   the matters set out at 8. below;

D.   none of the above.

5. Comparison Dates

The results of the comparisons required under section 13. of the Accountant's Report Checklist, at the dates selected by me were:

A. at: *(insert date 1)*

I.	Liabilities to clients as shown by client ledger accounts.	£
II.	Cash held in client account, and client money held in any account other than a client account, after allowance for lodgements cleared after the date and for outstanding cheques.	£
III.	Difference between I. and II. (if any). Details at 9. below.	£

B. at: *(insert date 2)*

I.	Liabilities to clients as shown by client ledger accounts.	£
II.	Cash held in client account, and client money held in any account other than a client account, after allowance for lodgements cleared after the date and for outstanding cheques.	£
III.	Difference between I. and II. (if any). Details at 9. below.	£

Notes:

The figure shown in 5.A.I. and 5.B.I. above is the total of credit balances, without adjustment for debit balances (unless capable of proper set-off, i.e. being in respect of the same client) or for receipts and payments not capable of allocation to individual ledger accounts.

ACCOUNTANT'S REPORT

6. Qualified Report
Have you found it necessary to qualify this report other than for trivial breaches?

Yes ☐

No ☐

If 'Yes' please complete 7. and/or 8. below.
If 'No' please proceed to 10.

7. Matter(s) in respect of which the Reporting Accountant has been unable to satisfy himself and the reason(s) he has been unable to do so, e.g. because a client's file is not available.

Please continue on a separate sheet if necessary.

8. Matter(s) (other than trivial breaches) in respect of which it appears to the Reporting Accountant that the Notary has not complied with the Notaries Accounts Rules.

Please continue on a separate sheet if necessary.

9. Details of the cause(s) of any differences shown at 5.A.III. and/or 5.B.III. above.

Please continue on a separate sheet if necessary.

ACCOUNTANT'S REPORT

10.   Accountant's Certificate

I confirm that I have read the Notaries Accounts Rules.

I confirm that I am the Reporting Accountant and that I have examined to the extent required by the Notaries Accounts Rules the details of all accounts kept or operated by the Notary in connection with the Notary's business at any bank or building society at any time during the Accounting Period to which the Accountant's Report relates, including client accounts, office accounts and accounts which are not client accounts but which contain client money.

I acknowledge that under Rule 11A of the Notaries Accounts Rules a copy of the Accountant's Report must be provided to the Registrar of the Faculty Office.

I acknowledge that information contained in the Accountant's Report (and any continuation sheets) will be relied upon by the Faculty Office and that I owe a duty of care to them in the preparation of this report.

I confirm that this is a true and complete copy of the Accountant's Report and has not been amended in any manner whatsoever – please delete if not applicable.

Name and address of Reporting Accountant:

Name and address of Reporting Accountant's firm:

Reporting Accountant's professional body:

Reporting Accountant's membership/registration number:

Do you have a current Practising Certificate?

Yes   ☐

No   ☐

Signature:

Date:

ACCOUNTANT'S REPORT
PART B: ACCOUNTANT'S REPORT CHECK LIST

Notes:
The following checks must be completed in order to satisfy the examination requirements under the Notaries Accounts Rules 1989 ('the Notaries Accounts Rules'). Where the result of the checks is found to be unsatisfactory, further details must be reported in section 14. of this check list or on a continuation sheet.

Name of notary who is the subject of this report ('the Notary'):

Results of the test checks for all client money required to be paid into client account:

		Satisfactory (please tick the appropriate column)		If 'No' should breaches be noted in the Accountant's Report?		Cross references to audit file documentation
		Yes	No	Yes	No	
1.	**Book-keeping system for every office: To ensure that the Notary has established and maintained proper accounting systems to enable compliance with the Notaries Accounts Rules.**					
1.1	The accounting records clearly distinguish between client and all other monies dealt with by the Notary.					
1.2	The particulars of all client money received, held or paid on account of each client are recorded in accordance with the Notaries Accounts Rules.					
1.3	The current balance on each client and office ledger account is shown or is readily ascertainable from the accounting records.					
1.4	The current balance shown on each client and office ledger account is correct.					
1.5	A written record or file of copies of all bills of costs distinguishing between profit costs and disbursements has been retained on a durable medium.					
1.6	Where it is possible to ascertain, the Notary has accounted to his clients as soon as possible after completion of any transaction or after retainers have been terminated.					

ACCOUNTANT'S REPORT

		Satisfactory (please tick the appropriate column)		If 'No' should breaches be noted in the Accountant's Report?		Cross references to audit file documentation
1.7	Where it is possible to ascertain, all monies held in client bank account have been paid promptly to the rightful recipient when due.					
2.	**Posting to ledger accounts and casts:** **To ensure that all dealings with client money have been appropriately and accurately recorded in accordance with the Notaries Accounts Rules.**	Yes	No	Yes	No	
2.1	All dealings with client money have been appropriately recorded in a clients' ledger or a clients' column of a ledger.					
2.2	Casts of client ledger accounts and receipts and payments records are correct.					
2.3	Postings have been recorded in chronological sequence with the date being that of the initiation of the transaction.					
3.	**Receipts and payments of client money:** **To ensure that sample receipts and payments of client money as shown in bank and building society statements are in accordance with the records of receipts and payments of client money.**	Yes	No	Yes	No	
3.1	Client money has been paid into client account without delay.					
3.2	Only client money that is required or permitted to be paid into client account has been paid into client account.					
3.3	Client money is only drawn from client account in accordance with Rule 7 of the Notaries Accounts Rules.					
3.4	Withdrawals from client bank account were made by payments other than in cash.					
3.5	Sample paid cheques have been obtained and details agreed to payment records.					

ACCOUNTANT'S REPORT

		Satisfactory (please tick the appropriate column)		If 'No' should breaches be noted in the Accountant's Report?		Cross references to audit file documentation
		Yes	No	Yes	No	
3.6	A test examination of client ledger accounts revealed that no withdrawals on behalf of any client exceeded the total money held for the time being to the credit of that client.	Yes	No	Yes	No	
3.7	If the test referred to in 3.6 above revealed that withdrawals on behalf of a client exceeded the total of the money held to the credit of that client, such overpayments were corrected without delay.					
3.8	Withdrawals from client bank account in respect of costs were properly required for or towards payment of the Notary's costs where there has been delivered to the client a bill of costs or other written intimation about the amount of costs.					
3.9	Withdrawals from client bank account in respect of disbursements were properly required for or towards the payment of a debt due to the Notary from the client or money already expended by the Notary on behalf of the client.					
4.	**System of recording costs and making transfers:** **To ensure that the system of recording costs and processing transfers is suitable.**	Yes	No	Yes	No	
4.1	The payments or liabilities mentioned in test 3.9 above were debited to the client ledger before the monies were withdrawn from client bank account.					
4.2	Transfers between client and office bank accounts have been recorded in both the client and office columns of appropriate client ledger accounts.					

ACCOUNTANT'S REPORT

		Satisfactory (please tick the appropriate column)		If 'No' should breaches be noted in the Accountant's Report?		Cross references to audit file documentation
4.3	Withdrawals from client bank account in respect of costs have been made by way of a cheque drawn in favour of the Notary or by way of a transfer to a bank or building society account in the name of the Notary, not being a client account.					
5.	**Examination of documents for verification of transactions and entries in accounting records: To ensure that the financial transactions evidenced by documents in the client files are recorded in a manner complying with the Notaries Accounts Rules.**	Yes	No	Yes	No	
5.1	A test examination of a number of client files has been made.					
5.2	All client files requested for examination were made available.					
5.3	If 5.2 above is not satisfactory details been provided in the Accountant's Report.					
6.	**Office accounts: To ensure that client money is identified and reflected in the client ledger in accordance with the Notaries Accounts Rules.**	Yes	No	Yes	No	
6.1	Checks have been made of such client office ledgers, cash books, bank and building society statements etc., as maintained by the Notary, with a view to ascertaining whether any client money has not been paid into client account.					
6.2	Office ledger credit balances have been investigated and such balances do not include client money incorrectly held in office account.					
6.3	In the event of office ledger credit balances existing on client ledger accounts, the position has been investigated and corrected without delay.					

ACCOUNTANT'S REPORT

		Satisfactory (please tick the appropriate column)		If 'No' should breaches be noted in the Accountant's Report?		Cross references to audit file documentation
		Yes	No	Yes	No	
7.	**Client money not held in client account: To ensure that Rule 9 of the Notaries Accounts Rules is complied with in respect of client money not paid into client account.**	Yes	No	Yes	No	
7.1	The Notary has disclosed any dealings in which money has been withheld from client bank account.					
7.2	Where money has been withheld from client account in accordance with Rule 9 of the Notaries Accounts Rules an appropriate written client instruction, acknowledgement or written authorisation has been received.					
8.	**Authorised withdrawals from client bank account(s): To ensure that all withdrawals from client account are made in accordance with Rule 7 of the Notaries Accounts Rules.**					
8.1	Cheques or other written instructions for withdrawal from client bank account have been signed by an approved person.					
8.2	Where electronic systems have been used to withdraw monies from client bank account the system has been operated by an approved person, or authorised electronically by an approved person.					
9.	**Client to client transfers: To ensure that transfers between client accounts are conducted in accordance with Rule 10 of the Notaries Accounts Rules.**	Yes	No	Yes	No	
9.1	All transfers of money from the ledger account of one client to that of another client have been effected in accordance with the Notaries Accounts Rules.					

215

ACCOUNTANT'S REPORT

		Satisfactory (please tick the appropriate column)		If 'No' should breaches be noted in the Accountant's Report?		Cross references to audit file documentation
10.	**Client ledger for borrower and lender:** **To ensure that when the Notary is acting for both the borrower and the lender that the transactions of each party are clearly distinguished in the client ledger.**	Yes	No	Yes	No	
10.1	When acting for both borrower and lender in a mortgage transaction between them and separate client ledger accounts for both clients have not been opened, the funds belonging to each client are clearly identifiable.					
11.	**Deposit interest:** **To ensure that the Notary has accounted to clients for deposit interest earned.**	Yes	No	Yes	No	
11.1	Where appropriate, the Notary has accounted to clients for interest earned.					
12.	**Reconciliations and extraction of client ledger balances:** **To ensure that client ledgers are reconciled to client bank accounts on a regular basis and that the reconciling items are dealt with promptly and accurately.**	Yes	No	Yes	No	
12.1	The client bank reconciliations have been checked on no fewer than two separate dates in the period covered in this report.					
12.2	All accounts, disclosed by the Notary or the Notary's bank or building society, containing client money have been included in the reconciliation.					
12.3	The client bank reconciliation total is complete and correct having been calculated by the closing client bank account balance plus an accurate and complete list of outstanding lodgements less an accurate and complete list of un-presented cheques.					

ACCOUNTANT'S REPORT

		Satisfactory (please tick the appropriate column)		If 'No' should breaches be noted in the Accountant's Report?		Cross references to audit file documentation
12.4	The cash book balances at each of the dates selected have been reconciled to the balances in client account and elsewhere as confirmed directly by the relevant banks and building societies.					
12.5	The client cash account balance is correctly calculated by the accurate and prompt recording of transactions.					
12.6	All client ledger account balances as at the reconciliation date have been listed and totalled and no debit balances have been included in the total.					
12.7	The total liabilities to clients as shown by such ledger accounts has been compared to the balance on the bank reconciliation statement and agreed.					
12.8	Where the comparison(s) in 12.6 and/or 12.7 above revealed differences, a reconciliation statement showing the cause of the differences had been prepared and differences had been promptly investigated and rectified.					
12.9	In the event of debit balances existing on client ledger accounts, the position has been investigated and corrected without delay.					
12.10	In the event of the reconciliations selected not being in agreement, the differences have been investigated and corrected promptly.					
12.11	Each reconciliation selected has been achieved by the comparison and agreement, without adjusting or balancing entries, of the client ledger balances total, the client cashbooks balances total, and the client bank accounts total.					
12.12	Reconciliations have been carried out not less than once in every three month period in accordance with Rule 11(4) of the Notaries Accounts Rules.					

ACCOUNTANT'S REPORT

		Satisfactory (please tick the appropriate column)		If 'No' should breaches be noted in the Accountant's Report?		Cross references to audit file documentation
12.13	Each reconciliation is in the form of a statement set out in logical format which is likely to reveal any discrepancies.					
12.14	The client bank reconciliation total has been compared with the balance on the client cash books.					
12.15	Reconciliation statements have been retained on a durable medium.					
Please give further details of unsatisfactory items in section 14. below.						
13.	**Information and explanations:**	Yes	No	Yes	No	
13.1	All information and explanations required have been received and satisfactorily cleared.					

Notes:
It is recommended that one of the review days selected coincides with the end date of the period covered by this report.

14.	**Details of unsatisfactory items.**

Please continue on a separate sheet if necessary.

Name and address of the Reporting Accountant:

Signature:

Date:

ACCOUNTANT'S REPORT

Please return the completed Accountant's Report Form and Accountant's Report Check List to:

The Registrar
The Faculty Office
1 The Sanctuary
Westminster
SW1P 3JT

or

The Registrar
The Faculty Office
DX: 145940 Westminster 4

PRACTICE RULES 1989
as amended by the Notarial Rules and Orders (Ratification and Citation) Rules 1991 and the Notaries (Access to Justice Act) (Consequential Provisions) Rules 1999

REVOKED BY THE NOTARIES PRACTICE RULES 2001 SUBJECT TO THE SAVINGS IN RULE 24.2

Citation and Commencement

These Rules may be cited as the Notaries' Practice Rules 1989 and shall come into operation on the 1st day of April 1990. Rule 1 (Practice of a Notary and obtaining instructions)

1. A Notary shall exercise his office in accordance with the Oath or Declaration made by him at the time of the grant of his Notarial Faculty, as set forth in the Public Notaries Act 1843, s.7;

2. A Notary shall not directly or indirectly obtain or attempt to obtain instructions for professional work or permit another person to do so on his behalf, or do anything in the course of practising as a Notary in any manner which compromises or impairs or is likely to compromise or impair any of the following:
    (a) the Notary's independence or integrity;
    (b) a person's freedom to instruct a Notary of his choice;
    (c) the Notary's duty to act in the best interests of the client;
    (d) the good repute of the Notary or of the Notary's profession;
    (e) the Notary's proper standard of work;
    (f) the Notary's duty of care to persons in all jurisdictions who may place legitimate reliance on the statements of fact contained in his notarial acts.

Rule 2 (Publicity)

A Notary may advertise his practice and seek to obtain directly or indirectly clients and business in any manner and through any medium whether informative or promotional with the exception of unsolicited telephone calls or unsolicited visits to persons or organisations, provided that:
    (a) the client's freedom to instruct a qualified person of the client's choice is not thereby unduly restricted;
    (b) the Notary's good reputation for integrity and professional standards of work is not thereby damaged;
    (c) he complies with the British Code of Advertising Practice, the Independent Broadcasting Authority Code of Advertising Standards and Practice and the Direct Mail Regulations. Provided, however, that nothing in this Rule shall be construed as authorising the use of the word "notaries" or any word designating or indicating notarial services in any publicity for activities which are not of a notarial nature.

Rule 2A (Scrivener Notaries)
No notary shall describe himself as a Scrivener or a Scrivener notary unless he holds the qualifications to practise as a Scrivener notary from time to time prescribed by the Incorporated Company of Scriveners of London.

Rule 3 (Introductions and referrals)
When a Notary enters into an arrangement with another person for the introduction of clients to the Notary or by the Notary to the other person he must ensure:

(a) that the client is informed in writing of the arrangement and of any commission or other benefit the Notary may be receiving or pay;

(b) that he obtains the client's written agreement as to the destination of the commission or else he shall account to the client for the commission;

(c) that he remains able to advise the client independently in accordance with these Rules and continues to do so regardless of his own interests.

Rule 4 (Employed Notaries)
1. (The general prohibitions)
A Notary who is the employee of a non-notary shall not perform any notarial act as part of his employment or do or perform any notarial act for his employer.

Provided, however, that nothing in this Rule shall prevent a Notary who is employed by a solicitor or is a member of a firm of solicitors from performing notarial acts for the clients of that solicitor or firm.

2. (Interpretation)
In this Rule:

(a) references to a Notary's employer include the employer's holding, associated or subsidiary company; and references to an employee include an employee of such holding, associated or subsidiary company; and

(b) "holding company" and "subsidiary company" have the meanings assigned to them by the Companies Acts 1985 and 1989, and two companies are "associated" where they are subsidiary companies of the same holding company.

Rule 5 (Offering services other than as a Notary)
1. (a) Subject to compliance with this Rule and provided there is no breach of Rule 1 or any other provision of these Rules, a Notary may engage in such lawful business activities as he may desire;

(b) Nothing in this Rule shall prevent a Notary, who is qualified as a solicitor, from practising as such; and such a practice shall not be subject to paragraph (3) of this Rule.

2. (Prohibition in respect of certain services)

A Notary shall not by himself or with any other person set up, operate, actively participate in or control any business, other than a Notary's practice, which engages in any activity reserved to Notaries (whether solely or together with other persons) or offers legal services customarily offered by a Notary as part of his practice.

3. (Safeguards for the public)

Where a Notary by himself or with any other person without breach of paragraph (2) of this Rule operates, actively participates in or controls any business, other than a Notary's practice, the Notary shall ensure:

(a) that the name of that business has no substantial element in common with the name of any practice of the Notary;

(b) that the words "notaries," "attorney(s)" or "lawyer(s)" or any words designating or indicating a notarial or legal practice are not used in connection with the Notary's involvement with that business;

(c) that any client referred by any practice of the Notary to the business is informed in writing that, as the customer of that business, he does not enjoy any protection attaching to the client of a Notary, and that where that business shares premises or reception staff with any practice of the Notary, every customer of the business is informed in writing that, as the customer of that business, he does not enjoy the protection attaching to the client of a Notary.

Rule 6 (Acceptance and refusal of instructions)

In the case of a transfer of any estate or interest in real or immovable property a Notary must not accept instructions from or continue to act for any person whose interests conflict with those of any other person by whom the Notary is at the material time also instructed. In particular, in the case of such a transfer, a Notary must not act for:

(a) both parties to a transaction save where it appears that there is no conflict of interest between the parties and both have consented in writing;

(b) any other party where the Notary himself or any member of his family or any associate of his or employee is a party to the transaction;

(c) any party where the Notary himself or any member of his family or any associate of his or employee, not being a party to the transaction, is interested in the transaction in a private capacity.

Provided, however, that nothing in this Rule shall prevent a Notary from acting for both a willing buyer and a willing seller in a transfer of any estate or interest in real or immovable property outside the United Kingdom provided that both parties have consented in writing.

Rule 7 (Fee sharing)

1. Subject to paragraph (2) of this Rule, a notary shall not share or agree to share his professional fees with any person not entitled to act as a notary; provided that this Rule shall not prohibit the payment of any allowance or allowances, sum or sums of money, that are or shall be agreed to be made

or paid to the widows or children of any deceased notary or notaries, by any surviving partner or partners of such deceased notary or notaries.

2.   A notary who also practises in partnership as a solicitor may share professional fees with his partners who are solicitors, provided that a notary who shares fees by virtue of this paragraph shall keep accounts which enable the income and expenditure arising from his practice as a notary to be distinguished from the income and expenditure arising from his practice as a solicitor, and shall furnish the Faculty Office with such additional information as to his partnership and accounting arrangements as may be prescribed in Rules or Orders of the Master.

Rule 8 (Name of a firm of Notaries)
The name of a firm of Notaries shall consist only of (a) the name or names of one or more present or former principals together with, if desired, conventional references to the firm and to such persons; (b) a firm name in use on 1st January 1989; or (c) the name of a firm of solicitors of which he be a partner; or (d) one approved in writing by the Master of the Faculties.

Rule 9 (Investment business)
1.   Without prejudice to the generality of the principles embodied in Rule 1 of these Rules, a Notary shall not in connection with investment business have any arrangement with another person under which the Notary could be constrained to recommend to clients or effect for them (or refrain from so doing) transactions in some investments but not others, with some persons but not others, or through the agency of some persons but not others; or to introduce or refer clients or other persons with whom he deals to some persons but not others; nor shall a Notary be an appointed representative.

2.   Notwithstanding any provision in Rule 5 of these Rules a Notary shall not by himself or with any other person set up, operate, actively participate in or control any separate business which is an appointed representative.

3.   This Rule shall have effect in relation to the conduct of investment business within or into any part of the United Kingdom.

4.   In this Rule "appointed representative," "investment" and "investment business" have the meanings assigned to them by the Financial Services Act 1986.

Rule 10 (Supervision of a Notary's Office)
1.   A Notary shall ensure that every office where he or his firm practises is and can reasonably be seen to be properly supervised. Such supervision shall be exercised by a Notary holding a Practising Certificate who shall spend sufficient time at such office to ensure adequate control of the staff employed there and afford requisite facilities for consultation with clients. Such Notary may be a principal, employee or consultant of the firm or a locum tenens.

2.	In determining whether or not there has been compliance with the requirement as to supervision in paragraph (1) of this Rule, account shall be taken of, inter alia, the arrangements for the principals to see or be apprised of incoming mail.

3.	Where supervision in accordance herewith is prevented by illness, accident or other sufficient or unforeseen cause for a prolonged period, suitable alternative arrangements shall be made without delay to ensure compliance.

4.	In cases where a Notary is not in attendance on days when his office is normally open to the public, he shall make adequate arrangements to ensure the provision of notarial services to persons requiring the same.

Rule 11 (Waivers)
In any particular case or cases the Master of the Faculties shall have power to waive in writing any of the provisions of these Rules for a particular purpose or purposes expressed in such waiver, and to revoke such waiver.

Rule 12 (Interpretation)
In these Rules, except where the context otherwise requires:
(a)	"arrangement" means any express or tacit agreement between a Notary and other person, whether contractually binding or not;
(b)	"firm" includes a sole practitioner;
(c)	"person" includes a body corporate or unincorporated association or group of persons;
(d)	"Notary" includes a firm of notaries; and
(e)	"solicitor" means a Solicitor of the Supreme Court of Judicature in England and Wales;
(f)	words importing the masculine gender include the feminine, words in the singular include the plural and words in the plural include the singular.

NOTARIES TRUST ACCOUNTS RULES 1989

Citation and Commencement

These Rules may be cited as the Notaries Trust Accounts Rules 1989 and shall come into operation on the 1st day of April, 1990.

1. These Rules may be cited as the Notaries Trust Accounts Rules 1989.

2. (1) In these Rules unless the context otherwise requires-
"Client account" shall mean a current or deposit account at a bank or deposit account with a building society, in the title of which the word "client" appears, kept and operated in accordance with the provisions of the Notaries Accounts Rules 1989.

      "Notary-trustee" shall mean a notary who is a sole trustee or co-trustee only with one or more of his partners or employees;

      "Trust account" shall mean a current or deposit account kept at a bank or deposit account kept with a building society in the title of which the word "trustee" or "executor" appears or which is otherwise clearly designated as a trust account, and kept solely for money subject to a particular trust of which the notary is a notary-trustee;

      "Bank" and "Building Society" shall have the meaning assigned to them by the Notaries Accounts Rules 1986;

      "Public officer" shall mean an officer whose remuneration is defrayed out of moneys provided by Parliament, the revenues of the Duchy of Cornwall or the Duchy of Lancaster, the general fund of the Church Commissioners, the Forestry or the Development Fund;

      "Statutory undertakers" shall mean any person authorised by or under an Act of Parliament, or an order having the force of an Act of Parliament, to construct, work, or carry on any railway, canal, inland navigation, dock, harbour, tramway, gas, electricity, water or other public undertaking;

      "Local authority" shall have the same meaning as is given to this expression by the Local Government Act 1972;

      "The Faculty Office" shall mean the Court of Faculties of the Lord Archbishop of Canterbury and the words "Master" and "Registrar" shall mean the Master and Registrar thereof respectively.

    (2) The Interpretation Act 1889 shall apply to these Rules in the same manner as it applies to an Act of Parliament.

3.   Subject to the provisions of Rule 9 of these Rules every notary-trustee who holds or receives money subject to a trust of which he is a notary-trustee, other than money which is paid into a client account as permitted by the Notaries Accounts Rules 1989, shall without delay pay such money into the trust account of the particular trust.

4.   There may be paid into a trust account-
     (a)   money subject to the particular trust
     (b)   such money belonging to the notary-trustee or to a co-trustee as may be necessary for the purpose of opening or maintaining the account; or
     (c)   money to replace any sum which for any reason may have been drawn from the account in contravention of Rule 8 of these Rules.

5.   Where a notary holds or receives a cheque or draft including money subject to a trust or trusts of which the notary is notary-trustee-
     (a)   he shall where practicable split such cheque or draft and, if he does so, shall deal with each part thereof as if he had received a separate cheque or draft in respect of that part; or
     (b)   if he does not split the cheque or draft, he may put it into a client account as permitted by the Notaries Accounts Rules 1989.

6.   No money, other than money which under the foregoing Rules a notary is required or permitted to pay into a trust account, shall be paid into a trust account, and it shall be the duty of a notary into whose trust account any money has been paid in contravention of this Rule to withdraw the same without delay on discovery.

7.   There may be drawn from a trust account-
     (a)   money properly required for a payment in the execution of the particular trust;
     (b)   money to be transferred to a client account;
     (c)   such money, not being money subject to the particular trust, as may have been paid into the account under paragraph (b) of Rule 4 of these Rules; or
     (d)   money which may for any reason have been paid into the account in contravention of Rule 6 of these Rules.

8.   No money other than money permitted by Rule 7 of these Rules to be drawn from a trust account shall be so drawn unless the Master upon an application made to him by the notary expressly authorise in writing its withdrawal.

9.   Notwithstanding the provisions of these Rules a notary shall not be under obligation to pay into a trust account money held or received by him which is subject to a trust of which he is notary trustee-
     (a)   if the money is received by him in the form of cash and is without delay paid in cash in the execution of the trust to a third party; or

(b)   if the money is received by him in the form of a cheque or draft which is without delay endorsed over in the execution of the trust to a third party and is not passed by the notary through a bank or building society account.

10.   (1)   Every notary-trustee shall at all times keep properly written up such accounts as may be necessary-

    (a)   to show separately in respect of each trust of which he is notary trustee all his dealings with money received, held or paid by him on account of that trust; and

    (b)   to distinguish the same from money received held or paid by him on any other account.

(2)   Every notary-trustee shall preserve for at least six years from the date of the last entry therein all accounts kept by him under this Rule.

11.   (1)   In order to ascertain whether these Rules have been complied with the Master acting either-

    (a)   on his own motion; or

    (b)   on a written statement and request transmitted to him by or on behalf of The Notaries' Society or The Society of Public Notaries of London; or

    (c)   on a written complaint lodged with him or his Registrar by a third party, may require any notary-trustee to produce at a time and place to be fixed by the Master, all books of account, bank and building society pass books, loose-leaf bank and building society statements, statements of account, vouchers and documents relating to all or any of the trusts of which he is a notary-trustee for the inspection of any person appointed by the Master, and to supply to such person any necessary information and explanations and such person shall be directed to prepare for the information of the Master a report on the result of such inspection. Such report may be used as a basis for proceedings in the Faculty office.

(2)   Upon being required so to do a notary-trustee shall produce such books of account, bank and building society pass books, loose-leaf bank and building society statements, statements of accounts, vouchers and documents at the time and place fixed.

(3)   In any case in which The Notaries' Society or The Society of Public Notaries of London are of opinion that an inspection should be made under this Rule of books of account, bank and building society pass books, loose-leaf bank and building society statements, statements of account, vouchers and documents relating to all or any of the trusts of which a notary is notary-trustee it shall be the duty of such Society to transmit to the Master a statement

containing all relevant information in their possession and a request that such an inspection be made.

(4) Before instituting an inspection on a written complaint lodged with them by a third party, the Master shall require prima facie evidence that a ground of complaint exists, and may require the payment by such party to the Master of a reasonable sum to be fixed by him to cover the costs of the inspection, and the costs of the notary-trustee against whom the complaint is made. The Master may deal with any sum so paid in such manner as he thinks fit.

12. Every requirement to be made by the Master of a notary-trustee under these Rules shall be made in writing and sent by recorded or registered delivery service to the last address of the notary-trustee appearing in the Roll or in the Register kept by the Faculty Office, and, when so made and sent, shall be deemed to have been received by the notary-trustee within 48 hours (excluding Saturdays, Sundays and Bank Holidays) of the time of posting.

13. Nothing in these Rules shall deprive a notary of any recourse Or right whether by way of lien, set-off, counterclaim, charge or otherwise, against money standing to the credit of a trust account.

14. These Rules shall not apply to a notary acting in the course of his employment as (a) a public officer, or (b) an officer of statutory undertakers, or (c) an officer of a local authority.

NOTARIES (NOTIFICATION OF ADDRESS) RULES 1982

All persons resident in England and Wales who have been admitted as Public Notaries in the Court of Faculties of the Archbishop of Canterbury shall notify the Registry of the Court in writing of any change in their principal place of business, or (in the case of persons not having a place of business) in their principal residential address.

NOTARIES (PRACTISING CERTIFICATES) RULES 1982
As amended by the Public Notaries (Practising Certificates) Rules 1991, the Public Notaries (Practising Certificates) (Amendment) Rules 1993, 1995 and 1999 and the Notaries (Access to Justice Act) (Consequential Provisions) Rules 1999

Citation and Commencement

1. These rules may be cited as the Public Notaries (Practising Certificates) Rules 1982 and shall come into operation on the 20th day of October 1982.

Entry of Solicitor's Practising Certificates in the Court of Faculties

2. A notary public having in force a practising certificate as a solicitor issued under the Solicitors Act 1974 may apply for the entry of the same in the Court of Faculties of the Archbishop of Canterbury by delivering the same at the Registry, either by post or in person, together with (a) a correctly completed and signed application in the form set out in the Schedule hereto; (b) a fee of £10.00 (or such other sum as the Master may from time to time by order prescribe) together with Value Added Tax thereon at the rate for the time being in force; (c) a contribution of £4.00 (or such other sum as the Master may from time to time by order prescribe) to the Contingency Fund; and (d) in the case of a notary to whom Rule 9 applies, evidence of indemnity insurance complying with the requirements of Rules 10 to 12 hereof.

3. On receipt of the documents referred to in the foregoing Rule, the Registrar shall, if he is satisfied that the name of the applicant is on the Roll of Notaries and that the requirements of these Rules have been met, enter upon a register kept by him for the purpose a note of the applicant's name and place of business, the date of issue of his solicitor's practising certificate and the date of its entry on the register; and shall return the certificate to the applicant after causing an indorsement to be made upon it in the form set out in the Schedule hereto or such other form as the Master may direct.

4. The date to be recorded as the date of entry for the purpose of the foregoing Rule shall be
   (a) 1st November, in any case in which the documents referred to in Rule 2 are received at the Registry between 1st November and 31st December inclusive in that year; OR
   (b) In any other case, the date on which such documents are received at the Registry.
   The date so recorded shall be taken for all purposes as the date on which the solicitor's practising certificate was entered in the Court of Faculties.

Issue of Notarial Practising Certificates

5. A person desiring to obtain a practising certificate as a public notary may apply for the same by delivering to the Registry, either by post or in person, a correctly completed and signed application in the form set out in

the Schedule hereto, together with (a) a fee of £10.00 (or such other sum as the Master may from time to time by order prescribe) together with Value Added Tax thereon at the rate for the time being in force; (b) a contribution of £4.00 (or such other sum as he Master may from time to time by order prescribe) to the Contingency Fund; and (c) in the case of a notary to whom Rule 9 applies evidence of indemnity insurance complying with the requirements of Rules 10 to 12 hereof.

6.   On receipt of the documents referred to in the foregoing Rule, the Registrar shall, if he is satisfied that the name of the applicant is on the Roll of Notaries and that the requirements of these Rules have been met, issue to the applicant a Practising Certificate in the form set out in the Schedule hereto, or such other form as the Master may direct, and enter upon a register kept by him for the purpose a note of the applicant's name and place of business and the date of issue of the certificate.

7.   The date to be recorded as the date of issue for the purpose of the foregoing Rule shall be
(a)   1st November, in any case in which the documents referred to in Rule 5 are received at the Registry between 1st October and 31st December inclusive in that year; OR
(b)   in any other case, the date on which such documents are received at the Registry.
The date so recorded shall be taken for all purposes as the date of issue of the notarial practising certificate.

8.   All notarial practising certificates shall expire on the 31st October next following the date of issue.

Insurance Requirements
9.   This Rule applies to any notary (a) who lodges a solicitor's practising certificate for entry but who is exempt under the Solicitors Indemnity Rules 1987 from holding solicitors' professional indemnity insurance provided by Solicitors Indemnity Fund Limited on the ground of a General or Specific Waiver granted by The Council of the Law Society OR (b) who lodges a solicitor's practising certificate for entry but to whom the Solicitors Indemnity Rules 1987 do not apply on the ground that he is engaged as a Solicitor in whole-time employment (other than private practice) and is not held out to the public as a principal; OR (c) who applies for the issue of a notarial practising certificate, unless he is a consultant or assistant solicitor with a firm of solicitors in private practice.

Provided that this Rule shall not apply to a solicitor holding a Specific Waiver of the Solicitors Indemnity Rules 1987 if the Master is satisfied that the circumstances in which the Specific Waiver was granted also justify a waiver of the requirement of insurance in practice as a notary.

10. An applicant to whom the foregoing Rule applies shall deliver to the Registry a current certificate of insurance against civil liability for professional negligence incurred by him in connection with his practice as a notary and a copy of the policy under which the insurance is provided. Such insurance shall provide cover, extending from the date on which the certificate of insurance is delivered to the Registry to the 31st October next following, in the sum of £100,000 (or such other sum as the Master of the Faculties may from time to time by order prescribe).

11. If the Registrar is of the opinion that by reason of the standing of the insurer, or by reason of the terms and conditions of the policy (including the circumstances in which liability of the insurer is excluded or modified), the cover provided is not adequate, he shall refer the application to the Master. In such a case the insurance shall be deemed not to comply with the requirements of these rules unless and until the Master declares himself satisfied that the cover provided is adequate, having regard to the nature of the applicant's practice.

12. An applicant required to provide evidence of indemnity insurance may, as an alternative to delivering the certificate referred to in Rule 10, do so (a) by supplying such documentary proof as the Registrar may require that he is similarly covered under the terms of a policy issued to another notary and complying with the requirements of these Rules, by reason of being a partner or employee of the policyholder; or (b) by delivering a current certificate of solicitors' professional indemnity insurance in his own name issued by Solicitors Indemnity Fund Limited.

13. (1) If the insurance cover of a notary public in force when his practising certificate was entered or issued (as the case may be) ceases, for any reason, before the normal expiry of the practising certificate, then the entry or the certificate (as the case may be) shall forthwith cease to have effect unless the Registrar is satisfied that alternative insurance cover complying with these Rules is already in force.

(2) In this Rule "insurance cover" means indemnity insurance and the insurance required by Rule 13A, and if the proviso to Rule 13A ceases to apply to a notary, his insurance cover shall be deemed to have ceased for the purposes of this Rule.

13A. An applicant shall (save as hereinafter provided) also deliver to the Registry a current certificate of insurance against financial loss suffered by a third party in consequence of any dishonest or fraudulent act or any omission by the applicant in connection with his practice as a Notary. Such insurance shall provide cover extending from the date on which the certificate of insurance was submitted to the Registry to the 31st October next following or such date as may be agreed by the Registrar. Provided that this requirement shall not apply if the applicant is a solicitor and third parties suffering such financial loss in connection with the applicant's practice as a Notary would be eligible to apply for compensation under the

Compensation Fund maintained by the Law Society pursuant to Section 36 of the Solicitors Act 1974.

False Statements

14.   The entry or issue of a practising certificate shall be void and of no effect if the holder was knowingly guilty of making any false material statement in, or in relation to, his application.

Interpretation and Revocation

15.   In these Rules:

"The Registry" shall mean the Registry of the Court of Faculties of the Archbishop of Canterbury, and "The Registrar" shall be construed accordingly.

"The Contingency Fund" shall mean the fund established by Order of the Master dated the 30th day of September 1981.

"The Master" shall mean the Commissary or Master of the Faculties.

"The 1975 Rules" shall mean the Solicitors' Indemnity Rules 1975, made under the authority of the Solicitors Act 1974. [See r.5 Public Notaries (Practising Certificates) Rules 1991].

16.   That part of the Master's Order dated the 30th day of September 1981, relating to the issue and registration of Practising Certificates, which requires the Registrar to be satisfied as to professional indemnity insurance is hereby revoked.

FACULTY OFFICE

Form of Application for entry or Issue of a Practising Certificate

UNDER THE PUBLIC NOTARIES (PRACTISING CERTIFICATES) RULES 1982 and 1991

FULL NAME:
PRIVATE ADDRESS:
PRINCIPAL PLACE OF NOTARIAL BUSINESS
PROFESSIONAL OR FIRM NAME USED IN NOTARIAL BUSINESS (if different from full name given above):
BUSINESS TELEPHONE NUMBER:
DOCUMENT EXCHANGE NUMBER, if any:
DATE OF ISSUE OF NOTARIAL FACULTY (or of appointment as a Welsh District Notary):
DO YOU ALSO PRACTISE AS A SOLICITOR? Yes/No
IF SO: IS YOUR SOLICITOR'S PRACTICE:
as a sole principal?
in partnership with other solicitors? as a consultant?
as an employee in private practice? as an employee not in private practice?

DO YOU SHARE NOTARIAL INCOME WITH YOUR SOLICITOR PARTNERS WHO ARE NOT NOTARIES?
Yes/No
IF SO: State the partnership name of your Solicitors' Practice
Do the accounts of the practice enable notarial income to be distinguished from other income?

IN ANY EVENT: IS YOUR NOTARIAL PRACTICE:
as a sole principal?
in partnership with other notaries?
as a consultant?
as an employee in private practice?
as an employee not in private practice? {1}

INDEMNITY INSURANCE
(delete as necessary)

Either

A)   I hold a current premium receipt issued by the Solicitors Indemnity Fund Limited, for professional indemnity insurance, on the strength of which my Solicitor's Practising Certificate was issued. I attach my Solicitors Practising Certificate or a certified copy thereof.

or

B)   I am employed as an assistant solicitor by, or engaged as a consultant to, a firm of solicitors in private practice covered by the professional indemnity fund of the Solicitors Indemnity Fund Limited. I attach my Solicitors Practising Certificate or a certified copy thereof.

or

C)   Although exempt from the requirements of the Solicitors' Indemnity Rules 1987 as amended, I hold a current certificate of insurance issued by the Solicitors Indemnity Fund Limited, which is attached to this application.

or

D)   I attach evidence of indemnity insurance complying with Rules 10 to 12 of the Public Notaries (Practising Certificate) Rules 1982, as amended.

FIDELITY INSURANCE
(delete as necessary)

Either

A)   I am covered by the Law Society's Compensation Fund or

B)   I am not covered by the law Society's Compensation Fund but I hereby undertake not to hold clients' money at any time

or

C)   I am not covered by the law Society's Compensation Fund. I do and will be holding clients' money. I attach evidence of Fidelity Insurance in compliance with Rule 13A of The Public Notaries' Certificate Rules 1982, as amended.

APPLICATION
(delete as necessary)

Either

A)   I hereby apply for entry in the Court of Faculties of the attached Solicitor's Practising Certificate issued to me for the year ending 31st October 199

or

B)   I hereby apply to the Court of Faculties for a Faculty Office Practising Certificate as a Public Notary for the year ending 31st October 199

APPLICANT'S SIGNATURE
DATE
DO NOT RETURN THIS FORM WITHOUT COMPLETING BOTH SIDES

THE COURT OF FACULTIES
OF
THE ARCHBISHOP OF CANTERBURY
PRACTISING CERTIFICATE FOR THE YEAR 199 /9
Pursuant to the Public Notaries (Practising Certificates) Rules 1982 and 1991 is duly enrolled as a Notary Public for England and Wales and is entitled to practise as such
Commencement Date: Termination
Date:
Registrar

235

NOTARIAL CONTINGENCY FUND RULES 1981
as amended by the Notarial Contingency Fund (Amendment) Rules 1993

1. A Fund, known as the "Contingency Fund" (hereafter called "The Fund") shall be maintained and administered by the Master and the Registrar of the Court of Faculties in accordance with the following provisions.

2. [revoked]

3. The Fund shall be maintained and administered by the Registrar of the Court of Faculties and shall be held by the Court of Faculties in Trust for the purposes aforesaid save that in the event of such Fund being no longer necessary in the opinion of the Master for such purposes then such Fund shall be held for such charitable purposes as the Archbishop of Canterbury for the time being shall direct.

4. Every Notary shall on each occasion on which he applies for a Practising Certificate pay the Registrar with the fee payable in respect of that certificate a contribution to the Fund of such amount as the Master may from time to time order together with any Value Added Tax payable in addition thereto.

5. All Annual Contributions received by the Registrar under this order shall be paid into the Fund.

6. The Registrar shall invest in securities in which Trustees are authorised by law to invest Trust Funds in their hands any money which forms part of the Fund.

7. The Registrar may insure with authorised Insurers and for such purposes and on such terms as the Master may direct against all liabilities and matters in relation to the Fund and this Order.

8. Subject to any requirements of law the Registrar at the direction of the Master may borrow for the purposes of the Fund from any lender and may charge any investments of the Fund by way of security for any such loan.

9. There shall be carried to the Fund:
    (a) all annual contributions paid to the Registrar in pursuance hereto.
    (b) all interest, dividends and other income and appreciative capital arising from the investment of the Fund or any part of it.
    (c) the proceeds of any realisation of any investment of the Fund.
    (d) all money borrowed for the purposes of the Fund in accordance with paragraph 8 above.
    (e) all sums received by the Registrar under any insurance effected by the Court of Faculties under paragraph 7 above.
    (f) all sums received by the Registrar in recompense by a Notary or any other person of any expenses paid out in respect of that Notary from the Fund.

(g)   any other money which may belong or accrue to the Fund or be received by the Registrar in respect of the Fund.

10.   All moneys from time to time forming part of the Fund and all investments of the Fund shall be applicable:

(i)   for payment of any costs, charges and expenses in establish-ing, maintaining, administering and applying the Fund.

(ii)   for payment of any premium on insurance effected by the Court under paragraph 7 above.

(iii)   for repayment of any money borrowed by the Registrar for the purpose of the Fund in accordance with paragraph 8 above and for payment of interest on any money so borrowed.

(iv)   for payment of all costs charges and expenses incurred by the Registrar his employees servants or agents as a result of proceedings brought in the Court by way of Memorial or Complaint against a Notary including all Court expenses and all expenses incurred as a result of proceedings brought both in the Court against the Court or in or before the Lord Chancellor in respect of any such Memorial or Complaint or for any act or omission done or made by the Court, its employees or agents or any of them in good faith and in execution or purported execution of the rights powers and duties of the Court.

(v)   for payment of any other sums properly payable out of the Fund by virtue of this Order.

(vi)   for the payment of any sum authorised by the provisions of or ordered by the Master to be paid pursuant to the Public Notaries (Conduct and Discipline) Rules 1993.

(vii)   for the payment of any costs of or expenses incurred by the Master, the Registrar or the Court in exercise of the powers contained in rule 12 of the Notaries Accounts Rules 1989.

(viii) for the payment of any costs of or expenses incurred by the Master, the Registrar or the Court in exercise of the powers contained in rule 11 of the Notaries Trust Accounts Rules 1989.

11.   The Master shall from time to time make rules concerning the Fund and the accounts in respect of it.

LEGISLATION RELEVANT TO NOTARIES

Public Notaries Act 1801

Public Notaries Act 1843

Powers of Attorney Act 1971

Bills of Exchange Act 1882

Mental Capacity Act 2005

Oaths Act 1978

Commissioner for Oaths Act 1889

Limited Liability Partnerships (Application of Companies Act 2006) Regulations 2009

Companies Act 2006

Consular Relations Act 1968

Access to Justice Act 1999

Courts and Legal Services Act 1990

Banking and Financial Dealings Act 1971

Statutory Declaration Act 1835

Courts and Legal Services Act 1990

Legal Services Act 2007

Law of Property (Miscellaneous Provisions) Act 1989

Law of Property Act 1925

Fraud Act 2006

The Perjury Act 1911

Public Notaries Act 1801
(Sections 1 & 4)

No person in England to act as a Public Notary unless duly admitted

1.   WHEREAS it is expedient, for the better preventing of illiterate and inexperienced persons being created to act as, or admitted to the faculty of Public Notaries, that the said faculty should be regulated in England: Be it therefore enacted &c., that from and after the first day of August, 1801, no person in England shall be created to act as a Public Notary, or use and exercise the office of a Notary, or do any notarial act, unless such person shall have been duly sworn, admitted, and enrolled in the court wherein Notaries have been accustomarily sworn, admitted and enrolled.

Act not to extend to proctors, secretaries to bishops, etc.

14.   Nothing in this Act contained shall extend, or be construed to extend, to any proctor in any ecclesiastical court in England; not to any secretary or secretaries to any bishop or bishops, merely practising as such secretary or secretaries; or to any other person or persons necessarily created a Notary Public for the purpose of holding or exercising any office or appointment, or occasionally performing any public duty or service under Government, and not as general practitioner or practitioners; anything hereinbefore contained to the contrary notwithstanding.

Public Notaries Act 1843
(Sections 4, 5, 7, 8 &10)

An Act for removing Doubts as to the Service of Clerks or Apprentices to Public Notaries, and for amending the Laws regulating the Admission of Public Notaries.

[Preamble recites the Public Notaries Act 1801.]

Master of the faculties may require testimonials of ability, etc.

4.   The master of the faculties for the time being may make any general rule or rules requiring testimonials, certificates, or proofs as the character, integrity, ability and competency of any person who shall hereafter apply for admission or readmission as a public notary to practise either in England or in any of her Majesty's foreign territories, colonies, settlements, dominions, forts, factories, or possessions, whether such person shall have served a clerkship or not, and from time to time alter and vary such rules as the master of the facilities shall seem meet, and may admit or reject any person applying, at his discretion, any law, custom, usage, or prescription to the contrary so withstanding.

Proceedings in case of refusal of master of faculties to grant a faculty

A1-04 5.   Provided always that if the master of the faculties shall refuse to grant any faculty to practise as a public notary to any person without just and reasonable cause, then the chancellor of England or the lord keeper of the great seal for the time being, upon complaint thereof being made, shall direct the Queen's writ to the said master of the faculties to the effect and shall proceed thereon according to the intent and meaning of the Act of Parliament of the twenty-fifth year of the reign of King Henry the Eighth, intituled "An Act concerning peterpence and dispensations", and in manner and form as is therein provided and set forth in case of the refusal of any licences, dispensations, faculties, instruments, or other writings, as fully and effectually, and with the same powers and authority, as if the same were here inserted and re-enacted.

Oath on admission of notary

A1-05 7.   Every person to be admitted and enrolled a public notary shall, before a faculty is granted to him authorising him to practise as such, make oath before the said master of the faculties, his surrogate or other proper officer, in substance and to the effect following:

"I A.B. do swear, that I will faithfully exercise the office of a public notary: I will faithfully make contracts or instruments for or between any party or parties requiring the same, and I will not add or diminish any thing without the knowledge and consent of such party or parties that may alter the substance of the fact; I will not make or attest any act, contract, or instrument in which I shall know there is violence or fraud; and in all things I will act uprightly and justly in the business of a public notary, according to the best of my skill and ability. So help me GOD."

Master of the faculties may issue commissions to take oaths, etc., required before the grant of faculties, marriage licences, etc.

A1-06   8.   The master of the faculties for the time being, or his surrogate, shall and he is hereby authorised and empowered to issue commissions to take any oaths, affidavits, affirmations, or declarations required by law to be taken before the grant of any faculty, marriage licence, or other instrument issuing from the said office of faculties; and all oaths, affidavits, affirmations, or declarations taken before the commissioner so appointed, and the faculty, marriage licence, or other instrument granted in pursuance thereof, shall be valid and effectual as if such oaths, affidavit, affirmation, or declaration was taken before the said master or his surrogate, anything in any Act or law to the contrary thereof notwithstanding.

Persons not duly authorised practising as notaries to be guilty of offence

A1-07   10.- (1)   In any case any person shall, in his own name or in the name of any other person, make, do, act, exercise, or execute or perform, any act, matter, or thing whatsoever of or in any wise appertaining or belonging to the office, function, or practice of a public notary, for or in expectation of any gain, fee, or reward, without being able to prove, if required, that he is duly authorised so to do, he shall be guilty of an offence and liable on summary conviction to a fine not exceeding level 3 on the standard scale.

(2)   Notwithstanding anything in section 127(1) of the Magistrates' Courts Act 1980, proceedings for an offence under this section may be commenced within 12 months from the time when the offence was committed.

Powers of Attorney Act 1971

An Act to make new provision in relation to powers of attorney and the delegation by trustees of their trusts, powers and discretions.   [12th May 1971]

BE IT ENACTED by the Queen's most Excellent Majesty, by and with the advice and consent of the Lords Spiritual and Temporal, and Commons, in this present Parliament assembled, and by the authority of the same, as follows:-

1.- (1) An instrument creating a power of attorney shall be signed and sealed by, or by direction and in the presence of, the donor of the power.

(2) Where such an instrument is signed and sealed by a person by direction and in the presence of the donor of the power, two other persons shall be present as witnesses and shall attest the instrument.

(3) This section is without prejudice to any requirement in, or having effect under, any other Act as to the witnessing of instruments creating powers of attorney and does not affect the rules relating to the execution of instruments by bodies corporate.

2.- (1) As from the commencement of this Act no instrument creating a power of attorney, and no copy of any such instrument, shall be deposited or filed at the central office of the Supreme Court or at the Land Registry under section 25 of the Trustee Act 1925, section 125 of the Law of Property Act 1925 or section 219 of the Supreme Court of Judicature (Consolidation) Act 1925.

(2) This section does not affect any right to search for, inspect or copy, or to obtain an office copy of, any such document which has been deposited or filed as aforesaid before the commencement of this Act.

3.- (1) The contents of an instrument creating a power of attorney may be proved by means of a copy which-

(a) is a reproduction of the original made with a photographic or other device for reproducing documents in facsimile; and

(b) contains the following certificate or certificates signed by the donor of the power or by a solicitor or stockbroker, that is to say-

(i) a certificate at the end to the effect that the copy is a true and complete copy of the original; and

(ii) if the original consists of two or more pages, a certificate at the end of each page of the copy to the effect that it is a true and complete copy of the corresponding page of the original.

(2) Where a copy of an instrument creating a power of attorney has been made which complies with subsection (1) of this section, the contents of the instrument may also be proved by means of a copy of that copy if the further copy itself complies with that sub-

section, taking references in it to the original as references to the copy from which the further copy is made.

(3) In this section "stockbroker" means a member of any stock exchange within the meaning of the Stock Transfer Act 1963 or the Stock Transfer Act (Northern Ireland) 1963.

(4) This section is without prejudice to section 4 of the Evidence and Powers of Attorney Act 1940 (proof of deposited instruments by office copy) and to any other method of proof authorised by law.

(5) For the avoidance of doubt, in relation to an instrument made in Scotland the references to a power of attorney in this section and in section 4 of the Evidence and Powers of Attorney Act 1940 include references to a factory and commission.

4.- (1) Where a power of attorney is expressed to be irrevocable and is given to secure-

    (a) a proprietary interest of the donee of the power; or

    (b) the performance of an obligation owed to the donee, then, so long as the donee has that interest or the obligation remains undischarged, the power shall not be revoked-

        (i) by the donor without the consent of the donee; or

        (ii) By the death, incapacity or bankruptcy of the donor or, if the donor is a body corporate, by its winding up or dissolution.

        (iii) by the death, incapacity or bankruptcy of the donor or,

(2) A power of attorney given to secure a proprietary interest may be given to the person entitled to the interest and persons deriving title under him to that interest, and those persons shall be duly be duly constituted donees of the power for all purposes of the power but without prejudice to any right to appoint substitutes given by the power.

(3) This section applies to powers of attorney whenever created.

5.- (1) A donee of a power of attorney who acts in pursuance Protection of the power at a time when it has been revoked shall not, by reason of the revocation, incur any liability (either to the donor or to any other person) if at that time he did not know that the of attorney power had been revoked.

(2) Where a power of attorney has been revoked and a person, without knowledge of the revocation, deals with the donee of the power, the transaction between them shall, in favour of that person, be as valid as if the power had then been in existence.

(3) Where the power is expressed in the instrument creating it to be irrevocable and to be given by way of security then, unless the person dealing with the donee knows that it was not in fact given by way of security, he shall be entitled to assume that the power is incapable of revocation except by the donor acting with the consent

of the donee and shall accordingly be treated for the purposes of subsection (2) of this section as having knowledge of the revocation only if he knows that it has been revoked in that manner.

(4) Where the interest of a purchaser depends on whether a transaction between the donee of a power of attorney and another person was valid by virtue of subsection (2) of this section, it shall be conclusively presumed in favour of the purchaser that that person did not at the material time know of the revocation of the power if-

(a) the transaction between that person and the donee was completed within twelve months of the date on which the power came into operation; or

(b) that person makes a statutory declaration, before or within three months after the completion of the purchase, that he did not at the material time know of the revocation of the power.

(5) Without prejudice to subsection (3) of this section, for the purposes of this section knowledge of the revocation of a power of attorney includes knowledge of the occurrence of any event (such as the death of the donor) which has the effect of revoking the power.

(6) In this section "purchaser" and "purchase" have the meanings specified in section 205(1) of the Law of Property Act 1925.

(7) This section applies whenever the power of attorney was created but only to acts and transactions after the commencement of this Act.

6.- (1) Without prejudice to section 5 of this Act, where-

(a) the donee of a power of attorney executes, as transferor, an instrument transferring registered securities; and

(b) the instrument is executed for the purposes of a stock exchange transaction, it shall be conclusively presumed in favour of the transferee that the power had not been revoked at the date of the instrument if a statutory declaration to that effect is made by the donee of the power on or within three months after that date.

(2) In this section "registered securities" and "stock exchange transaction" have the same meanings as in the Stock Transfer Act 1963.

7.- (1) The donee of a power of attorney may, if he thinks fit-

(a) execute any instrument with his own signature and, where of attorney sealing is required, with his own seal, and

(b) do any other thing in his own name, by the authority of the donor of the power; and any document executed or thing done in that manner shall be as effective as if executed or done by the donee with the signature and seal, or, as the case may be, in the name, of the donor of the power.

(2) For the avoidance of doubt it is hereby declared that an instrument to which subsection (3) or (4) of section 74 of the Law of Property

Act 1925, applies may be executed either as provided in those subsections or as provided in this section.

(3) This section is without prejudice to any statutory direction requiring an instrument to be executed in the name of an estate owner within the meaning of the said Act of 1925.

(4) This section applies whenever the power of attorney was created.

8. Section 129 of the Law of Property Act 1925 (which contains provisions, now unnecessary, in respect of powers of attorney granted by married women) shall cease to have effect.

9. - (1) Section 25 of the Trustee Act 1925 (power to delegate trusts etc., during absence abroad) shall be amended as follows.

(2) For subsections (1) to (8) of that section there shall be substituted the following subsections-

"(1) Notwithstanding any rule of law or equity to the contrary, a trustee may, by power of attorney, delegate for Powers of Attorney Act 1971 c. 27 a period not exceeding twelve months the execution or exercise of all or any of the trusts, powers and discretions vested in him as trustee either alone or jointly with any other person or persons.

(2) The persons who may be donees of a power of attorney under this section include a trust corporation but not (unless a trust corporation) the only other co-trustee of the donor of the power.

(3) An instrument creating a power of attorney under this section shall be attested by at least one witness.

(4) Before or within seven days after giving a power of attorney under this section the donor shall give written notice thereof (specifying the date on which the power comes into operation and its duration, the donee of the power, the reason why the power is given and, where some only are delegated, the trusts, powers and discretions delegated) to-

(a) each person (other than himself), if any, who under any instrument creating the trust has power (whether alone or jointly) to appoint a new trustee; and

(b) each of the other trustees, if any;

but failure to comply with this subsection shall not, in favour of a person dealing with the donee of the power, invalidate any act done or instrument executed by the donee.

(5) The donor of a power of attorney given under this section shall be liable for the acts or defaults of the donee in the same manner as if they were the acts or defaults of the donor."

(3) Subsections (9) and (10) of the said section 25 shall stand as subsections (6) and (7) and for subsection (11) of that section there shall be substituted the following subsection-

"(8) This section applies to a personal representative, tenant for life and statutory owner as it applies to a trustee except that subsection (4) shall apply as if it required the notice there mentioned to be given-

245

(a) in the case of a personal representative, to each of the other personal representatives, if any, except any executor who has renounced probate;

(b) in the case of a tenant for life, to the trustees of the settlement and to each person, if any, who together with the person giving the notice constitutes the tenant for life;

(c) in the case of a statutory owner, to each of the persons, if any, who together with the person giving the notice constitute the statutory owner and, in the case of a statutory owner by virtue of section 23(1)(a) of the Settled Land Act 1925, to the trustees of the settlement."

(4) This section applies whenever the trusts, powers or discretions in question arose but does not invalidate anything done by virtue of the said section 25 as in force at the commencement of this Act.

10. - (1) Subject to subsection (2) of this section, a general power of attorney in the form set out in Schedule 1 to this Act, of attorney in or in a form to the like effect but expressed to be made under specified form this Act, shall operate to confer-

(a) on the donee of the power; or

(b) if there is more than one donee, on the donees acting jointly or acting jointly or severally, as the case may be,

authority to do on behalf of the donor anything which he can lawfully do by an attorney.

(2) This section does not apply to functions which the donor has as a trustee or personal representative or as a tenant for life or statutory owner within the meaning of the Settled Land Act 1925.

11.- (1) This Act may be cited as the Powers of Attorney Act 1971.

(2) The enactments specified in Schedule 2 to this Act are hereby repealed to the extent specified in the third column of that Schedule.

(3) In section 125(2) of the Law of Property Act 1925 for the words "as aforesaid" there shall be substituted the words "under the Land Registration Act 1925"; and in section 219(2) of the Supreme Court of Judicature (Consolidation) Act 1925 for the words "so deposited" there shall be substituted the words "deposited under this section before the commencement of the Powers of Attorney Act 1971."

(4) This Act shall come into force on 1st October 1971.

(5) Section 3 of this Act extends to Scotland and Northern Ireland but, save as aforesaid, this Act extends to England and Wales only.

SCHEDULES

Schedule 1 – Section 10

Form of General Power of Attorney for Purposes of Section 10

THIS GENERAL POWER OF ATTORNEY is made this   day of   19
by AB of   .
I appoint CD of   .
[or CD of   and
EF of   jointly
or

     jointly and severally] to be my attorney[s] in accordance with section 10 of
the Powers of Attorney Act 1971.

In Witness etc,

Schedule 2 – Section 11(2)

REPEALS

Chapter	Short Title	Extent of Repeal
15 & 16 Geo. 5. c. 19.	The Trustee Act 1925.	Section 29.
15 & 16 Geo. 5. c. 20.	The Law of Property Act 1925.	Sections 123 and 124. Section 125(1) Sections 126 to 129.
15 & 16 Geo. 5. c. 49.	The Supreme Court of Judicature (Consolidation) Act 1925.	Section 219(1).
4 & 5 Eliz. 2. c. 46.	The Administration of Justice Act 1956.	Section 18.

PART III.
CHEQUES ON A BANKER.

PART IV.
PROMISSORY NOTES.

PART V.
SUPPLEMENTARY.

An Act to codify the law relating to Bills of Exchange, Cheques, and Promissory Notes.

[18th August 1882.]

BE it enacted by the Queen's most Excellent Majesty, by and with the advice and consent of the Lords Spiritual and Temporal, and Commons, in this present Parliament assembled, and by the authority of the same, as follows:

PART I.
PRELIMINARY.

1.   This Act may be cited as the Bills of Exchange Act, 1882.

2.   In this Act, unless the context otherwise requires,-

" Acceptance " means an acceptance completed by delivery or notification.

" Action " includes counter claim and set off.

" Banker " includes a body of persons whether incorporated or not who carry on the business of banking.

" Bankrupt " includes any person whose estate is vested in a trustee or assignee under the law for the time being in force relating to bankruptcy.

" Bearer " means the person in possession of a bill or note which is payable to bearer.

" Bill " means bill of exchange, and "note " means promissory note.

" Delivery " means transfer of possession, actual or constructive from one person to another.

" Holder " means the payee or indorsee of a bill or note who is in possession of it, or the bearer thereof.

251

" Indorsement " means an indorsement completed by delivery.

" Issue " means the first delivery of a bill or note, complete in form to a person who takes it as a holder.

" Person " includes a body of persons whether incorporated or not.

" Value " means valuable consideration.

" Written " includes printed, and " writing " includes print.

PART II.
BILLS OF EXCHANGE.

Form and Interpretation.

3.   (1.)   A bill of exchange is an unconditional order in writing, addressed by one person to another, signed by the person giving it, requiring the person to whom it is addressed to pay on demand or at a fixed or determinable future time a sum certain in money to or to the order of a specified person, or to bearer.

(2.)   An instrument which does not comply with these conditions, or which orders any act to be done in addition to the payment of money, is not a bill of exchange.

(3.)   An order to pay out of a particular fund is not unconditional within the meaning of this section; but an unqualified order to pay, coupled with (a) an indication of a particular fund out of which the drawee is to re-imburse himself or a particular account to be debited with the amount, or (b) a statement of the transaction which gives rise to the bill, is unconditional.

(4)   A bill is not invalid by reason-
   (a.)   That it is not dated;
   (b.)   That it does not specify the value given, or that any value has been given therefor;
   (c.)   That it does not specify the place where it is drawn or the place where it is payable.

4.   (1.)   An inland bill is a bill which is or on the face of it purports to be (a) both drawn and payable within the British Islands, or (b) drawn within the British Islands upon some person resident therein. Any other bill is a foreign bill.

For the purposes of this Act " British Islands " mean any part of the United Kingdom of Great Britain and Ireland, the islands of Man, Guernsey, Jersey, Alderney, and Sark, and the islands adjacent to any of them being part of the dominions of Her Majesty.

	(2.)	Unless the contrary appear on the face of the bill the holder may treat it as an inland bill.
5.	(1.)	A bill may be drawn payable to, or to the order of, the drawer; or it may be drawn payable to, or to the order of, the drawee.
	(2.)	Where in a bill drawer and drawee are the same person, or where the drawee is a fictitious person or a person not having capacity to contract, the holder may treat the instrument, at his option, either as a bill of exchange or as a promissory note.
6.	(1.)	The drawee must be named or otherwise indicated in a bill with reasonable certainty.
	(2.)	A bill may be addressed to two or more drawees whether they are partners or not, but an order addressed to two drawees in the alternative or to two or more drawees in succession is not a bill of exchange.
7.	(1.)	Where a bill is not payable to bearer, the payee must be named or otherwise indicated therein with reasonable certainty.
	(2.)	A bill may be made payable to two or more payees jointly, or it may be made payable in the alternative to one of two, or one or some of several payees. A bill may also be made payable to the holder of an office for the time being.
	(3.)	Where the payee is a fictitious or non-existing person the bill may be treated as payable to bearer.
8.	(1.)	When a bill contains words prohibiting transfer, or indicating an intention that it should not be transferable, it is valid as between the parties thereto, but is not negotiable.
	(2.)	A negotiable bill may be payable either to order or to bearer.
	(3.)	A bill is payable to bearer which is expressed to be so payable, or on which the only or last indorsement is an indorsement in blank.
	(4.)	A bill is payable to order which is expressed to be so payable, or which is expressed to be payable to a particular person, and does not contain words prohibiting transfer or indicating an intention that it should not be transferable.
	(5.)	Where a bill, either originally or by indorsement, is expressed to be payable to the order of a specified person, and not to him or his order, it is nevertheless payable to him or his order at his option.

9. (1.) The sum payable by a bill is a sum certain within the meaning of this Act, although it is required to be paid-
   - (a.) With interest.
   - (b.) By stated instalments.
   - (c.) By stated instalments, with a provision that upon default in payment of any instalment the whole shall become due.
   - (d.) According to an indicated rate of exchange or according to a rate of exchange to be ascertained as directed by the bill.

   (2.) Where the sum payable is expressed in words and also in figures, and there is a discrepancy between the two, the sum denoted by the words is the amount payable.

   (3.) Where a bill is expressed to be payable with interest, unless the instrument otherwise provides, interest runs from the date of the bill, and if the bill is undated from the issue thereof.

10. (1.) A bill is payable on demand-
   - (a.) Which is expressed to be payable on demand, or at sight, or on presentation; or
   - (b.) In which no time for payment is expressed.

   (2.) Where a bill is accepted or indorsed when it is overdue, it shall, as regards the acceptor who so accepts, or any indorser who so indorses it, be deemed a bill payable on demand.

11. A bill is payable at a determinable future time within the meaning of this Act which is expressed to be payable-

   (1.) At a fixed period after date or sight.
   (2.) On or at a fixed period after the occurrence of a specified event which is certain to happen, though the time of happening may be uncertain.

   An instrument expressed to be payable on a contingency is not a bill, and the happening of the event does not cure the defect.

12. Where, a bill expressed to be payable at a fixed period after date is issued undated, or where the acceptance of a bill payable at a fixed period after sight is undated, any holder may insert therein the true date of issue or acceptance, and the bill shall be payable accordingly.

   Provided that (1) where the holder in good faith and by mistake inserts a wrong date, and (2) in every case where a wrong date is inserted, if the bill subsequently comes into the hands of a holder in due course the bill shall not be avoided thereby, but shall operate and be payable as if the date so inserted had been the true date.

13.   (1.)   Where a bill or an acceptance or any indorsement on a bill is dated, the date shall, unless the contrary be proved, be deemed to be the true date of the drawing, acceptance, or indorsement, as the case may be.

    (2.)   A bill is not invalid by reason only that it is ante-dated or post-dated, or that it bears date on a Sunday.

14.   Where a bill is not payable on demand the day on which it falls due is determined as follows:

    (1.)   Three days, called days of grace, are, in every case where the bill itself does not otherwise provide, added to the time of payment as fixed by the bill, and the bill is due and payable on the last day of grace: Provided that-
        (a.)   When the last day of grace falls on Sunday, Christmas Day, Good Friday, or a day appointed by Royal proclamation as a public fast or thanksgiving day, the bill is, except in the case herein-after provided for, due and payable on the preceding business day;
        (b.)   When the last day of grace is a bank holiday (other than Christmas Day or Good Friday) under the Bank Holidays Act, 1871, and Acts amending or extending it, or when the last day of grace is a Sunday and the second day of grace is a Bank Holiday, the bill is due and payable on the succeeding business day.

    (2.)   Where a bill is payable at a fixed period after date, after sight, or after the happening of a specified event, the time of payment is determined by excluding the day from which the time is to begin to run and by including the day of payment.

    (3.)   Where a bill is payable at a fixed period after sight, the time begins to run from the date of the acceptance if the bill be accepted, and from the date of noting or protest if the bill be noted or protested for non-acceptance, or for non-delivery.

    (4.)   The term " month " in a bill means calendar month.

15.   The drawer of a bill and any indorser may insert therein the name of a person to whom the holder may resort in case of need, that is to say, in case the bill is dishonoured by non-acceptance or non-payment. Such person is called the referee in case of need. It is in the option of the holder to resort to the referee in case of need or not as he may think fit.

16.   The drawer of a bill, and any indorser, may insert therein an express stipulation-

    (1.)   Negativing or limiting his own liability to the holder:

(2.)   Waiving as regards himself some or all of the holder's duties.

17.   (1.)   The acceptance of a bill is the signification by the drawee of his assent to the order of the drawer.

(2.)   An acceptance is invalid unless it complies with the following conditions, namely: -
(a.)   It must be written on the bill and be signed by the drawee. The mere signature of the drawee without additional words is sufficient.
(b.)   It must not express that the drawee will perform his promise by any other means than the payment of money.

18.   A bill may be accepted-

(1.)   before it has been signed by the drawer, or while otherwise incomplete:

(2.)   When it is overdue, or after it has been dishonoured by a previous refusal to accept, or by non-payment:

(3.)   When a bill payable after sight is dishonoured by non-acceptance, and the drawee subsequently accepts it, the holder, in the absence of any different agreement, is entitled to have the bill accepted as of the date of first presentment to the drawee for acceptance.

19.   (1.)   An acceptance is either (a) general or (b) qualified.

(2.)   A general acceptance assents without qualification to the order of the drawer. A qualified acceptance in express terms varies the effect of the bill as drawn.

In particular an acceptance is qualified which is-
(a.)   conditional, that is to say, which makes payment by the acceptor dependent on the fulfilment of a condition therein stated:
(b.)   partial, that is to say, an acceptance to pay part only of the amount for which the bill is drawn:
(c.)   local, that is to say, an acceptance to pay only at a particular specified place:

An acceptance to pay at a particular place is a general acceptance, unless it expressly states that the bill is to be paid there only and not elsewhere:
(d.)   qualified as to time:
(e.)   the acceptance of some one or more of the drawees, but not of all.

20. (1.) Where a simple signature on a blank stamped paper is delivered by the signer in order that it may be converted into a bill, it operates as a prima facie authority to fill it up as a complete bill for any amount the stamp will cover, using the signature for that of the drawer, or the acceptor, or an indorser; and, in like manner, when a bill is wanting in any material particular, the person in possession of it has a prima facie authority to fill up the omission in any way he thinks fit.

(2.) In order that any such instrument when completed may be enforceable against any person who became a party thereto prior to its completion, it must be filled up within a reasonable time, and strictly in accordance with the authority given. Reasonable time for this purpose is a question of fact.

Provided that if any such instrument, after completion is negotiated, to a holder in due course it shall be valid and effectual for all purposes in his hands, and he may enforce it as if it had been filled up within a reasonable time and strictly in accordance with the authority given.

21. (1.) Every contract on a bill, whether it be the drawer's, the acceptor's, or an indorser's, is incomplete and revocable, until delivery of the instrument in order to give effect thereto.

Provided that where acceptance is written on a bill, and the drawee gives notice to or according to the directions of the person entitled to the bill that he has accepted it, the acceptance then becomes complete and irrevocable.

(2.) As between immediate parties, and as regards a remote party other than a holder in due course, the delivery-
(a.) in order to be effectual must be made either by or under the authority of the party drawing, accepting, or indorsing, as the case may be:
(b.) may be shown to have been conditional or for a special purpose only, and not for the purpose of transferring the property in the bill.

But if the bill be in the hands of a holder in due course a valid delivery of the bill by all parties prior to him so as to make them liable to him is conclusively presumed.

(3.) Where a bill is no longer in the possession of a party who has signed it as drawer, acceptor, or indorser, a valid and unconditional delivery by him is presumed until the contrary is proved.

Capacity and Authority of Parties.

22. (1.) Capacity to incur liability as a party to a bill is co-extensive with capacity to contract.

Provided that nothing in this section shall enable a corporation to make itself liable as drawer, acceptor, or indorser of a bill unless it is competent to it so to do under the law for the time being in force relating to corporations.

(2.) Where a bill is drawn or indorsed by an infant, minor, or corporation having no capacity or power to incur liability on a bill, the drawing or indorsement entitles the holder to receive payment of the bill, and to enforce it against any other party thereto.

23. No person is liable as drawer, indorser, or acceptor of a bill who has not signed it as such: Provided that

(1.) Where a person signs a bill in a trade or assumed name, he is liable thereon as if he had signed it in his own name:

(2.) The signature of the name of a firm is equivalent to the signature by the person so signing of the names of all persons liable as partners in that firm.

24. Subject to the provisions of this Act, where a signature on a bill is forged or placed thereon without the authority of the person whose signature it purports to be, the forged or unauthorised signature is wholly inoperative, and no right to retain the bill or to give a discharge therefor or to enforce payment thereof against any party thereto can be acquired through or under that signature, unless the party against whom it is sought to retain or enforce payment of the bill is precluded from setting up the forgery or want of authority.

Provided that nothing in this section shall affect the ratification of an unauthorised signature not amounting to a forgery.

25. A signature by procuration operates as notice that the agent has but a limited authority to sign, and the principal is only bound by such signature if the agent in so signing was acting within the actual limits of his authority.

26. (1.) Where a person signs a bill as drawer, indorser, or acceptor, and adds words to his signature, indicating that he signs or in representative for or on behalf of a principal, or in a representative character, he is not personally liable thereon; but the mere addition to his signature of words describing him as an agent, or as filling a representative character, does not exempt him from personal liability.

(2.) In determining whether a signature on a bill is that of the principal or that of the agent by whose hand it is written, the construction most favourable to the validity of the instrument shall be adopted.

The Consideration for a Bill.

27. (1.) Valuable consideration for a bill may be constituted by,-

    (a.) Any consideration sufficient to support a simple contract;

    (b.) An antecedent debt or liability. Such a debt or liability is deemed valuable consideration whether the bill is payable on demand or at a future time.

(2.) Where value has at any time been given for a bill the holder is deemed to be a holder for value as regards the acceptor and all parties to the bill who became parties prior to such time.

(3.) Where the holder of a bill has a lien on it, arising either from contract or by implication of law, he is deemed to be a holder for value to the extent of the sum for which he has a lien.

28. (1.) An accommodation party to a bill is a person who has signed a bill as drawer, acceptor, or indorser, without receiving value therefor, and for the purpose of lending his name to some other person.

(2.) An accommodation party is liable on the bill to a holder for value; and it is immaterial whether, when such holder took the bill, he knew such party to be an accommodation party or not.

29. (1.) A holder in due course is a holder who has taken a bill, complete and regular on the face of it, under the following conditions; namely,

    (a.) That he became the holder of it before it was overdue, and without notice that it had been previously dishonoured, if such was the fact:

    (b.) That he took the bill in good faith and for value, and that at the time the bill was negotiated to him he had no notice of any defect in the title of the person, who negotiated it.

(2.) In particular the title of a person who negotiates a bill is defective within the meaning of this Act when he obtained the bill, or the acceptance thereof, by fraud, duress, or force and fear, or other unlawful means, or for an illegal consideration, or when he negotiates it in breach of faith, or under such circumstances as amount to a fraud.

(3.) A holder (whether for value or not), who derives his title to a bill through a holder in due course, and who is not himself a party to any fraud or illegality affecting it, has all the rights of that holder in due course as regards the acceptor and all parties to the bill prior to that holder.

30. (1.) Every party whose signature appears on a bill is prima facie deemed to have become a party thereto for value.

(2.) Every holder of a bill is prima facie deemed to be a holder in due course; but if in an action on a bill it is admitted or proved that the acceptance, issue, or subsequent negotiation of the bill is affected with fraud, duress, or force and fear, or illegality, the burden of proof is shifted, unless and until the holder proves that, subsequent to the alleged fraud or illegality, value has in good faith been given for the bill.

Negotiation of Bills.

31. (1.) A bill is negotiated when it is transferred from one person to another in such a manner as to constitute the transferee the holder of the bill.

(2.) A bill payable to bearer is negotiated by delivery.

(3.) A bill payable to order is negotiated by the indorsement of the holder completed by delivery.

(4.) Where the holder of a bill payable to his order transfers it for value without indorsing it, the transfer gives the transferee such title as the transferor had in the bill, and the transferee in addition acquires the right to have the indorsement of the transferor.

(5.) Where any person is under obligation to indorse a bill in a representative capacity, he may indorse the bill in such terms as to negative personal liability.

32. An indorsement in order to operate as a negotiation must comply with the following conditions, namely:-

(1.) It must be written on the bill itself and be signed by the indorser. The simple signature of the indorser on the bill, without additional words, is sufficient.

An indorsement written on an allonge, or on a " copy " of a bill issued or negotiated in a country where " copies " are recognised, is deemed to be written on the bill itself.

(2.) It must be an indorsement of the entire bill. A partial endorsement, that is to say, an indorsement which purports to transfer to the indorsee a part only of the amount payable, or which purports to transfer the bill to two or more indorsees severally, does not operate as a negotiation of the bill.

260

(3.) Where a bill is payable to the order of two or more payees or indorsees who are not partners all must indorse, unless the one indorsing has authority to indorse for the others.

(4.) Where, in a bill payable to order, the payee or indorsee is wrongly designated, or his name is mis-spelt, he may indorse the bill as therein described, adding, if he think fit, his proper signature.

(5.) Where there are two or more indorsements on a bill, each indorsement is deemed to have been made in the order in which it appears on the bill, until the contrary is proved.

(6.) An indorsement may be made in blank or special. It may also contain terms making it restrictive.

33. Where a bill purports to be indorsed conditionally the condition may be disregarded by the payer, and payment to the indorsee is valid whether the condition has been fulfilled or not.

34. (1.) An indorsement in blank specifies no indorsee, and a bill so indorsed becomes payable to bearer.

(2.) A special indorsement specifies the person to whom, or to whose order, the bill is to be payable.

(3.) The provisions of this Act relating to a payee apply with the necessary modifications to an indorsee under a special indorsement.

(4.) When a bill has been indorsed in blank, any holder may convert the blank indorsement into a special indorsement by writing above the indorser's signature a direction to pay the bill to or to the order of himself or some other person.

35. (1.) An indorsement is restrictive which prohibits the further negotiation of the bill or which expresses that it is a mere authority to deal with the bill as thereby directed and not a transfer of the ownership thereof, as, for example, if a bill be indorsed " Pay D. only," or " Pay D. for the account of X.," or " Pay D. or order for collection."

(2.) A restrictive indorsement gives the indorsee the right to receive payment of the bill and to sue any party thereto that his indorser could have sued, but gives him no power to transfer his rights as indorsee unless it expressly authorise him to do so.

(3.) Where a restrictive indorsement authorises further transfer, all subsequent indorsees take the bill with the same rights and subject to the same liabilities as the first indorsee under the restrictive indorsement.

36.   (1.)   Where a bill is negotiable in its origin it continues to be negotiable until it has been (a) restrictively indorsed or (b) discharged by payment or otherwise.

(2.)   Where an overdue bill is negotiated, it can only be negotiated subject to any defect of title affecting it at its maturity, and thenceforward no person who takes it can acquire or give a better title than that which the person from whom he took it had.

(3.)   A bill payable on demand is deemed to be overdue within the meaning and for the purposes of this section, when it appears on the face of it to have been in circulation for an unreasonable length of time. What is an unreasonable length of time for this purpose is a question of fact.

(4.)   Except where an endorsement bears date after the maturity of the bill, every negotiation is prima facie deemed to have been effected before the bill was overdue.

(5.)   Where a bill which is not overdue has been dishonoured any person who takes it with notice of the dishonour takes it subject to any defect of title attaching thereto at the time of dishonour, but nothing in this sub-section shall affect the rights of a holder in due course.

37.   Where a bill is negotiated back to the drawer, or to a prior indorser or to the acceptor, such party may, subject to the provisions of this Act, re-issue and further negotiate the bill, but he is not entitled to enforce payment of the bill against any intervening party to whom he was previously liable.

38.   The rights and powers of the holder of a bill are as follows:

(1.)   He may sue on the bill in his own name:

(2.)   Where he is a holder in due course, he holds the bill free from any defect of title of prior parties, as well as from mere personal defences available to prior parties among themselves, and may enforce payment against all parties liable on the bill:

(3.)   Where his title is defective (a) if he negotiates the bill to a holder in due course, that holder obtains a good and complete title to the bill, and (b) if he obtains payment of the bill the person who pays him in due course gets a valid discharge for the bill.

General duties of the Holder.

39.   (1.)   Where a bill is payable after sight, presentment for acceptance is necessary in order to fix the maturity of the instrument.

(2.)   Where a bill expressly stipulates that it shall be presented for acceptance, or where a bill is drawn payable elsewhere than at the residence or place of business of the drawee it must be presented for acceptance before it can be presented for payment.

(3.) In no other case is presentment for acceptance necessary in order to render liable any party to the bill.

(4.) Where the holder of a bill, drawn payable elsewhere than at the place of business or residence of the drawee, has not time, with the exercise of reasonable diligence, to present the bill for acceptance before presenting it for payment on the day that it falls due, the delay caused by presenting the bill for acceptance before presenting it for payment is excused, and does not discharge the drawer and indorsers.

40. (1.) Subject to the provisions of this Act, when a bill payable after sight is negotiated, the holder must either present it for acceptance or negotiate it within a reasonable time.

(2.) If he do not do so, the drawer and all indorsers prior to that holder are discharged.

(3.) In determining what is a reasonable time within the meaning of this section, regard shall be had to the nature of the bill, the usage of trade with respect to similar bills, and the facts of the particular case.

41. (1.) A bill is duly presented for acceptance which is presented in accordance with the following rules:
    (a.) The presentment must be made by or on behalf of the holder to the drawee or to some person authorised to accept or refuse acceptance on his behalf at a reasonable hour on a business day and before the bill is overdue:
    (b.) Where a bill is addressed to two or more drawees, who are not partners, presentment must be made to them all, unless one has authority to accept for all, then presentment may be made to him only:
    (c.) Where the drawee is dead, presentment may be made to his personal representative:
    (d.) Where the drawee is bankrupt, presentment may be made to him or to his trustee:
    (e.) Where authorised by agreement or usage, a presentment through the post office is sufficient.

(2.) Presentment in accordance with these rules is excused, and a bill may be treated as dishonoured by non-acceptance-
    (a.) Where the drawee is dead or bankrupt, or is a fictitious person or a person not having capacity to contract by bill:
    (b.) Where, after the exercise of reasonable diligence, such presentment cannot be effected:

(c.) Where although the presentment has been irregular, acceptance has been refused on some other ground.

(3.) The fact that the holder has reason to believe that the bill, on presentment, will be dishonoured does not excuse presentment.

2. (1.) When a bill is duly presented for acceptance and is not accepted within the customary time, the person presenting it must treat it as dishonoured by non-acceptance. If he do not, the holder shall lose his right of recourse against the drawer and indorsers.

43. (1.) A bill is dishonoured by non-acceptance-
(a.) when it is duly presented for acceptance, and such an acceptance as is prescribed by this Act is refused or cannot be obtained; or
(b.) when presentment for acceptance is excused and the bill is not accepted.

(2.) Subject to the provisions of this Act when a bill is dishonoured by non-acceptance, an immediate right of recourse against the drawer and indorsers accrues to the holder, and no presentment for payment is necessary.

44. (1.) The holder of a bill may refuse to take a qualified acceptance, and if he does not obtain an unqualified acceptance may treat the bill as dishonoured by non-acceptance.

(2.) Where a qualified acceptance is taken, and the drawer or an indorser has not expressly or impliedly authorised the holder to take a qualified acceptance, or does not subsequently assent thereto, such drawer or indorser is discharged from his liability on the bill.

The provisions of this sub-section do not apply to a partial acceptance, whereof due notice has been given. Where a foreign bill has been accepted as to part, it must be protested as to the balance.

(3.) When the drawer or indorser of a bill receives notice of a qualified acceptance, and does not within a reasonable time express his dissent to the holder he shall be deemed to have assented thereto.

45. Subject to the provisions of this Act a bill must be duly presented for payment. If it be not so presented the drawer and indorsers shall be discharged.

A bill is duly presented for payment which is presented in accordance with the following rules:-

(1.)   Where the bill is not payable on demand, presentment must be made on the day it falls due.

(2.)   Where the bill is payable on demand, then, subject to the provisions of this Act, presentment must be made within a reasonable time after its issue in order to render the drawer liable, and within a reasonable time after its indorsement, in order to render the indorser liable.

         In determining what is a reasonable time, regard shall be had to the nature of the bill, the usage of trade with regard to similar bills, and the facts of the particular case.

(3.)   Presentment must be made by the holder or by some person authorised to receive payment on his behalf at a reasonable hour on a business day, at the proper place as herein-after defined, either to the person designated by the bill as payer, or to some person authorised to pay or refuse payment on his behalf if with the exercise of reasonable diligence such person can there be found.

(4.)   A bill is presented at the proper place:-
         (a.)   Where a place of payment is specified in the bill and the bill is there presented.
         (b.)   Where no place of payment is specified, but the address of the drawee or acceptor is given in the bill, and the bill is there presented.
         (c.)   Where no place of payment is specified and no address given, and the bill is presented at the drawee's or acceptor's place of business if known, and if not, at his ordinary residence if known.
         (d.)   In any other case if presented to the drawee or acceptor wherever he can be found, or if presented at his last known place of business or residence.

(5.)   Where a bill is presented at the proper place, and after the exercise of reasonable diligence no person authorised to pay or refuse payment can be found there, no further presentment to the drawee or acceptor is required.

(6.)   Where a bill is drawn upon, or accepted by two or more persons who are not partners, and no place of payment is specified, presentment must be made to them all.

(7.)   Where the drawee or acceptor of a bill is dead, and no place of payment is specified, presentment must be made to a personal representative, if such there be, and with the exercise of reasonable diligence he can be found.

(8.)   Where authorised by agreement or usage a presentment through the post office is sufficient.

46.   (1.)   Delay in making presentment for payment is excused when the delay is caused by circumstances beyond the control of the holder, and not imputable to his default, misconduct, or negligence. When the cause of delay ceases to operate presentment must be made with reasonable diligence.

(2.)   Presentment for payment is dispensed with, -
       (a.)   Where, after the exercise of reasonable diligence presentment, as required by this Act, cannot be effected.
               The fact that the holder has reason to believe that the bill will, on presentment, be dishonoured, does not dispense with the necessity for presentment.
       (b.)   Where the drawee is a fictitious person.
       (c.)   As regards the drawer where the drawee or acceptor is not bound, as between himself and the drawer, to accept or pay the bill, and the drawer has no reason to believe that the bill would be paid if presented.
       (d.)   As regards an indorser, where the bill was accepted or made for the accommodation of that indorser, and he has no reason to expect that the bill would be paid if presented.
       (e.)   By waiver of presentment, express or implied.

47.   (1.)   A bill is dishonoured by non-payment (a) when it is duly presented for payment and payment is refused or cannot be obtained, or (b) when presentment is excused and the bill is overdue and unpaid.

(2.)   Subject to the provisions of this Act, when a bill is dishonoured by non-payment, an immediate right of recourse against the drawer and indorsers accrues to the holder.

48.   Subject to the provisions of this Act, when a bill has been dishonoured by non-acceptance or by non-payment, notice of dishonour must be given to the drawer and each indorser, and any drawer or indorser to whom such notice is not given is discharged;

Provided that—
(1.)   Where a bill is dishonoured by non-acceptance, and notice of dishonour is not given, the rights of a holder in due course subsequent to the omission, shall not be prejudiced by the omission.

(2.)   Where a bill is dishonoured by non-acceptance and due notice of dishonour is given, it shall not be necessary to give notice of a

266

subsequent dishonour by non-payment unless the bill shall in the meantime have been accepted.

49. Notice of dishonour in order to be valid and effectual must be given in accordance with the following rules:-

(1.) The notice must be given by or on behalf of the holder, or by or on behalf of an indorser who, at the time of giving it, is himself liable on the bill.

(2.) Notice of dishonour may be given by an agent either in his own name, or in the name of any party entitled to give notice whether that party be his principal or not.

(3.) Where the notice is given by or on behalf of the holder, it enures for the benefit of all subsequent holders and all prior indorsers who have a right of recourse against the party to whom it is given.

(4.) Where notice is given by or on behalf of an indorser entitled to give notice as herein-before provided, it enures for the benefit of the holder and all indorsers subsequent to the party to whom notice is given.

(5.) The notice may be given in writing or by personal communication, and may be given in any terms which sufficiently identify the bill, and intimate that the bill has been dishonoured by non-acceptance or non-payment.

(6.) The return of a dishonoured bill to the drawer or an indorser is, in point of form, deemed a sufficient notice of dishonour.

(7.) A written notice need not be signed, and an insufficient written notice may be supplemented and validated by verbal communication. A mis-description of the bill shall not vitiate the notice unless the party to whom the notice is given is in fact misled thereby.

(8.) Where notice of dishonour is required to be given to any person, it may be given either to the party himself, or to his agent in that behalf.

(9.) Where the drawer or indorser is dead, and the party giving notice knows it, the notice must be given to a personal representative if such there be, and with the exercise of reasonable diligence he can be found.

(10.) Where the drawer or indorser is bankrupt, notice may be given either to the party himself or to the trustee.

(11.) Where there are two or more drawers or indorsers who are not partners, notice must be given to each of them, unless one of them has authority to receive such notice for the others.

(12.) The notice may be given as soon as the bill is dishonoured and must be given within a reasonable time thereafter.

In the absence of special circumstances notice is not deemed to have been given within a reasonable time, unless-
(a.) where the person giving and the person to receive notice reside in the same place, the notice is given or sent off in time to reach the latter on the day after the dishonour of the bill.
(b.) where the person giving and the person to receive notice reside in different places, the notice is sent off on the day after the dishonour of the bill, if there be a post at a convenient hour on that day, and if there be no such post on that day then by the next post thereafter.

(13.) Where a bill when dishonoured is in the hands of an agent, he may either himself give notice to the parties liable on the bill, or he may give notice to his principal. If he give notice to his principal, he must do so within the same time as if he were the holder, and the principal upon receipt of such notice has himself the same time for giving notice as if the agent had been an independent holder.

(14.) Where a party to a bill receives due notice of dishonour, he has after the receipt of such notice the same period of time for giving notice to antecedent parties that the holder has after the dishonour.

(15.) Where a notice of dishonour is duly addressed and posted, the sender is deemed to have given due notice of dishonour, notwithstanding any miscarriage by the post office.

50. (1.) Delay in giving notice of dishonour is excused where the delay is caused by circumstances beyond the control of the party giving notice, and not imputable to his default, misconduct, or negligence. When the cause of delay ceases to operate the notice must be given with reasonable diligence.

(2.) Notice of dishonour is dispensed with-
(a.) When, after the exercise of reasonable diligence, notice as required by this Act cannot be given to or does not reach the drawer or indorser sought to be charged:
(b.) By waiver express or implied. Notice of dishonour may be waived before the time of giving notice has arrived, or after the omission to give due notice:
(c.) As regards the drawer in the following cases, namely, (1) where drawer and drawee are the same person, (2) where the

drawee is a fictitious person or a person not having capacity to contract, (3) where the drawer is the person to whom the bill is presented for payment, (4) where the drawee or acceptor is as between himself and the drawer under no obligation to accept or pay the bill, (5) where the drawer has countermanded payment:

(d.) As regards the indorser in the following cases, namely, (1) where the drawee is a fictitious person or a person not having capacity to contract and the indorser was aware of the fact at the time he indorsed the bill, (2) where the indorser is the person to whom the bill is presented for payment, (3) where the bill was accepted or made for his accommodation.

51. (1.) Where an inland bill has been dishonoured it may, if the holder think fit, be noted for non-acceptance or non-payment, as the case may be; but it shall not be necessary to note or protest any such bill in order to preserve the recourse against the drawer or indorser.

(2.) Where a foreign bill, appearing on the face of it to be such, has been dishonoured by non-acceptance it must be duly protested for non-acceptance, and where such a bill, which has not been previously dishonoured by non-acceptance, is dishonoured by non-payment it must be duly protested for non-payment. If it be not so protested the drawer and indorsers are discharged. Where a bill does not appear on the face of it to be a foreign bill, protest thereof in case of dishonour is unnecessary.

(3.) A bill which has been protested for non-acceptance may be subsequently protested for non-payment.

(4.) Subject to the provisions of this Act, when a bill is noted or protested, it must be noted on the day of its dishonour. When a bill has been duly noted, the protest may be subsequently extended as of the date of the noting.

(5.) Where the acceptor of a bill becomes bankrupt or insolvent or suspends payment before it matures, the holder may cause the bill to be protested for better security against the drawer and indorsers.

(6.) A bill must be protested at the place where it is dishonoured:

Provided that-

(a.) When a bill is presented through the post office, and returned by post dishonoured, it may be protested at the place to which it is returned and on the day of its return if received during business hours, and if not received during business hours, then not later than the next business day:

<table>
<tr><td></td><td>(b.)</td><td>When a bill drawn payable at the place of business or residence of some person other than the drawee, has been dishonoured by non-acceptance, it must be protested for n-payment at the place where it is expressed to be payable, and no further presentment for payment to, or demand on, the drawee is necessary.</td></tr>
</table>

(7.)   A protest must contain a copy of the bill, and must be signed by the notary making it, and must specify-

(a.)   The person at whose request the bill is protested:

(b.)   The place and date of protest, the cause or reason for protesting the bill, the demand made, and the answer given, if any, or the fact that the drawee or acceptor could not be found.

(8.)   Where a bill is lost or destroyed, or is wrongly detained from the person entitled to hold it, protest may be made on a copy or written particulars thereof.

(9.)   Protest is dispensed with by any circumstance which would dispense with notice of dishonour. Delay in noting or protesting is excused when the delay is caused by circumstances beyond the control of the holder, and not imputable to his default, misconduct, or negligence. When the cause of delay ceases to operate the bill must be noted or protested with reasonable diligence.

52.   (1.)   When a bill is accepted generally presentment for payment is not necessary in order to render the acceptor liable.

(2.)   When by the terms of a qualified acceptance presentment for payment is required, the acceptor, in the absence of an express stipulation to that effect, is not discharged by the omission to present the bill for payment on the day that it matures.

(3.)   In order to render the acceptor of a bill liable it is not necessary to protest it, or that notice of dishonour should be given to him.

(4.)   Where the holder of a bill presents it for payment, he shall exhibit the bill to the person from whom he demands payment, and when a bill is paid the holder shall forthwith deliver it up to the party paying it.

Liabilities of Parties.

53.   (1.)   A bill, of itself, does not operate as an assignment of funds in the hands of the drawee available for the payment thereof, and the drawee of a bill who does not accept as required by this Act is not liable on the instrument. This sub-section shall not extend to Scotland.

(2.) In Scotland, where the drawee of a bill has in his hands funds available for the payment thereof, the bill operates as an assignment of the sum for which it is drawn in favour of the holder, from the time when the bill is presented to the drawee.

54. The acceptor of a bill, by accepting it—
(1.) Engages that he will pay it according to the tenor of his acceptance:

(2.) Is precluded from denying to a holder in due course:
(a.) The existence of the drawer, the genuineness of his signature, and his capacity and authority to draw the bill;
(b.) In the case of a bill payable to drawer's order, the then capacity of the drawer to indorse, but not the genuineness or validity of his indorsement;
(c.) In the case of a bill payable to the order of a third person, the existence of the payee and his then capacity to indorse, but not the genuineness or validity of his endorsement.

55. (1.) The drawer of a bill by drawing it—
(a.) Engages that on due presentment it shall be accepted and paid according to its tenor, and that if it be dishonoured he will compensate the holder or any indorser who is compelled to pay it, provided that the requisite proceedings on dishonour be duly taken;
(b.) Is precluded from denying to a holder in due course the existence of the payee and his then capacity to indorse.

(2.) The indorser of a bill by indorsing it-
(a.) Engages that on due presentment it shall be accepted and paid according to its tenor, and that if it be dishonoured he will compensate the holder or a subsequent endorser who is compelled to pay it, provided that the requisite proceedings on dishonour be duly taken;
(b.) Is precluded from denying to a holder in due course the genuineness and regularity in all respects of the drawer's signature and all previous indorsements;
(c.) Is precluded from denying to his immediate or a subsequent indorsee that the bill was at the time of his indorsement a valid and subsisting bill, and that he had then a good title thereto.

56. Where a person signs a bill otherwise than as drawer or acceptor, he thereby incurs the liabilities of an indorser to a holder as in due course.

57. Where a bill is dishonoured, the measure of damages, which shall be deemed to be liquidated damages, shall be as, follows:

(1.) The holder may recover from any party liable on the bill, and the drawer who has been compelled to pay the bill may recover from

271

the acceptor, and an indorser who has been compelled to pay the bill may recover from the acceptor or from the drawer or from a prior indorser-

(a.)   The amount of the bill:

(b.)   Interest thereon from the time of presentment for payment if the bill is payable on demand, and from the maturity of the bill in any other case:

(c.)   The expenses of noting, or, when protest is necessary, and the protest has been extended, the expenses of protest.

(2.)   In the case of a bill which has been dishonoured abroad, in lieu of the above damages, the holder may recover from the drawer or an indorser, and the drawer or an indorser who has been compelled to pay the bill may recover from any party liable to him, the amount of the re-exchange with interest thereon until the time of payment.

(3.)   Where by this Act interest may be recovered as damages, such interest may, if justice require it, be withheld wholly or in part, and where a bill is expressed to be payable with interest at a given rate, interest as damages may or may not be given at the same rate as interest proper.

58.   (1.)   Where the holder of a bill payable to bearer negotiates it by delivery without indorsing it, he is called a "transferor by delivery".

(2.)   A transferor by delivery is not liable on the instrument.

(3.)   A transferor by delivery who negotiates a bill thereby warrants to his immediate transferee being a holder for value that the bill is what it purports to be, that he has a right to transfer it, and that at the time of transfer he is not aware of any fact which renders it valueless.

59.   (1.)   A bill is discharged by payment in due course by or on behalf of the drawee or acceptor.

"Payment in due course" means payment made at or after the maturity of the bill to the holder thereof in good faith and without notice that his title to the bill is defective.

(2.)   Subject to the provisions herein-after contained, when a bill is paid by the drawer or an indorser it is not discharged; but

(a.)   Where a bill payable to, or to the order of, a third party is paid by the drawer, the drawer may enforce payment thereof against the acceptor, but may not re-issue the bill.

(b.)   Where a bill is paid by an indorser, or where a bill payable to drawer's order is paid by the drawer, the party paying it is remitted to his former rights as regards the acceptor or antecedent parties, and he may, if he thinks fit, strike out his own and subsequent indorsements, and again negotiate the bill.

(3.)   Where an accommodation bill is paid in due course by the party accommodated the bill is discharged.

60.   When a bill payable to order on demand is drawn on a banker, and the banker on whom it is drawn pays the bill in good faith and in the ordinary course of business, it is not incumbent on the banker to show that the indorsement of the payee or any subsequent indorsement was made by or under the authority of the person whose indorsement it purports to be, and the banker is deemed to have paid the bill in due course, although such indorsement has been forged or made without authority.

61.   When the acceptor of a bill is or becomes the holder of it at or after its maturity, in his own right, the bill is discharged.

62.   (1.)   When the holder of a bill at or after its maturity absolutely and unconditionally renounces his rights against the acceptor the bill is discharged.

                The renunciation must be in writing, unless the bill is delivered up to the acceptor.

        (2.)   The liabilities of any party to a bill may in like manner be renounced by the holder before, at, or after its maturity; but nothing in this section shall affect the rights of a holder in due course without notice of the renunciation.

63.   (1.)   Where a bill is intentionally cancelled by the holder or his agent, and the cancellation is apparent thereon, the bill is discharged.

        (2.)   In like manner any party liable on a bill may be discharged by the intentional cancellation of his signature by the holder or his agent. In such case any indorser who would have had a right of recourse against the party whose signature is cancelled, is also discharged.

        (3.)   A cancellation made unintentionally, or under a mistake, or without the authority of the holder is inoperative; but where a bill or any signature thereon appears to have been cancelled the burden of proof lies on the party who alleges that the cancellation was made unintentionally, or under a mistake, or without authority.

64.   (1.)   Where a bill or acceptance is materially altered without the assent of all parties liable on the bill, the bill is avoided except as against a party who has himself made, authorised, or assented to the alteration, and subsequent indorsers.

Provided that,

Where a bill has been materially altered, but the alteration is not apparent, and the bill is in the hands of a holder in due course, such holder may avail himself of the bill as if it had not been altered, and may enforce payment of it according to its original tenour.

(2.) In particular the following alterations are material, namely, any alteration of the date, the sum payable, the time of payment, the place of payment, and, where a bill has been accepted generally, the addition of a place of payment without the acceptor's assent.

Acceptance and Payment for Honour.

65. (1.) Where a bill of exchange has been protested for dishonour by non-acceptance, or protested for better security, and is, not overdue, any person, not being a party already liable thereon, may, with the consent of the holder, intervene and accept the bill supra protest, for the honour of any party liable thereon, or for the honour of the person for whose account the bill is drawn.

(2.) A bill may be accepted for honour for part only of the sum for which it is drawn.

(3.) An acceptance for honour supra protest in order to be valid must-
  (a.) be written on the bill, and indicate that it is an acceptance for honour:
  (b.) be signed by the acceptor for honour:

(4.) Where an acceptance for honour does not expressly state for whose honour it is made, it is deemed to be an acceptance for the honour of the drawer.

(5.) Where a bill payable after sight is accepted for honour, its maturity is calculated from the date of the noting for non-acceptance, and not from the date of the acceptance for honour.

66. (1.) The acceptor for honour of a bill by accepting it engages that he will, on due presentment, pay the bill according to the tenor of his acceptance, if it is not paid by the drawee, provided it has been duly presented for payment, and protested for non-payment, and that he receives notice of these facts.

(2.) The acceptor for honour is liable to the holder and to all parties to the bill subsequent to the party for whose honour he has accepted.

67. (1.) Where a dishonoured bill has been accepted for honour supra protest, or contains a reference in case of need, it must be protested for non payment before it is presented for payment to the acceptor for honour, or referee in case of need.

(2.) Where the address of the acceptor for honour is in the same place where the bill is protested for non-payment, the bill must be presented to him not later than the day following its maturity; and where the address of the acceptor for honour is in some place other than the place where it was protested for non-payment, the bill must be forwarded not later than the day following its maturity for presentment to him.

(3.) Delay in presentment or non-presentment is excused by any circumstance, which would excuse delay in presentment for payment or non-presentment for payment.

(4.) When a bill of exchange is dishonoured by the acceptor for honour it must be protested for non-payment by him.

68. (1.) Where a bill has been protested for non-payment, any person may intervene and pay it supra protest for the honour of any party liable thereon, or for the honour of the person for whose account the bill is drawn.

(2.) Where two or more persons offer to pay a bill for the honour of different parties, the person whose payment will discharge most parties to the bill shall have the preference.

(3.) Payment for honour supra protest, in order to operate as such and not as a mere voluntary payment, must be attested by a notarial act of honour which may be appended to the protest or form an extension of it.

(4.) The notarial act of honour must be founded on a declaration made by the payer for honour, or his agent in that behalf, declaring his intention to pay the bill for honour, and for whose honour he pays.

(5.) Where a bill has been paid for honour, all parties subsequent to the party for whose honour it is paid are discharged, but the payer for honour is subrogated for, and succeeds to both the rights and duties of, the holder as regards the party for whose honour he pays, and all parties liable to that party.

(6.) The payer for honour on paying to the holder the amount of the bill and the notarial expenses incidental to its dishonour is entitled to receive both the bill itself and the protest. If the holder do not on demand deliver them up he shall be liable to the payer for honour in damages.

(7.) Where the holder of a bill refuses to receive payment supra protest he shall lose his right of recourse against any party who would have been discharged by such payment.

Lost Instruments.

69.   Where a bill has been lost before it is overdue, the person who was the holder of it may apply to the drawer to give him another bill of the same tenor, giving security to the drawer if required to indemnify him against all persons whatever in case the bill alleged to have been lost shall be found again.

If the drawer on request as aforesaid refuses to give such duplicate bill, he may be compelled to do so.

70.   In any action or proceeding upon a bill, the court or a judge may order that the loss of the instrument shall not be set up, provided an indemnity be given to the satisfaction of the court or judge against the claims of any other person upon the instrument in question.

Bill in a Set.

71.   (1.)   Where a bill is drawn in a set, each part of the set being numbered, and containing a reference to the other parts, the whole of the parts constitute one bill.

    (2.)   Where, the holder of a set indorses two or more parts to different persons, he is liable on every such part, and every indorser subsequent to him is liable on the part he has himself indorsed as if the said parts were separate bills.

    (3.)   Where two or more parts of a set are negotiated to different holders in due course, the holder whose title first accrues is as between such holders deemed the true owner of the bill; but nothing in this sub-section shall affect the rights of a person who in due course accepts or pays the part first presented to him.

    (4.)   The acceptance may be written on any part, and it must be written on one part only.

If the drawee accepts more than one part, and such accepted parts get into the hands of different holders in due course, he is liable on every such part as if it were a separate bill.

    (5.)   When the acceptor of a bill drawn in a set pays it without requiring the part bearing his acceptance to be delivered up to him, and that part at maturity is outstanding in the hands of a holder in due course, he is liable to the holder thereof.

    (6.)   Subject to the preceding rules, where any one part of a bill drawn in a set is discharged by payment or otherwise, the whole bill is discharged.

Conflict of Laws.

72.   Where a bill drawn in one country is negotiated, accepted, or payable in another, the rights, duties, and liabilities of the parties thereto are determined as follows:

(1.)   The validity of a bill as regards requisites in form is determined by the law of the place of issue, and the validity as regards requisites in form of the supervening contracts, such as acceptance, or indorsement, or acceptance supra protest, is determined by the law of the place where such contract was made.

Provided that-
(a.)   Where a bill is issued out of the United Kingdom it is not invalid by reason only that it is not stamped in accordance with the law of the place of issue:
(b.)   Where a bill, issued out of the United Kingdom, conforms, as regards requisites in form, to the law of the United Kingdom, it may, for the purpose of enforcing payment thereof, be treated as valid as between all persons who negotiate, hold, or become parties to it in the United Kingdom.

(2.)   Subject to the provisions of this Act, the interpretation of the drawing, indorsement, acceptance, or acceptance supra protest of a bill, is determined by the law of the place where such contract is made.

Provided that where an inland bill is indorsed in a foreign country the indorsement shall as regards the payer be interpreted according to the law of the United Kingdom.

(3.)   The duties of the holder with respect to presentment for acceptance or payment and the necessity for or sufficiency of a protest or notice of dishonour, or otherwise, are determined by the law of the place where the act is done or the bill is dishonoured.

(4.)   Where a bill is drawn out of but payable in the United Kingdom and the sum payable is not expressed in the currency of the United Kingdom, the amount shall, in the absence of some express stipulation, be calculated according to the rate of exchange for sight drafts at the place of payment on the day the bill is payable.

(5.)   Where a bill is drawn in one country and is payable in another, the due date thereof is determined according to the law of the place where it is payable.

PART III.
CHEQUES ON A BANKER.

73.   A cheque is a bill of exchange drawn on a banker payable on demand. Except as otherwise provided in this Part, the provisions of this Act applicable to a bill of exchange payable on demand apply to a cheque.

74.   Subject to the provisions of this Act-

(1.)   Where a cheque is not presented for payment within a reasonable time of its issue, and the drawer or the person on whose account it is drawn had the right at the time of such presentment as between him and the banker to have the cheque paid and suffers actual damage through the delay, he is discharged to the extent of such damage, that is to say, to the extent to which such drawer or person is a creditor of such banker to a larger amount than he would have been had such cheque been paid.

(2.)   In determining what is a reasonable time regard shall be had to the nature of the instrument, the usage of trade and of bankers, and the facts of the particular case.

(3.)   The holder of such cheque as to which such drawer or person is discharged shall be a creditor, in lieu of such drawer or person, of such banker to the extent of such discharge, and entitled to recover the amount from him.

75.   The duty and authority of a banker to pay a cheque drawn on him by his customer are determined by-

(1.)   Countermand of payment:

(2.)   Notice of the customer's death.

Crossed Cheques.

76.   (1.)   Where a cheque bears across its face an addition of-

(a.)   The words " and company " or any abbreviation thereof between two parallel transverse lines, either with or without the words " not negotiable "; or

(b.)   Two parallel transverse lines simply, either with or without the words " not negotiable ";

that addition constitutes a crossing, and the cheque is crossed generally.

(2.)   Where a cheque bears across its face an addition of the name of a banker, either with or without the words " not negotiable " that addition constitutes a crossing, and the cheque is crossed specially and to that banker.

77.   (1.)   A cheque may be crossed generally or specially by the drawer.

(2.)   Where a cheque is uncrossed, the holder may cross it generally or specially.

(3.)   Where a cheque is crossed generally the holder may cross it specially.

(4.)   Where a cheque is crossed generally or specially, the holder may add the words " not negotiable ".

(5.)   Where a cheque is crossed specially, the banker to whom it is crossed may again cross it specially to another banker for collection.

(6.)   Where an uncrossed cheque, or a cheque crossed generally, is sent to a banker for collection, he may cross it specially to himself.

78.   A crossing authorised by this Act is a material part of the cheque; it shall not be lawful for any person to obliterate or, except as authorised by this Act, to add to or alter the crossing.

79.   (1.)   Where a cheque is crossed specially to more than one banker except when crossed to an agent for collection being a banker, the banker on whom it is drawn shall refuse payment thereof.

(2.)   Where the banker on whom a cheque is drawn which is so crossed nevertheless pays the same, or pays a cheque crossed generally otherwise than to a banker, or if crossed specially otherwise than to the banker to whom it is crossed, or his agent for collection being a banker, he is liable to the true owner of the cheque for any loss he may sustain owing to the cheque having been so paid.

Provided that where a cheque is presented for payment which does not at the time of presentment appear to be crossed, or to have had a crossing which has been obliterated, or to have been added to or altered otherwise than as authorised by this Act, the banker paying the cheque in good faith and without negligence shall not be responsible or incur any liability, nor shall the payment be questioned by reason of the cheque having being crossed, or of the crossing having been obliterated or having been added to or altered otherwise than as authorised by this Act, and of payment having been made otherwise than to a banker or to the banker to whom the cheque is or was crossed, or to his agent for collection being a banker, as the case may be.

80.   Where the banker, on whom a crossed cheque is drawn, in good faith and without negligence pays it, if crossed generally, to a banker, and if crossed specially, to the banker to whom it is crossed, or his agent for collection being a banker, the banker paying the cheque, and, if the cheque has come

279

into the hands of the payee, the drawer, shall respectively be entitled to the same rights and be placed in the same position as if payment of the cheque had been made to the true owner thereof.

81.   Where a person takes a crossed cheque which bears on it the words " not negotiable " he shall not have and shall not be capable of giving a better title to the cheque than that which the person from whom he took it had.

82.   Where a banker in good faith and without negligence receives payment for a customer of a cheque crossed generally specially to himself, and the customer has no title or a defective title thereto, the banker shall not incur any liability to the true owner of the cheque by reason only of having received such payment.

PART IV.
PROMISSORY NOTES.

83.   (1.)   A promissory note is an unconditional promise in writing made by one person to another signed by the maker, engaging to pay, on demand or at a fixed or determinable future time, a sum certain in money, to, or to the order of, a specified person or to bearer.

         (2.)   An instrument in the form of a note payable to maker's order is not a note within the meaning of this section unless and until it is indorsed by the maker.

         (3.)   A note is not invalid by reason only that it contains also a pledge of collateral security with authority to sell or dispose thereof.

         (4.)   A note which is, or on the face of it purports to be, both made and payable within the British Islands is an inland note. Any other note is a foreign note.

84.   A promissory note is inchoate and incomplete until delivery thereof to the payee or bearer.

85.   (1.)   A promissory note may be made by two or more makers, and they may be liable thereon jointly, or jointly and severally according to its tenour.

         (2.)   Where a note runs " I promise to pay " and is signed by two or more persons it is deemed to be their joint and several note.

86.   (1.)   Where a note payable on demand has been indorsed, it must be presented for payment within a reasonable time of the indorsement. If it be not so presented the indorser is discharged.

         (2.)   In determining what is a reasonable time, regard shall be had to the nature of the instrument, the usage of trade, and the facts of the particular case.

(3.)   Where a note payable on demand is negotiated, it is not deemed to be overdue, for the purpose of affecting the holder with defects of title of which he had no notice, by reason that it appears that a reasonable time for presenting it for payment has elapsed since its issue.

87.   (1.)   Where a promissory note is in the body of it made payable at a particular place, it must be presented for payment at that place in order to render the maker liable. In any other case, presentment for payment is not necessary in order to render the maker liable.

   (2.)   Presentment for payment is necessary in order to render the indorser of a note liable.

   (3.)   Where a note is in the body of it made payable at a particular place, presentment at that place is necessary in order to render an indorser liable; but when a place of payment is indicated by way of memorandum only, presentment at that place is sufficient to render the indorser liable, but a presentment to the maker elsewhere, if sufficient in other respects, shall also suffice.

88.   The maker of a promissory note by making it-
   (1.)   Engages that he will pay it according to its tenour;
   (2.)   Is precluded from denying to a holder in due course the existence of the payee and his then capacity to indorse.

89.   (1.)   Subject to the provisions in this part and, except as by this section provided, the provisions of this Act relating to bills of exchange apply, with the necessary modifications, to promissory notes.

   (2.)   In applying those provisions the maker of a note shall be deemed to correspond with the acceptor of a bill, and the first indorser of a note shall be deemed to correspond with the drawer of an accepted bill payable to drawer's order.

   (3.)   The following provisions as to bills do not apply to notes;

namely, provisions relating to-
   (a.)   Presentment for acceptance;
   (b.)   Acceptance;
   (c.)   Acceptance supra protest;
   (d.)   Bills in a set.

   (4.)   Where a foreign note is dishonoured, protest thereof is unnecessary.

PART V.
SUPPLEMENTARY.

90. A thing is deemed to be done in good faith, within the meaning of this Act, where it is in fact done honestly, whether it is done negligently or not.

91. (1.) Where, by this Act, any instrument or writing is required to be signed by any person, it is not necessary that he should sign it with his own hand, but it is sufficient if his signature is written thereon by some other person by or under his authority.

(2.) In the case of a corporation, where, by this Act, any instrument or writing is required to be signed, it is sufficient if the instrument or writing be sealed with the corporate seal.

But nothing in this section shall be construed as requiring the bill or note of a corporation to be under seal.

92. Where, by this Act, the time limited for doing any act or thing is less than three days, in reckoning time, non-business days are excluded.

" Non-business days " for the purposes of this Act mean-
(a.) Sunday, Good Friday, Christmas Day:
(b.) A bank holiday under the Bank Holidays Act, 1871, or Acts amending it:
(c.) A day appointed by Royal proclamation as a public fast or thanksgiving day.
Any other day is a business day.

93. For the purposes of this Act, where a bill or note is required to be protested within a specified time or before some further proceeding is taken, it is sufficient that the bill has been noted for protest before the expiration of the specified time or the taking of the proceeding; and the formal protest may be extended at any time thereafter as of the date of the noting.

94. Where a dishonoured bill or note is authorised or required to be protested, and the services of a notary cannot be obtained at the place where the bill is dishonoured, any householder or substantial resident of the place may, in the presence of two witnesses, give a certificate, signed by them, attesting the dishonour of the bill, and the certificate shall in all respects operate as if it were a formal protest of the bill.

The form given in Schedule 1 to this Act may be used with necessary modifications, and if used shall be sufficient.

95. The provisions of this Act as to crossed cheques shall apply to a warrant for payment of dividend.

96. The enactments mentioned in the second schedule to this Act are hereby repealed as from the commencement of this Act to the extent in that schedule mentioned.

Provided that such repeal shall not affect anything done or suffered, or any right, title, or interest acquired or accrued before the commencement of this Act, or any legal proceeding or remedy in respect of any such thing, right, title, or interest.

97. (1.) The rules in bankruptcy relating to bills of exchange, promissory notes, and cheques, shall continue to apply thereto notwithstanding anything in this Act contained.

(2.) The rules of common law including the law merchant, save in so far as they are inconsistent with the express provisions of this Act, shall continue to apply to bills of exchange, promissory notes, and cheques.

(3.) Nothing in this Act or in any repeal effected thereby shall affect-

(a.) The provisions of the Stamp Act, 1870, or Acts amending it, or any law or enactment for the time being in force relating to the revenue:

(b.) The provisions of the Companies Act, 1862, or Acts amending it, or any Act relating to joint stock banks or companies:

(c.) The provisions of any Act relating to or confirming the privileges of the Bank of England or the Bank of Ireland respectively:

(d.) The validity of any usage relating to dividend warrants, or the indorsements thereof.

98. Nothing in this Act or in any repeal effected thereby shall extend or restrict, or in any way alter or affect the law and practice in Scotland in regard to summary diligence.

99. Where any Act or document refers to any enactment repealed by this Act, the Act or document shall be construed, and shall operate, as if it referred to the corresponding provisions of this Act.

100. In any judicial proceeding in Scotland, any fact relating to a bill of exchange, bank cheque, or promissory note, which is relevant to any question of liability thereon, may be proved by parole evidence: Provided that this enactment shall not in any way affect the existing law and practice whereby the party who is, according to the tenour of any bill of exchange, bank cheque, or promissory note, debtor to the holder in the

amount thereof, may be required, as a condition of obtaining a sist of diligence, or suspension of a charge, or threatened charge, to make such consignation, or to find such caution as the court or judge before whom the cause is depending may require.

This section shall not apply to any case where the bill of exchange, bank cheque, or promissory note has undergone the sesennial prescription.

SCHEDULES

FIRST SCHEDULE

Form of protest which may be used when the services of a notary cannot be obtained.

Know all men that I, *A.B.* [householder], of   in the county of

in the United Kingdom, at the request of *C.D.*, there being no notary public available, did on the
         Day of   188   at   demand   payment
[*or* acceptance]of the bill of exchange hereunder written, from *E.F.,* to which demand he made answer [state answer, if any] wherefore I now, in the presence of *G.H.* and *J.K.* do protest the said bill of exchange.

          (Signed)   A.B.

                        G.H. (Witness)
                        J.K.   (Witness)

NB.   The Bill itself should be annexed, or a copy of the bill and all that is written thereon should be underwritten.

SECOND SCHEDULE
ENACTMENTS REPEALED

Session and Chapter.	Title of Act and extent of Repeal
9 Will. 3. c. 17.	An Act for the better payment of Inland Bills of Exchange.
3 & 4 Anne, c. 8.	An Act for giving like remedy upon Promissory Notes as is now used upon Bills of Exchange, and for the better payment of Inland Bills of Exchange.
17 Geo. 3. c. 30.	An Act for further restraining the negotiation of promissory notes and inland bills of exchange under a limited sum within that part of Great Britain called England.
39 & 40 Geo. 3. c. 42.	An Act for the better observance of Good Friday in certain cases therein mentioned.
48 Geo. 3. c. 88.	An Act to restrain the Negotiation of Promissory Notes and Inland Bills of Exchange under a Limited sum in England.
1 & 2 Geo. 4. c. 78.	An Act to regulate Acceptances of Bills of Exchange.
7 & 8 Geo. 4. c. 15.	An Act for declaring the law in relation to Bills of Exchange and Promissory Notes becoming payable on Good Friday or Christmas Day.
9 Geo. 4. c. 24.	An Act to repeal certain Acts, and to consolidate and amend the laws relating to bills of exchange and promissory notes in Ireland. in part; that is to say, Section two, four, seven, eight, nine, ten, eleven.
2 & 3 Will. 4. c. 98.	An Act for regulating the protesting for non-payment of Bills of Exchange drawn payable at a place not being the place of the residence of the drawee or drawees of the same.

6 & 7 Will. 4. c. 58.	An Act for declaring the law as to the day on which it is requisite to present for payment to Acceptor, or Acceptors supra protest for honour, or to the Referee or Referees, in case of need, Bills of Exchange which have been dishonoured.
8 & 9 Vict. c. 37. in part.	An Act to regulate the issue of bank notes in Ireland, and to regulate the repayment of certain sums advanced by the Governor and Company of the Bank of Ireland for the public service, in part; that is to say, Section twenty-four.
19 & 20 Vict. c. 97. in part.	The Mercantile Law Amendment Act, 1856, in part; that is to say, Sections six and seven.
23 & 24 Vict. c. 111. in part.	An Act for granting to Her Majesty certain duties of stamps, and to amend the laws relating to the stamp duties, in part; that is to say, Section nineteen.
34 & 35 Vict. c. 74.	An Act to abolish days of grace in the case of bills of exchange and promissory notes payable at sight or on presentation.
39 & 40 Vict. c. 81.	The Crossed Cheques Act, 1876.
41 & 42 Vict. c. 13.	The Bills of Exchange Act, 1878.

ENACTMENT REPEALED AS TO SCOTLAND

19 & 20 Vict. c. 60. in part.	The Mercantile Law (Scotland) Amendment Act, 1856, in part; that is to say, Sections ten, eleven, twelve, thirteen, fourteen, fifteen, and sixteen.

SECTION 1

Persons who lack mental capacity

The principles

1. **The principles**
   (1)   The following principles apply for the purposes of this Act.
   (2)   A person must be assumed to have capacity unless it is established that he lacks capacity.
   (3)   A person is not to be treated as unable to make a decision unless all practicable steps to help him to do so have been taken without success.
   (4)   A person is not to be treated as unable to make a decision merely because he makes an unwise decision.
   (5)   An act done, or decision made, under this Act for or on behalf of a person who lacks capacity must be done, or made, in his best interests.
   (6)   Before the act is done, or the decision is made, regard must be had to whether the purpose for which it is needed can be as effectively achieved in a way that is less restrictive of the person's rights and freedom of action.

Preliminary

2. **People who lack capacity**
   (1)   For the purposes of this Act, a person lacks capacity in relation to a matter if at the material time he is unable to make a decision for himself in relation to the matter because of an impairment of, or a disturbance in the functioning of, the mind or brain.

   (2)   It does not matter whether the impairment or disturbance is permanent or temporary.

   (3)   A lack of capacity cannot be established merely by reference to—
           (a)   a person's age or appearance, or
           (b)   a condition of his, or an aspect of his behaviour, which might lead others to make unjustified assumptions about his capacity.

   (4)   In proceedings under this Act or any other enactment, any question whether a person lacks capacity within the meaning of this Act must be decided on the balance of probabilities.

   (5)   No power which a person ("D") may exercise under this Act—
           (a)   in relation to a person who lacks capacity, or
           (b)   where D reasonably thinks that a person lacks capacity, is exercisable in relation to a person under 16.

(6)   Subsection (5) is subject to section 18(3).

3.   **Inability to make decisions**
(1)   For the purposes of section 2, a person is unable to make a decision for himself if he is unable—
    (a)   to understand the information relevant to the decision,
    (b)   to retain that information,
    (c)   to use or weigh that information as part of the process of making the decision, or
    (d)   to communicate his decision (whether by talking, using sign language or any other means).

(2)   A person is not to be regarded as unable to understand the information relevant to a decision if he is able to understand an explanation of it given to him in a way that is appropriate to his circumstances (using simple language, visual aids or any other means).

(3)   The fact that a person is able to retain the information relevant to a decision for a short period only does not prevent him from being regarded as able to make the decision.

(4)   The information relevant to a decision includes information about the reasonably foreseeable consequences of—
    (a)   deciding one way or another, or
    (b)   failing to make the decision.

4.   **Best interests**
(1)   In determining for the purposes of this Act what is in a person's best interests, the person making the determination must not make it merely on the basis of—
    (a)   the person's age or appearance, or
    (b)   a condition of his, or an aspect of his behaviour, which might lead others to make unjustified assumptions about what might be in his best interests.

(2)   The person making the determination must consider all the relevant circumstances and, in particular, take the following steps.

(3)   He must consider—
    (a)   whether it is likely that the person will at some time have capacity in relation to the matter in question, and
    (b)   if it appears likely that he will, when that is likely to be.

(4)   He must, so far as reasonably practicable, permit and encourage the person to participate, or to improve his ability to participate, as fully as possible in any act done for him and any decision affecting him.

(5)   Where the determination relates to life-sustaining treatment he must not, in considering whether the treatment is in the best interests of the person concerned, be motivated by a desire to bring about his death.

(6)   He must consider, so far as is reasonably ascertainable—
   (a)   the person's past and present wishes and feelings (and, in particular, any relevant written statement made by him when he had capacity),
   (b)   the beliefs and values that would be likely to influence his decision if he had capacity, and
   (c)   the other factors that he would be likely to consider if he were able to do so.

(7)   He must take into account, if it is practicable and appropriate to consult them, the views of—
   (a)   anyone named by the person as someone to be consulted on the matter in question or on matters of that kind,
   (b)   anyone engaged in caring for the person or interested in his welfare,
   (c)   any donee of a lasting power of attorney granted by the person, and
   (d)   any deputy appointed for the person by the court,

as to what would be in the person's best interests and, in particular, as to the matters mentioned in subsection (6).

(8)   The duties imposed by subsections (1) to (7) also apply in relation to the exercise of any powers which—
   (a)   are exercisable under a lasting power of attorney, or
   (b)   are exercisable by a person under this Act where he reasonably believes that another person lacks capacity.

(9)   In the case of an act done, or a decision made, by a person other than the court, there is sufficient compliance with this section if (having complied with the requirements of subsections (1) to (7)) he reasonably believes that what he does or decides is in the best interests of the person concerned.

Lasting powers of attorney
9.   Lasting powers of attorney
   (1)   A lasting power of attorney is a power of attorney under which the donor ("P") confers on the donee (or donees) authority to make decisions about all or any of the following—
   (a)   P's personal welfare or specified matters concerning P's personal welfare, and
   (b)   P's property and affairs or specified matters concerning P's property and affairs, and which includes authority to make

such decisions in circumstances where P no longer has capacity.

(2)   A lasting power of attorney is not created unless—
    (a)   section 10 is complied with,
    (b)   an instrument conferring authority of the kind mentioned in subsection (1) is made and registered in accordance with Schedule 1, and
    (c)   at the time when P executes the instrument, P has reached 18 and has capacity to execute it.

(3)   An instrument which—
    (a)   purports to create a lasting power of attorney, but
    (b)   does not comply with this section, section 10 or Schedule 1,
confers no authority.

(4)   The authority conferred by a lasting power of attorney is subject to—
    (a)   the provisions of this Act and, in particular, sections 1 (the principles) and 4 (best interests), and
    (b)   any conditions or restrictions specified in the instrument.

10.   Appointment of donees
(1)   A donee of a lasting power of attorney must be—
    (a)   an individual who has reached 18, or
    (b)   if the power relates only to P's property and affairs, either such an individual or a trust corporation.

(2)   An individual who is bankrupt may not be appointed as donee of a lasting power of attorney in relation to P's property and affairs.

(3)   Subsections (4) to (7) apply in relation to an instrument under which two or more persons are to act as donees of a lasting power of attorney.

(4)   The instrument may appoint them to act—
    (a)   jointly,
    (b)   jointly and severally, or
    (c)   jointly in respect of some matters and jointly and severally in respect of others.

(5)   To the extent to which it does not specify whether they are to act jointly or jointly and severally, the instrument is to be assumed to appoint them to act jointly.

(6)   If they are to act jointly, a failure, as respects one of them, to comply with the requirements of subsection (1) or (2) or Part 1 or 2 of Schedule 1 prevents a lasting power of attorney from being created.

(7)   If they are to act jointly and severally, a failure, as respects one of them, to comply with the requirements of subsection (1) or (2) or Part 1 or 2 of Schedule 1—

      (a)   prevents the appointment taking effect in his case, but

      (b)   does not prevent a lasting power of attorney from being created in the case of the other or others.

(8)   An instrument used to create a lasting power of attorney—

      (a)   cannot give the donee (or, if more than one, any of them) power to appoint a substitute or successor, but

      (b)   may itself appoint a person to replace the donee (or, if more than one, any of them) on the occurrence of an event mentioned in section 13(6)(a) to (d) which has the effect of terminating the donee's appointment.

11.   Lasting powers of attorney: restrictions

(1)   A lasting power of attorney does not authorise the donee (or, if more than one, any of them) to do an act that is intended to restrain P, unless three conditions are satisfied.

(2)   The first condition is that P lacks, or the donee reasonably believes that P lacks, capacity in relation to the matter in question.

(3)   The second is that the donee reasonably believes that it is necessary to do the act in order to prevent harm to P.

(4)   The third is that the act is a proportionate response to—

      (a)   the likelihood of P's suffering harm, and

      (b)   the seriousness of that harm.

(5)   For the purposes of this section, the donee restrains P if he—

      (a)   uses, or threatens to use, force to secure the doing of an act which P resists, or

      (b)   restricts P's liberty of movement, whether or not P resists,

    or if he authorises another person to do any of those things.

(6)   But the donee does more than merely restrain P if he deprives P of his liberty within the meaning of Article 5(1) of the Human Rights Convention.

(7)   Where a lasting power of attorney authorises the donee (or, if more than one, any of them) to make decisions about P's personal welfare, the authority—

      (a)   does not extend to making such decisions in circumstances other than those where P lacks, or the donee reasonably believes that P lacks, capacity,

      (b)   is subject to sections 24 to 26 (advance decisions to refuse treatment), and

       (c)   extends to giving or refusing consent to the carrying out or continuation of a treatment by a person providing health care for P.

(8)   But subsection (7)(c)—
       (a)   does not authorise the giving or refusing of consent to the carrying out or continuation of life-sustaining treatment, unless the instrument contains express provision to that effect, and
       (b)   is subject to any conditions or restrictions in the instrument.

12.   **Scope of lasting powers of attorney: gifts**

(1)   Where a lasting power of attorney confers authority to make decisions about P's property and affairs, it does not authorise a donee (or, if more than one, any of them) to dispose of the donor's property by making gifts except to the extent permitted by subsection (2).

(2)   The donee may make gifts—
       (a)   on customary occasions to persons (including himself) who are related to or connected with the donor, or
       (b)   to any charity to whom the donor made or might have been expected to make gifts,
if the value of each such gift is not unreasonable having regard to all the circumstances and, in particular, the size of the donor's estate.

(3)   "Customary occasion" means—
       (a)   the occasion or anniversary of a birth, a marriage or the formation of a civil partnership, or
       (b)   any other occasion on which presents are customarily given within families or among friends or associates.

(4)   Subsection (2) is subject to any conditions or restrictions in the instrument

13.   **Revocation of lasting powers of attorney etc.**

(1)   This section applies if—
       (a)   P has executed an instrument with a view to creating a lasting power of attorney, or
       (b)   a lasting power of attorney is registered as having been conferred by P,
and in this section references to revoking the power include revoking the instrument.

(2)   P may, at any time when he has capacity to do so, revoke the power.

(3)   P's bankruptcy revokes the power so far as it relates to P's property and affairs.

(4)   But where P is bankrupt merely because an interim bankruptcy restrictions order has effect in respect of him, the power is suspended, so far as it relates to P's property and affairs, for so long as the order has effect.

(5)   The occurrence in relation to a donee of an event mentioned in subsection (6)—
     (a)   terminates his appointment, and
     (b)   except in the cases given in subsection (7), revokes the power.

(6)   The events are—
     (a)   the disclaimer of the appointment by the donee in accordance with such requirements as may be prescribed for the purposes of this section in regulations made by the Lord Chancellor,
     (b)   subject to subsections (8) and (9), the death or bankruptcy of the donee or, if the donee is a trust corporation, its winding-up or dissolution,
     (c)   subject to subsection (11), the dissolution or annulment of a marriage or civil partnership between the donor and the donee,
     (d)   the lack of capacity of the donee.

(7)   The cases are—
     (a)   the donee is replaced under the terms of the instrument,
     (b)   he is one of two or more persons appointed to act as donees jointly and severally in respect of any matter and, after the event, there is at least one remaining donee.

(8)   The bankruptcy of a donee does not terminate his appointment, or revoke the power, in so far as his authority relates to P's personal welfare.

(9)   Where the donee is bankrupt merely because an interim bankruptcy restrictions order has effect in respect of him, his appointment and the power are suspended, so far as they relate to P's property and affairs, for so long as the order has effect.

(10)   Where the donee is one of two or more appointed to act jointly and severally under the power in respect of any matter, the reference in subsection (9) to the suspension of the power is to its suspension in so far as it relates to that donee.

(11)   The dissolution or annulment of a marriage or civil partnership does not terminate the appointment of a donee, or revoke the power, if the instrument provided that it was not to do so.

14.   Protection of donee and others if no power created or power revoked

(1)   Subsections (2) and (3) apply if—
   (a)   an instrument has been registered under Schedule 1 as a lasting power of attorney, but
   (b)   a lasting power of attorney was not created, whether or not the registration has been cancelled at the time of the act or transaction in question.

(2)   A donee who acts in purported exercise of the power does not incur any liability (to P or any other person) because of the non-existence of the power unless at the time of acting he—
   (a)   knows that a lasting power of attorney was not created, or
   (b)   is aware of circumstances which, if a lasting power of attorney had been created, would have terminated his authority to act as a donee.

(3)   Any transaction between the donee and another person is, in favour of that person, as valid as if the power had been in existence, unless at the time of the transaction that person has knowledge of a matter referred to in subsection (2).

(4)   If the interest of a purchaser depends on whether a transaction between the donee and the other person was valid by virtue of subsection (3), it is conclusively presumed in favour of the purchaser that the transaction was valid if—
   (a)   the transaction was completed within 12 months of the date on which the instrument was registered, or
   (b)   the other person makes a statutory declaration, before or within 3 months after the completion of the purchase, that he had no reason at the time of the transaction to doubt that the donee had authority to dispose of the property which was the subject of the transaction.

(5)   In its application to a lasting power of attorney which relates to matters in addition to P's property and affairs, section 5 of the Powers of Attorney Act 1971 (c. 27) (protection where power is revoked) has effect as if references to revocation included the cessation of the power in relation to P's property and affairs.

(6)   Where two or more donees are appointed under a lasting power of attorney, this section applies as if references to the donee were to all or any of them.

Oaths Act 1978

An Act to consolidate the Oaths Act 1838 and the Oaths Acts 1888 to 1977, and to repeal, as obsolete, section 13 of the Circuit Courts (Scotland) Act 1828.
[30th June 1978]

BE IT ENACTED by the Queen's most Excellent Majesty, by and with the advice and consent of the Lords Spiritual and Temporal, and Commons, in this present Parliament assembled, and by the authority of the same, as follows:-

PART I
ENGLAND, WALES AND NORTHERN IRELAND

1.- (1) Any oath may be administered and taken in England, Wales or Northern Ireland in the following form and manner:-

The person taking the oath shall hold the New Testament, or, in the case of a Jew, the Old Testament, in his uplifted hand, and shall say or repeat after the officer administering the oath the words " I swear by Almighty God that ...... ", followed by the words of the oath prescribed by law.

(2) The officer shall (unless the person about to take the oath voluntarily objects thereto, or is physically incapable of so taking the oath) administer the oath in the form and manner aforesaid without question.

(3) In the case of a person who is neither a Christian nor a Jew, the oath shall be administered in any lawful manner.

(4) In this section "officer" means any person duly authorised to administer oaths.

2.- In the following provisions, namely-

(a) section 28(1) of the Children and Young Persons Act 1963; and

(b) section 56(1) of the Children and Young Persons Act (Northern Ireland) 1968

(each of which prescribes the form of oath for use in juvenile courts and by children and young persons in other courts) for the words " section 2 of the Oaths Act 1909 " there shall be substituted the words "section 1 of the Oaths Act 1978".

PART II
UNITED KINGDOM

Oaths

3.- If any person to whom an oath is administered desires to swear with uplifted hand, in the form and manner in which an oath is usually administered in Scotland, he shall be permitted so to do, and the oath shall be administered to him in such form and manner without further question.

4.- (1) In any case in which an oath may lawfully be and has been administered to any person, if it has been administered in a form and manner other than that prescribed by law, he is bound by it if it has been administered in such form and with such ceremonies as he may have declared to be binding.

(2) Where an oath has been duly administered and taken, the fact that the person to whom it was administered had, at the time of taking it, no religious belief, shall not for any purpose affect the validity of the oath.

Solemn affirmations

5.- (1) Any person who objects to being sworn shall be permitted to make his solemn affirmation instead of taking an oath.

(2) Subsection (1) above shall apply in relation to a person to whom it is not reasonably practicable without inconvenience or delay to administer an oath in the manner appropriate to his religious belief as it applies in relation to a person objecting to be sworn.

(3) A person who may be permitted under subsection (2) above to make his solemn affirmation may also be required to do so.

(4) A solemn affirmation shall be of the same force and effect as an oath.

6.- (1) Subject to subsection (2) below, every affirmation shall be as follows: -

" I   do solemnly, sincerely and truly declare and affirm,"

and then proceed with the words of the oath prescribed by law, omitting any words of imprecation or calling to witness.

(2) Every affirmation in writing shall commence: -

" I,   of , do solemnly and sincerely affirm," and the form in lieu of jurat shall be "Affirmed at this day of 19 , Before me."

Supplementary

7.- (1) The enactments specified in Part I of the Schedule to this Act (consequential repeals) and Part II of that Schedule (enactment obsolete since the Oaths Act 1888) are hereby repealed to the extent specified in the third column of that Schedule.

(2) In so far as anything done under an enactment repealed by this Act could have been done under a corresponding provision of this Act, it shall not be invalidated by the repeal but shall have effect as if done under that provision.

(3) Where any instrument or document refers, either expressly or by implication, to an enactment repealed by this Act, the reference shall, except where the context otherwise requires, be construed as, or as including, a reference to the corresponding provision of this Act.

(4) The court-martial enactments (which make provision in relation to the use of affirmations at courts-martial corresponding to that made by subsection (2) of section 1 of the Oaths Act 1961) shall not be affected by the repeal of subsection (3) of that section (by virtue of which each of them was inserted in the section in which it appears).

(5) In this Act "the court-martial enactments" means
section 102(2) of the Army Act 1955;
section 102(2) of the Air Force Act 1955;
section 60(6) of the Naval Discipline Act 1957.

(6) Nothing in this Act shall be taken as prejudicing the operation of section 38 of the Interpretation Act 1889 (which relates to the effect of repeals).

8.- (1) This Act may be cited as the Oaths Act 1978.

(2) Part I of this Act does not extend to Scotland.

(3) It is hereby declared that this Act extends to Northern Ireland.

(4) In their application to each of the court-martial enactments subsections (4) and (5) of section 7 above extend to any territory to which that enactment extends.

(5) This Act shall come into force on the expiration of the period of one month from the date on which it is passed.

SCHEDULE   Section 7

Repeals

Part I
Consequential Repeals

Chapter	Short Title	Extent of Repeal
1 & 2 Vict. c. 105.	Oaths Act 1838.	The whole Act.
51 & 52 Vict. c. 46.	Oaths Act 1888.	The whole Act.
9 Edw. 7 c. 39.	Oaths Act 1909.	The whole Act.
9 & 10 Eliz. 2 c. 21.	Oaths Act 1961.	The whole Act.
1977 c. 38.	Administration of Justice Act 1977.	Section 8. Section 32(2)

Part II
Repeal of an Obsolete Enactment

Chapter	Short Title	Extent of Repeal
1 & 2 Vict. c. 105.	Oaths Act 1838.	The whole Act.
51 & 52 Vict. c. 46.	Oaths Act 1888.	The whole Act.
9 Edw. 7 c. 39.	Oaths Act 1909.	The whole Act.
9 & 10 Eliz. 2 c. 21.	Oaths Act 1961.	The whole Act.
1977 c. 38.	Administration of Justice Act 1977.	Section 8. Section 32(2)

Commissioner for Oaths Act 1889

An Act for amending and consolidating enactments relating to the administration of Oaths.

[31st May 1889.]

BE it enacted by the Queen's most Excellent Majesty, by and with the advice and consent of the Lords Spiritual and Temporal, and Commons, in this present Parliament assembled, and by the authority of the same, as follows:

1.-   (1.)   The Lord Chancellor may from time to time, by commission signed by him, appoint persons being practising solicitors or other fit and proper persons to be commissioners for oaths, and may revoke any such appointment.

(2.)   A commissioner for oaths may, by virtue of his commission, in England or elsewhere, administer any oath or take any affidavit for the purposes of any court or matter in England, including any of the ecclesiastical courts or jurisdictions, matters ecclesiastical, matters relating to applications for notarial faculties, and matters relating to the registration of any instrument, whether under an Act of Parliament or otherwise, and take any bail or recognizance in or for the purpose of any civil proceeding in the Supreme Court, including all proceedings on the revenue side of the Queen's Bench Division.

(3.)   Provided that a commissioner for oaths shall not exercise any of the powers given by this section in any proceeding in which he is solicitor to any of the parties to the proceeding, or clerk to any such solicitor, or in which he is interested.

2.   Every person who, being an officer of or performing duties in relation to any court, is for the time being so authorised by a judge of the court, or by or in pursuance of any rules or orders regulating the procedure of the court, and every person directed to take an examination in any cause or matter in the Supreme Court, shall have authority to administer any oath or take any affidavit required for any purpose connected with his duties.

3.-   (1.)   Any oath or affidavit required for the purpose of any court or matter in England, or for the purpose of the registration of any instrument in any part of the United Kingdom, may be taken or made in any place out of England before any person having authority to administer an oath in that place.

(2.)   In the case of a person having such authority otherwise than by the law of a foreign country, judicial and official notice shall be taken of his seal or signature affixed, impressed, or subscribed to or on any such oath or affidavit.

4. The Lord Chancellor may, whenever it appears to him necessary to do so, authorise any person to administer oaths and take oaths for affidavits for any purpose relating to prize proceedings in the Supreme Court, whilst that person is on the high seas or out of Her Majesty's dominions, and it shall not be necessary to affix any stamp to the document by which he is so authorised.

5. Every commissioner before whom any oath or affidavit is taken or made under this Act shall state truly in the jurat or attestation at what place and on what date the oath or affidavit is taken or made.

6.- (1.) Every British ambassador, envoy, minister, chargé d'affaires, and secretary of embassy or legation exercising his functions in any foreign country, and every British consul-general, consul, vice-consul, acting- consul, pro-consul, and consular agent exercising his functions in any foreign place may, in that country or place, administer any oath and take any affidavit, and also do any notarial act which any notary public can do within the United Kingdom; and every oath, affidavit, and notarial act administered, sworn, or done by or before any such person shall be as effectual as if duly administered, sworn, or done by or before any lawful authority in any part of the United Kingdom.

(2.) Any document purporting to have affixed, impressed, or subscribed thereon or thereto the seal and signature of any person authorised by this section to administer an oath in testimony of any oath, affidavit, or act being administered, taken, or done by or before him, shall be admitted in evidence without proof of the seal or signature being the seal or signature of that person, or of the official character of that person.

7. Whoever wilfully and corruptly swears falsely in any oath or affidavit taken or made in accordance with the provisions of this Act, shall be guilty of perjury in every case where if he had so sworn in a judicial proceeding before a court of competent jurisdiction he would be guilty of perjury.

8. Whoever forges, counterfeits, or fraudulently alters the seal or signature of any person authorised by or under this Act to administer an oath, or tenders in evidence, or otherwise uses, any affidavit having any seal or signature so forged or counterfeited or fraudulently altered, knowing the same to be forged, counterfeited, or fraudulently altered, shall be guilty of felony, and liable on conviction to penal servitude for any term not exceeding seven years and not less than five years, or to imprisonment with or without hard labour for any term not exceeding two years.

9. Any offence under this Act, whether committed within or without Her Majesty's dominions, may be inquired of, dealt with, tried, and punished in any county or place in the United Kingdom in which the person charged with the offence was apprehended or is in custody, and for all purposes

incidental to or consequential on the trial or punishment the offence shall be deemed to have been committed in that county or place.

10.   Where any offence under this Act is alleged to have been committed with respect to any affidavit, a judge of any court before which the affidavit is produced may order the affidavit to be impounded and kept in such custody and for such time and on such conditions as he thinks fit.

11.   In this Act, unless the context otherwise requires,-
" Oath " includes affirmation and declaration

" Affidavit " includes affirmation, statutory or other declaration, acknowledgment, examination, and attestation or protestation of honour

" Swear " includes affirm, declare, and protest

" Supreme Court " means the Supreme Court of Judicature in England.

12.   The enactments specified in the schedule to this Act are hereby repealed to the extent specified in that schedule.

Provided that this repeal shall not affect-
(a.)   anything done or suffered under any enactment repealed by this Act; nor
(b.)   any appointment made under or authority given by or in pursuance of any enactment so repealed; nor
(c.)   any punishment incurred or to be incurred in respect of any offence committed before the commencement of this Act against any enactment so repealed; nor
(d.)   any legal proceeding for enforcing any such punishment;

and any such legal proceeding may be instituted or continued and any such punishment may be imposed as if this Act had not been passed.

13.   A commissioner authorised before the commencement of this Act to administer oaths in the Supreme Court shall be deemed to be a commissioner for oaths within the meaning of this Act.

14.   This Act shall commence and come into operation on the first day of January one thousand eight hundred and ninety.

15.   This Act may be cited as the Commissioners for Oaths Act, 1889.

SCHEDULE

A description or citation of a portion of an Act is inclusive of the words, sections, or other parts, first and last mentioned, or otherwise referred to as forming the beginning, or as forming the end respectively, of the portion comprised in the description or citation.

Session and Chapter.	Title of Act and extent of Repeal	Extent of Repeal.
16 & 17 Chas. 2. c. 9.	An Act to empower the Chancellor of the duchy to grant commissions for taking affidavits within the duchy liberty.	The whole Act.
17 Geo. 2. c. 7.	An Act for taking and swearing affidavits to be made use of in any of the courts of the county palatine of Lancaster.	The whole Act.
4 Geo. 3. c. 21.	An Act for taking and swearing affidavits to be made use of in any of the courts of the county palatine of Durham.	The whole Act.
6 Geo. 4. c. 87.	An Act to regulate the payment of salaries and allowances to British consuls at foreign ports, and the disbursements at such ports for certain public purposes.	Section twenty.
3 & 4 Will. 4. c. 42.	An Act for the further amendment of the law and the better advancement of justice.	Section forty-two.
4 & 5 Will. 4. c. 42.	An Act to facilitate the taking of affidavits and affirmations in the court of the Vice Warden of the Stannaries of Cornwall.	The whole Act.
2 & 3 Vict. c. 58.	An Act to make further provision for the administration of justice and for improving the	Section six from "and that any "commissioner".

	practice and proceedings in the courts of the Stannaries of Cornwall.	
5 & 6 Vict. c. 103.	An Act for abolishing certain offices of the High Court of Chancery in England.	Sections seven and eight.
6 & 7 Vict. c. 82.	An Act the title of which begins with the words "An Act for extending," and ends with the words "examination of witnesses."	Sections one to four.
11 & 12 Vict. c. 10.	An Act for empowering certain officers of the High Court of Chancery to administer oaths and take declarations and affirmations.	The whole Act.
15 & 16 Vict. c. 76.	The Common Law Procedure Act, 1852.	Section twenty-three.
15 & 16 Vict. c. 86.	An Act to amend the practice and course of proceeding in the High Court of Chancery.	Sections twenty-two, twenty-three, and twenty-four.
16 & 17 Vict. c. 70.	The Lunacy Regulation Act, 1853.	Section fifty-seven.
16 & 17 Vict. c. 78.	An Act relating to the appointment of persons to administer oaths in Chancery, and to affidavits made for purposes connected with registration.	The whole Act.
17 & 18 Vict. c. 78.	The Admiralty Court Act, 1854.	Section six from "and any examiner" to the end of the section. Sections seven to eleven.
18 & 19 Vict. c. 42.	An act to enable British diplomatic and consular agents abroad to	The whole Act.

	administer oaths and do notarial acts.	
18 & 19 Vict. c. 134.	An Act the title of which begins with the words "An Act to make "further provision," and ends with the words "leasing and "sale therefore".	Section fifteen.
20 & 21 Vict. c. 77.	An Act to amend the law relating to probates and letters of administration in England.	Section twenty-seven to "Provided that" and from "any person who" to end of section.
21 & 22 Vict. c. 95.	An Act to amend the Act of the twentieth and twenty-first Victoria, chapter seventy-seven.	Sections thirty to thirty-four.
21 & 22 Vict. c. 108.	An Act to amend the Act of the twentieth and twenty-first Victoria, chapter eighty-five.	Sections twenty to twenty-three.
22 Vict. c. 16.	An Act the title of which begins with the words "An Act to enable," and ends with the words "of the Exchequer."	The whole Act except section five.
28 & 29 Vict. c. 104.	The Crown Suits, &c. Act, 1865.	Sections eighteen, nineteen, forty-three, and forty-four.
32 & 33 Vict. c. 38.	The Bails Act, 1869	The whole Act.
40 & 41 Vict. c. 25.	The Solicitors Act, 1877	Section eighteen.

FORMALITIES OF DOING BUSINESS

Formalities of doing business under the law of England and Wales or Northern Ireland
4.   Sections 43 to 47 apply to LLPs, modified so that they read as follows—

"LLP contracts

43.— (1)   Under the law of England and Wales or Northern Ireland a contract may be made—
            (a)   by an LLP, by writing under its common seal, or
            (b)   on behalf of an LLP, by a person acting under its authority, express or implied.

(2)   This is without prejudice to section 6 of the Limited Liability Partnerships Act 2000 (c. 12) (members as agents).

(3)   Any formalities required by law in the case of a contract made by an individual also apply, unless a contrary intention appears, to a contract made by or on behalf of an LLP.

Execution of documents
44.— (1)   Under the law of England and Wales or Northern Ireland a document is executed by an LLP—
            (a)   by the affixing of its common seal, or
            (b)   by signature in accordance with the following provisions.

(2)   A document is validly executed by an LLP if it is signed on behalf of the LLP—
            (a)   by two members, or
            (b)   by a member of the LLP in the presence of a witness who attests the signature.

(3)   A document signed in accordance with subsection (2) and expressed, in whatever words, to be executed by the LLP has the same effect as if executed under the common seal of the LLP.

(4)   In favour of a purchaser a document is deemed to have been duly executed by an LLP if it purports to be signed in accordance with subsection (2).

A "purchaser" means a purchaser in good faith for valuable consideration and includes a lessee, mortgagee or other person who for valuable consideration acquires an interest in property.

(5)   Where a document is to be signed by a person on behalf of more than one LLP, or on behalf of an LLP and a company, it is not duly signed by that person for the purposes of this section unless he signs it separately in each capacity.

(6)   References in this section to a document being (or purporting to be) signed by a member are to be read, in a case where that member is a firm, as references to its being (or purporting to be) signed by an individual authorised by the firm to sign on its behalf.

(7)   This section applies to a document that is (or purports to be) executed by an LLP in the name of or on behalf of another person whether or not that person is also an LLP.

Common seal
45.— (1)   An LLP may have a common seal, but need not have one.

(2)   An LLP which has a common seal shall have its name engraved in legible characters on the seal.

(3)   If an LLP fails to comply with subsection (2) an offence is committed by—
(a)   the LLP, and
(b)   every member of the LLP who is in default.

(4)   A member of an LLP, or a person acting on behalf of an LLP, commits an offence if he uses, or authorises the use of, a seal purporting to be a seal of the LLP on which its name is not engraved as required by subsection (2).

(5)   A person guilty of an offence under this section is liable on summary conviction to a fine not exceeding level 3 on the standard scale.

(6)   This section does not form part of the law of Scotland.

Execution of deeds
46.— (1)   A document is validly executed by an LLP as a deed for the purposes of section 1(2)(b) of the Law of Property (Miscellaneous Provisions) Act 1989 (c. 34) and for the purposes of the law of Northern Ireland if, and only if—
(a)   it is duly executed by the LLP, and
(b)   it is delivered as a deed.

(2)   For the purposes of subsection (1)(b) a document is presumed to be delivered upon its being executed, unless a contrary intention is proved.

Execution of deeds or other documents by attorney

47.— (1) Under the law of England and Wales or Northern Ireland an LLP may, by instrument executed as a deed, empower a person, either generally or in respect of specified matters, as its attorney to execute deeds or other documents on its behalf.

(2) A deed or other document so executed, whether in the United Kingdom or elsewhere, has effect as if executed by the LLP.".

Companies Act 2006
(Sections 43, 44, 45, 46, 47, 48 & 49)

Formalities of doing business under the law of England and Wales or Northern Ireland

43   Company contracts

(1)   Under the law of England and Wales or Northern Ireland a contract may be made—

(a)   by a company, by writing under its common seal, or

(b)   on behalf of a company, by a person acting under its authority, express or implied.

(2)   Any formalities required by law in the case of a contract made by an individual also apply, unless a contrary intention appears, to a contract made by or on behalf of a company.

44   Execution of documents

(1)   Under the law of England and Wales or Northern Ireland a document is executed by a company—

(a)   by the affixing of its common seal, or

(b)   by signature in accordance with the following provisions.

(2)   A document is validly executed by a company if it is signed on behalf of the company—

(a)   by two authorised signatories, or

(b)   by a director of the company in the presence of a witness who attests the signature.

(3)   The following are "authorised signatories" for the purposes of subsection (2)—

(a)   every director of the company, and

(b)   in the case of a private company with a secretary or a public company, the secretary or any joint secretary) of the company.

(4)   A document signed in accordance with subsection (2) and expressed, in whatever words, to be executed by the company has the same effect as if executed under the common seal of the company.

(5)   In favour of a purchaser a document is deemed to have been duly executed by a company if it purports to be signed in accordance with subsection (2). A "purchaser" means a purchaser in good faith for valuable consideration and includes a lessee, mortgagee or other person who for valuable consideration acquires an interest in property.

(6) Where a document is to be signed by a person on behalf of more than one company, it is not duly signed by that person for the purposes of this section unless he signs it separately in each capacity.

(7) References in this section to a document being (or purporting to be) signed by a director or secretary are to be read, in a case where that office is held by a firm, as references to its being (or purporting to be) signed by an individual authorised by the firm to sign on its behalf.

(8) This section applies to a document that is (or purports to be) executed by a company in the name of or on behalf of another person whether or not that person is also a company.

45 Common seal
(1) A company may have a common seal, but need not have one.

(2) A company which has a common seal shall have its name engraved in legible characters on the seal.

(3) If a company fails to comply with subsection (2) an offence is committed by—
   (a) the company, and
   (b) every officer of the company who is in default.

(4) An officer of a company, or a person acting on behalf of a company, commits an offence if he uses, or authorises the use of, a seal purporting to be a seal of the company on which its name is not engraved as required by subsection (2).

(5) A person guilty of an offence under this section is liable on summary conviction to a fine not exceeding level 3 on the standard scale.

(6) This section does not form part of the law of Scotland.

46 Execution of deeds
(1) A document is validly executed by a company as a deed for the purposes of section 1(2)(b) of the Law of Property (Miscellaneous Provisions) Act 1989 (c. 34) and for the purposes of the law of Northern Ireland if, and only if—
   (a) it is duly executed by the company, and
   (b) it is delivered as a deed.

(2) For the purposes of subsection (1)(b) a document is presumed to be delivered upon its being executed, unless a contrary intention is proved.

47 Execution of deeds or other documents by attorney

(1)   Under the law of England and Wales or Northern Ireland a company may, by instrument executed as a deed, empower a person, either generally or in respect of specified matters, as its attorney to execute deeds or other documents on its behalf.

(2)   A deed or other document so executed, whether in the United Kingdom or elsewhere, has effect as if executed by the company.

Formalities of doing business under the law of Scotland

48 Execution of documents by companies

(1)   The following provisions form part of the law of Scotland only.

(2)   Notwithstanding the provisions of any enactment, a company need not have a company seal.

(3)   For the purposes of any enactment—
    (a)   providing for a document to be executed by a company by affixing its common seal, or
    (b)   referring (in whatever terms) to a document so executed,

a document signed or subscribed by or on behalf of the company in accordance with the provisions of the Requirements of Writing (Scotland) Act 1995 (c. 7) has effect as if so executed.

Other matters

49 Official seal for use abroad

(1)   A company that has a common seal may have an official seal for use outside the United Kingdom.

(2)   The official seal must be a facsimile of the company's common seal, with the addition on its face of the place or places where it is to be used.

(3)   The official seal when duly affixed to a document has the same effect as the company's common seal.

This subsection does not extend to Scotland.

(4)   A company having an official seal for use outside the United Kingdom may—
    (a)   by writing under its common seal, or
    (b)   as respects Scotland, by writing subscribed in accordance with the Requirements of Writing (Scotland) Act 1995, authorise any person appointed for the purpose to affix the official seal to any deed or other document to which the company is party.

(5) As between the company and a person dealing with such an agent, the agent's authority continues—
  (a) during the period mentioned in the instrument conferring the authority, or
  (b) if no period is mentioned, until notice of the revocation or termination of the agent's authority has been given to the person dealing with him.

(6) The person affixing the official seal must certify in writing on the deed or other document to which the seal is affixed the date on which, and place at which, it is affixed.

Consular Relations Act 1968
(Section 10)

10.-   (1)   A diplomatic agent or consular officer of any State may, if authorised to do so under the laws of that State, administer oaths, take affidavits and do notarial acts-

        (a)   required by a person for use in that State or under the laws thereof; or

        (b)   otherwise required by a national of that State but not for use in the United Kingdom except under the laws of some other country.

  (2)   Her Majesty may by Order in Council exclude or restrict the provisions of the preceding subsection in relation to the diplomatic agents or consular officers of any State if it appears to Her that in any territory of that State diplomatic agents or consular officers of the United Kingdom are not permitted to perform functions corresponding in nature and extent to those authorised by that subsection.

  (3)   Her Majesty may by Order in Council make provision for applying section 6 of the Commissioners for Oaths Act 1889 (powers as to oaths and notarial acts abroad) to countries within the Commonwealth or the Republic of Ireland by requiring the section to be construed as if-

        (a)   the references therein to a foreign country or place included such country or place as may be specified in the Order; and

        (b)   the diplomatic ranks specified in that section included such ranks of any United Kingdom mission in a country specified in the Order as may be so specified in relation to that country.

  (4)   In this section "diplomatic agent" has the same meaning as in the Diplomatic Privileges Act 1964.

Access to Justice Act 1999
(Section 53)

Public notaries

Abolition of scriveners' monopoly
53. A public notary may practise as a notary in, or within three miles of, the City of London whether or not he is a member of the Incorporated Company of Scriveners of London (even if he is admitted to practise only outside that area).

Courts and Legal Services Act 1990
(Sections 57 and 66)

Notaries

57.— (1)   Public notaries shall no longer be appointed to practise only within particular districts in England, or particular districts in Wales.

(2)   It shall no longer be necessary to serve a period of apprenticeship before being admitted as a public notary.

(3)   Accordingly, the following enactments relating to public notaries shall cease to have effect—
   (a)   section 2 of the Public Notaries Act 1801 (which provides that no person shall be admitted as a public notary unless he has served as an apprentice for seven years);
   (b)   section 1 of the Public Notaries Act 1833 (which restricts the requirement to serve an apprenticeship to London and an area of ten miles from the Royal Exchange);
   (c)   section 2 of the Public Notaries Act 1833 (appointment of public notaries to practise within particular districts in England);
   (d)   section 3 of the Public Notaries Act 1843 (which reduced the period of apprenticeship to five years);
   (e)   section 37 of the Welsh Church Act 1914 (appointment of public notaries to practise within particular districts in Wales); and
   (f)   section 29 of the Administration of Justice Act 1969 (which reduced the period of apprenticeship for public notaries in London).

(4)   The Master may by rules make provision—
   (a)   as to the educational and training qualifications which must be satisfied before a person may be granted a faculty to practise as a public notary;
   (b)   as to further training which public notaries are to be required to undergo;
   (c)   for regulating the practice, conduct and discipline of public notaries;
   (d)   supplementing the provision made by subsections (8) and (9);
   (e)   as to the keeping by public notaries of records and accounts;
   (f)   as to the handling by public notaries of clients' money;
   (g)   as to the indemnification of public notaries against losses arising from claims in respect of civil liability incurred by them;

(h) as to compensation payable for losses suffered by persons in respect of dishonesty on the part of public notaries or their employees; and

(i) requiring the payment, in such circumstances as may be prescribed, of such reasonable fees as may be prescribed, including in particular fees for—

(i) the grant of a faculty;

(ii) the issue of a practising certificate by the Court of Faculties of the Archbishop of Canterbury; or

(iii) the entering in that court of a practising certificate issued under the Solicitors Act 1974.

(5) The repeal of section 2 of the Act of 1833 and section 37 of the Act of 1914 by this Act shall not affect any appointment made under either of those sections; but the Master may by rules make such provision as he considers necessary or expedient in consequence of either, or both, of those repeals.

(6) Rules made under subsection (5) may, in particular, provide for the grant by the Master of a new faculty for any person to whom the Notary Public (Welsh Districts) Rules 1924 applied immediately before the commencement of this section, in place of the faculty granted to him by the Clerk of the Crown in Chancery.

(7) Subsections (4) to (6) shall not be taken to prejudice—

(a) any other power of the Master to make rules; or

(b) any rules made by him under any such power.

(8) With effect from the operative date, any restriction placed on a qualifying district notary, in terms of the district within which he may practise as a public notary, shall cease to apply.

(9) In this section—

"Master" means the Master of the Faculties;

"the operative date" means the date on which subsection (1) comes into force or, if on that date the notary concerned is not a qualifying district notary (having held his faculty for less than five years)—

(a) the date on which he becomes a qualifying district notary; or

(b) such earlier date, after the commencement of subsection (1), as the Master may by rules prescribe for the purpose of this subsection;

"prescribed" means prescribed by rules made under this section; and

"qualifying district notary" means a person who—

(a) holds a faculty as a notary appointed under section 2 of the Act of 1833 or section 37 of the Act of 1914; and

(b) has held it for a continuous period of at least five years.

(10) Section 5 of the Ecclesiastical Licences Act 1533 (which amongst other things now has the effect of requiring faculties to be registered by the Clerk of the Crown in Chancery) shall not apply in relation to any faculty granted to a public notary.

(11) Nothing in this section shall be taken—

(a) to authorise any public notary to practise as a notary or to perform or certify any notarial act within the jurisdiction of the Incorporated Company of Scriveners of London or to affect the jurisdiction or powers of the Company; or

(b) to restrict the power of the Company to require a person seeking to become a public notary within its jurisdiction to serve a period of apprenticeship.

66.— (1) Section 39 of the Solicitors Act 1974 (which, in effect, prevents Multi-disciplinary solicitors entering into partnership with persons who are not solicitors) and multi-national shall cease to have effect. practices.

(2) Nothing in subsection (1) prevents the Law Society making rules which prohibit solicitors from entering into any unincorporated association with persons who are not solicitors, or restrict the circumstances in which they may do so.

(3) Section 10 of the Public Notaries Act 1801 (which, in effect, prevents notaries entering into partnership with persons who are not notaries) shall cease to have effect.

(4) Nothing in subsection (3) prevents the Master of the Faculties making rules which prohibit notaries from entering into any unincorporated association with persons who are not notaries, or restrict the circumstances in which they may do so.

(5) It is hereby declared that no rule of common law prevents barristers from entering into any unincorporated association with persons who are not barristers.

(6) Nothing in subsection (5) prevents the General Council of the Bar from making rules which prohibit barristers from entering into any such unincorporated association, or restrict the circumstances in which they may do so.

Banking and Financial Dealings Act 1971
(Sections 1, 3 and 4 and Schedule 1)

Bank Holidays

1. - (1)   Subject to subsection (2) below, the days specified in Schedule 1 to this Act shall be bank holidays in England and Wales, in Scotland and Northern Ireland as indicated in the Schedule.

Bills of Exchange and promissory notes

3. -   (1)   Section 92 of the Bills of Exchange Act 1882 (which, in a case in which the time limited by that Act for doing any act or thing is less than three days, excludes non-business days from the reckoning of that time, and defines such days for the purposes of the Act) shall have the effect as if, in paragraph (a) of the definition of non-business days, "Saturday" were inserted immediately before "Sunday".

This subsection shall not operate to extend to any period expiring at or before the time it comes into force.

(2)   For section 14(1) of the Bills of Exchange Act 1882 (under or by virtue of which the date of maturity of a bill or promissory note that does not say otherwise is arrived at by adding three days of grace to the time of payment as fixed by the bill or note, but is advanced or postponed if the last day of grace is a non-business day) there shall be substituted, except in its application to bills drawn and notes made before this subsection comes into force, the following paragraph –

"(1)   The bill is due and payable in all cases on the last day of the time of payment as fixed by the bill or, if that is a non-business day, on the succeeding business day."

4.   (4)   Accordingly in section 92 of the Bills of Exchange Act 1882, in the definition of "non-business days," for the words "the Bank Holidays Act 1871 or Acts amending it" in paragraph (b) there shall be substituted the words "the Banking and Financial Dealings Act 1971," and there shall be added as a new paragraph (d):-

"(d)   a day declared by an order under section 2 of the Banking and Financial Dealings Act 1971 to be a non-business day."

SCHEDULE 1

Bank Holidays
A1-127 1.   The following are to be bank holidays in England and Wales:

Easter Monday.
The last Monday in May.
The last Monday in August.
26th December, if it be not a Sunday.
27th December in a year in which 25th or 26th December is a Sunday.

Statutory Declarations Act 1835

An Act to repeal an Act for the present Session of Parliament, intituled An Act for the more effectual Abolition of Oaths and Affirmations taken and made in various Departments of the State, and to substitute Declarations in lieu thereof, and for the more entire Suppression of voluntary and extra-judicial oaths and Affidavits; and to make other Provisions for the Abolition of unnecessary Oaths.

[9th September 1833.]

WHEREAS an Act was passed in the present Session of Parliament, intituled An Act for the more effectual Abolition of Oaths and Affirmations taken and made in various Departments of the State, and to substitute Declarations in lieu thereof; and for the more entire Suppression of voluntary and extra-judicial Oaths and Affidavits; and it was thereby enacted that the said Act should commence and take effect from and after the First Day of June in this present Year, the Year of our Lord One thousand eight hundred and thirty-five, it not being intended that the said recited Act should take effect before the same received the Royal Assent: And whereas the said recited Act did not receive the Royal Assent till after the said First Day of June One thousand eight hundred and thirty-five: And where it was enacted by the said recited Act, that from and after the First Day of June next ensuing it should not be lawful for any Justice of the Peace to ad minister or receive such voluntary Oaths as are therein mentioned, it being intended that the said Prohibition should talk effect from the Time of the Commencement of the said recited Act: And whereas it is expedient to amend the said Act, and to make some further Provisions for the better effecting the Object thereof, and to consolidate all the Provisions relating thereto into One Act: Be it therefore enacted by the King's most Excellent Majesty, by and with the Advice and Consent of the Lords Spiritual and Temporal, and Commons, in this present Parliament assembled, and by the Authority of the same, That from and after the passing of this Act the said recited Act shall be and the same is hereby repealed.

II.   And be it further enacted, That in any Case where, by any Act or Acts made or to be made relating to the Revenues of Customs or Excise, the Post Office, the Office of Stamps and Taxes, the Office of Woods and Forests, Land Revenues, Works, and Buildings, the War Office, the Army Pay Office, the Office of the Treasurer of the Navy, the Accountant General of the Navy, or the Ordnance, His Majesty's Treasury, Chelsea Hospital, Greenwich Hospital, the Board of Trade, or any of the Offices of His Majesty's Principal Secretaries of State, the India Board, the Office for auditing the Public Accounts, the National Debt Office, or any Office under the Control, Direction, or Superintendence of the Lords Commissioners of His Majesty's Treasury, or by any official Regulation in any Department, any Oath, solemn Affirmation, or Affidavit might, but for the passing of this Act, be required to be taken or made by any Person on the doing of any Act, Matter, or Thing, or for the Purpose of verifying any Book, Entry, or Return, or for any other Purpose whatsoever, it shall be lawful for the Lords Commissioners of, His Majesty's Treasury or any Three of them, if they shall so think fit, by Writing under their Hands and Seals, to substitute a Declaration to the same Effect as the Oath, solemn Affirmation, or Affidavit which might but for the passing of this Act be required to be taken or made; and the Person who might under the Act or Acts imposing the same be required to take or make such Oath, solemn Affirmation, or Affidavit shall, in Presence of the Commissioners, Collector, other Officer or Person empowered by such Act or Acts to administer such Oath, solemn Affirmation, or Affidavit, make and subscribe such Declaration, and every such Commissioner, Collector, other Officer or Person is hereby empowered and required to administer the same accordingly.

III.   And be it enacted, That when the said Lords Commissioners of His Majesty's Treasury or any Three of them shall, in any such Case as herein-before mentioned, have substituted, in Writing under their Hands and Seals, a Declaration in lieu of an Oath, solemn Affirmation, or Affidavit, such Lords Commissioners shall, so soon as conveniently may be, cause a Copy of the Instrument substituting such Declaration to be inserted and published in the London Gazette; and from and after the Expiration of Twenty-one Days next following the Day of the Date of the Gazette wherein the Copy of such Instrument shall have been published, the Provisions of this Act shall extend and apply to each and every Case specified in such Instrument, as well and in the same Manner as if the same were specified and named in this Act.

IV.   And be it enacted, That after the Expiration of the said Twenty-one Days it shall not be lawful for any Commissioner, Collector, Officer, or other Person to administer or cause to be administered, or receive or cause to be received, any Oath, solemn Affirmation, or Affidavit, in the lieu of which such Declaration as aforesaid shall have been directed by the Lords Commissioners of His Majesty's Treasury to be substituted.

V.   And be it enacted, That if any Person, shall make and subscribe any such Declaration as herein-before mentioned in lieu of any Oath, solemn Affirmation, or Affidavit by any Act or Acts relating to the Revenues of Customs or Excise, Stamps and Taxes, or Post Office, required to be made on the doing of any Act, Matter, or Thing, or for verifying any Book, Account, Entry, or Return, or for any Purpose whatsoever, and shall wilfully make therein any false Statements as to any material Particular, the Person making the same shall be deemed guilty of a Misdemeanor.

VI.   Provided always, and be it enacted, That nothing in this Act contained shall extend or apply to the Oath of Allegiance in any Case in which the same now is or may be required to be taken by any Person who may be appointed to any Office, but that such Oath of Allegiance shall continue to be required, and shall be administered and taken, as well and in the same Manner as if this Act had not been passed.

VII.   Provided also, and be it enacted, That nothing in this Act contained shall extend or apply to any Oath, solemn Affirmation, or Affidavit which now is or hereafter may be made or taken, or be required to be made or taken, in any Judicial Proceeding in any Court of Justice, or in any Proceeding for or by way of summary Conviction before any Justice or Justices of the Peace, but all such

Oaths, Affirmations, and Affidavits shall continue to be required, and to be administered, taken, and made, as well and in the same Manner as if this Act had not been passed.

VIII.   And be it enacted, That it shall be lawful for the Universities of Oxford and Cambridge, and for all other Bodies Corporate and Politic, and for all Bodies now by Law or Statute, or by any valid Usage, authorized to administer or receive any Oath, solemn Affirmation, or Affidavit, to make Statutes, Bye Laws, or Orders authorizing and directing the Substitution of a Declaration in lieu of any Oath, solemn Affirmation, or Affidavit now required to be taken or made: Provided always, that such Statutes, Bye Laws, or Orders be otherwise duly made and passed according to the Charter, Laws, or Regulations of the particular University, other Body Corporate and Politic, or other Body so authorized as aforesaid.

IX.   And whereas Persons serving the Offices of Churchwarden and Sidesman are at present required to take an Oath of Office before entering upon the Execution thereof, and also an Oath on quitting such Office, and it is expedient that a Declaration shall be substituted for such Oath of Office, and that the Oath on quitting the same shall be abolished; be it enacted, That in future every Person entering upon the Office of Churchwarden or Sidesman, before beginning to discharge the Duties thereof, shall, in lieu of such Oath of Office, make and subscribe, in the Presence of the Ordinary or other Person before whom he would, but for the passing of this Act, be required to take such Oath, a Declaration that he will faithfully and diligently perform the Duties of his Office, and such Ordinary or other Person is hereby empowered and required to administer the same accordingly: Provided always, that no Churchwarden or Sidesman shall in future be required to take any Oath on quitting Office, as has heretofore been practised.

X.   And be it enacted, That in any Case where, under any Act or Acts for making, maintaining, or regulating any Highway, or any Road, or any Turnpike Road, or for paving, lighting, watching, or improving any City, Town, or Place, or touching any Trust relating thereto, any Oath, solemn Affirmation, or Affidavit might, but for the passing of this Act, be required to be taken or made by any Person whomsoever, no such Oath, solemn Affirmation, or Affidavit shall in future be required to be or be taken or made, but the Person who might under the Act or Acts imposing the same be required to take or make such Oath, solemn Affirmation, or Affidavit shall, in lieu thereof, in the Presence of the Trustee, Commissioner, or other Person before whom he might under such Act or facts be required to take or make the same, make and subscribe a Declaration to the same Effect as such Oath, solemn Affirmation, or Affidavit, and such Trustee, Commissioner, or other Person is hereby empowered and required to administer and receive the same.

XI.   And be it enacted, That whenever any Person or Persons shall seek to obtain any Patent under the Great Seal for any Discovery or Invention, such Person or Persons shall, in lieu of any Oath, Affirmation, or Affidavit which heretofore has or might be required to be, taken or made upon or before obtaining any such Patent, make and subscribe, in the Presence of the Person before whom he might, but for the passing of this Act, be required to take or make such Oath, Affirmation, or Affidavit, a Declaration to the same Effect as such Oath, Affirmation, or Affidavit; and such Declaration, when duly made and subscribed, shall be to all Intents and Purposes as valid and effectual as the Oath, Affirmation, or Affidavit in lieu whereof it shall have been so made and subscribed.

XII.   And be it enacted, That where by any Act or Acts at the Time in force for regulating the Business of Pawnbrokers any Oath, Affirmation, or Affidavit might, but for the passing of this Act, be required to be taken or made, the Person who by or under such Act or Acts might be required to take or make such Oath, Affirmation, or Affidavit shall in lieu thereof make and subscribe a Declaration to the same Effect; and such Declaration shall be made and subscribed at the same Time, and on the same Occasion, and in the Presence of the same Person or Persons, as the Oath, Affirmation, or Affidavit in lieu whereof it shall be made and subscribed would by the Act or Acts directing or requiring the same be directed or required to be taken or made; and all and every the Enactments, Provisions, and Penalties contained in or imposed by any such Act to such or Acts, as to any Oath, Affirmation, or Affidavit thereby directed or required to be taken or made, shall extend and apply to any Declaration in lieu thereof, as well and in the same Manner as if the same were herein expressly enacted with reference thereto.

XIII.   And whereas a Practice has prevailed of administering and receiving Oaths and Affidavits voluntarily taken and made in Matters not the Subject of any Judicial Inquiry, nor in anywise pending or at issue before the Justice of the Peace or other Person by whom such Oaths or Affidavits have been administered or received: And whereas Doubts have arisen whether or not such Proceeding is illegal; for the more effectual Suppression of such Practice and removing such Doubts, be it enacted, That from and after the Commencement of this Act it shall not be lawful for any Justice of the Peace or other Person to administer, or cause or allow to be administered, or to receive, or cause or allow to be received, any Oath, Affidavit, or solemn Affirmation touching any Matter or Thing whereof such Justice or other Person hath not Jurisdiction or Cognizance by some Statute in force at the Time being: Provided always, that nothing herein contained shall be construed to extend to any Oath, Affidavit, or solemn Affirmation before any Justice in any Matter or Thing touching the Preservation of the Peace, or the Prosecution, Trial, or Punishment of Offences, or touching any Proceedings before either of the Houses of Parliament or any Committee thereof respectively, nor to any Oath, Affidavit, or Affirmation which may be required by the Laws of any Foreign Country to give Validity to Instruments in Writing designed to be used in such Foreign Countries respectively.

XIV.   And be it further enacted, That in any Case in which it has been the usual Practice of the Bank of England to receive Affidavits on Oath to prove the Death of any Proprietor of any Stocks or Funds transferrable there, or to identify the Person of any such Proprietor, or to remove any other Impediment to the Transfer of any such Stocks or Funds, or relating to the Loss, Mutilation, or Defacement of any Bank Note or Bank Post Bill, no such Oath or Affidavit shall in future be required to be taken or made, but in lieu thereof the Person who might have been required to take or make such Oath or Affidavit shall make and subscribe a Declaration to the same Effect as such Oath or Affidavit.

XV.   And whereas an Act was passed in the Fifth Year of the Reign of His late Majesty King George the Second, intituled An Act for the more easy Recovery of Debts in His Majesty's Plantations and Colonies in America: And whereas another Act was passed in the Fifty-fourth Year of the Reign of His late Majesty King George the Third, intituled An Act for the more easy Recovery of Debts in His Majesty's Colony of New South Wales: And whereas it is expedient that in future a Declaration should be substituted in lieu of the Affidavit on Oath authorised and required by the said recited Acts; be it therefore enacted, That from and after the Commencement of this Act, in any Action or Suit then depending or thereafter to be brought or intended to be brought in any Court of Law or Equity within any of the Territories, Plantations, Colonies, or Dependencies Abroad, being within and Part of His Majesty's Dominions, for or relating to any Debt or Account wherein any Person residing in Great Britain and Ireland shall be a Party, or for or relating to any Lands, Tenements, or Hereditaments or other Property situate, lying, and being in the said Places respectively, it shall and may be lawful to and for the Plaintiff or Defendant, and also to and for any Witness to be examined or made use of in such Action or Suit, to verify or prove any Matter or Thing relating thereto by solemn Declaration or Declarations in Writing in the Form in the Schedule hereunto annexed, made before any Justice of the Peace, Notary Public, or other Officer now by Law authorized to administer an Oath, and certified and transmitted under the Signature and Seal of any such Justice, Notary Public duly admitted and practising, or other Officer, which Declaration, and every Declaration relative to such Matter or Thing as aforesaid, in any Foreign Kingdom or State, or to the Voyage of any Ship or Vessel, every such Justice of the Peace, Notary Public, or other Officer shall be and he is hereby authorized and empowered to administer or receive; and every Declaration so made, certified, and transmitted shall in all such Actions and Suits be allowed to be of the same Force and Effect as if the Person or Persons making the same had appeared and sworn or affirmed the Matters contained in such Declaration viva voce in open Court , or upon a commission issued for the Examination of Witnesses or of any Party in such Action or Suit respectively; provided that in every such Declaration there shall be expressed the Addition of the Party making such Declaration, and the particular Place of his or her Abode.

XVI.   And be it further enacted, That it shall and may be lawful to and for any attesting Witness to the Execution of any Will or Codicil, Deed or Instrument in Writing, and to and for any other competent Person, to verify and prove the signing, sealing, Publication, or Delivery of any such Will, Codicil, Deed, or Instrument in Writing, made as aforesaid, and every such Justice, Notary, or other Officer shall be and is hereby authorized and empowered to administer or receive such Declaration.

XVII. And be it further enacted, That in all Suits now depending or hereafter to be brought in any Court of Law or Equity by or on behalf of His Majesty, His Heirs and Successors, in any of His said Majesty 's Territories, Plantations, Colonies, Possessions or Dependencies, for or relating to any Debt or Account, that His Majesty, His Heirs and Successors, shall and may prove His and their Debts and Accounts and examine His or their Witness or Witnesses by Declaration, in like Manner as any Subject or Subjects is or are impowered or may do by this present Act.

XVIII. And whereas it may be necessary and proper in many Cases not herein specified to require Confirmation of written Instruments or Allegations, or Proof of Debts, or of the Execution of Deeds or other Matters; be it therefore further enacted, That it shall and may be lawful for any Justice of the Peace, Notary Public, or other Officer now by Law authorized to administer an Oath, to take and receive the Declaration of any Person voluntarily making the same before him in the Form in the Schedule to this Act annexed; and if any Declaration so made shall be false or untrue in any material Particular the Person wilfully making such false Declaration shall be deemed guilty of a Misdemeanor.

XIX. And be it enacted, That whenever any Declaration shall be made and subscribed by any Person or Persons under or in pursuance of the Provisions of this Act, or any of them, all and every such Fees or Fee as would have been due and payable on the taking or making any legal Oath, solemn Affirmation, or Affidavit shall be in like Manner due and payable upon making and subscribing such Declaration.

XX. And be it further enacted, That in all Cases where a Declaration in lieu of an Oath shall have been substituted by this Act, or by virtue of any Power or Authority hereby given, or where a Declaration is directed or authorized to be made and subscribed under the Authority of this Act, or of any Power hereby given, although the same be not substituted in lieu of an Oath heretofore legally taken, such Declaration unless otherwise directed under the Powers hereby given, shall be in the Form prescribed in the Schedule hereunto annexed.

XXI. And be it further enacted, That in any Case where a Declaration is substituted for an Oath under the Authority of this Act, or by virtue of any Power or Authority hereby given, or is directed and authorized to be made and subscribed under the Authority of this Act, or by virtue of any Power hereby given, any Person who shall wilfully and corruptly make and subscribe any such Declaration, knowing the same to be untrue in any material Particular, shall be deemed guilty of a Misdemeanor.

XXII. And be it enacted, That this Act shall commence and take effect from and after the First Day of October in this present Year, the Year of our Lord One thousand eight hundred and thirty-five.

XXIII. And be it further enacted, That this Act may be amended, altered, or repealed by any Act to be passed in this present Session of Parliament.

SCHEDULE referred to by the foregoing Act.

I, A. B. do solemnly and sincerely declare, That
and I make this solemn Declaration conscientiously believing the same to be true,
and by virtue of the Provisions of an Act made and passed in the
Year of the Reign of His present Majesty, intituled An Act [here insert
the Title of this Act].

Courts and Legal Services Act 1990
(Section 113)

113.- (1) In this section—

"authorised person" means—

    (a)   any authorised advocate or authorised litigator, other than one who is a solicitor (in relation to whom provision similar to that made by this section is made by section 81 of the Solicitors Act 1974); or

    (b)   any person who is a member of a professional or other body prescribed by the Lord Chancellor for the purposes of this section; and

"general notary" means any public notary other than—

    (a)   an ecclesiastical notary; or

    (b)   one who is a member of the Incorporated Company of Scriveners (in relation to whom provision similar to that made by this section is made by section 65 of the Administration of Justice Act 1985).

(2) Section 1(1) of the Commissioners for Oaths Act 1889 (appointment of commissioners by Lord Chancellor) shall cease to have effect.

(3) Subject to the provisions of this section, every authorised person shall have the powers conferred on a commissioner for oaths by the Commissioners for Oaths Acts 1889 and 1891 and section 24 of the Stamp Duties Management Act 1891; and any reference to such a commissioner in an enactment or instrument (including an enactment passed or instrument made after the commencement of this Act) shall include a reference to an authorised person unless the context otherwise requires.

(4) Subject to the provisions of this section, every general notary shall have the powers conferred on a commissioner for oaths by the Commissioners for Oaths Acts 1889 and 1891; and any reference to such a commissioner in an enactment or instrument (including an enactment passed or instrument made after the commencement of this Act) shall include a reference to a general notary unless the context otherwise requires.

(5) No person shall exercise the powers conferred by this section in any proceedings in which he is interested.

(6) A person exercising such powers and before whom any oath or affidavit is taken or made shall state in the jurat or attestation at which place and on what date the oath or affidavit is taken or made.

(7)   A document containing such a statement and purporting to be sealed or signed by an authorised person or general notary shall be admitted in evidence without proof of the seal or signature, and without proof that he is an authorised person or general notary.

(8)   The Lord Chancellor may, with the concurrence of the Lord Chief Justice and the Master of the Rolls, by order prescribe the fees to be charged by authorised persons exercising the powers of commissioners for oaths by virtue of this section in respect of the administration of an oath or the taking of an affidavit.

(9)   In this section "affidavit" has the same meaning as in the Commissioners for Oaths Act 1889.

(10)   Every—
        (a)   solicitor who holds a practising certificate which is in force;
        (b)   authorised person;
        (c)   general notary; and
        (d)   member of the Incorporated Company of Scriveners ("the Company") who has been admitted to practise as a public notary within the jurisdiction of the Company, shall have the right to use the title "Commissioner for Oaths".

Legal Services Act 2007
(Sections 12, 13, 14, 18 and 20, Schedules 2 and 4)

Reserved legal activities

12   Meaning of "reserved legal activity" and "legal activity"

(1)   In this Act "reserved legal activity" means—

    (a)   the exercise of a right of audience;

    (b)   the conduct of litigation;

    (c)   reserved instrument activities;

    (d)   probate activities;

    (e)   notarial activities;

    (f)   the administration of oaths.

(2)   Schedule 2 makes provision about what constitutes each of those activities.

(3)   In this Act "legal activity" means—

    (a)   an activity which is a reserved legal activity within the meaning of this Act as originally enacted, and

    (b)   any other activity which consists of one or both of the following—

        (i)   the provision of legal advice or assistance in connection with the application of the law or with any form of resolution of legal disputes;

        (ii)   the provision of representation in connection with any matter concerning the application of the law or any form of resolution of legal disputes.

(4)   But "legal activity" does not include any activity of a judicial or quasi-judicial nature (including acting as a mediator).

(5)   For the purposes of subsection (3) "legal dispute" includes a dispute as to any matter of fact the resolution of which is relevant to determining the nature of any person's legal rights or liabilities.

(6)   Section 24 makes provision for adding legal activities to the reserved legal activities.

Carrying on the activities

13   Entitlement to carry on a reserved legal activity

(1)   The question whether a person is entitled to carry on an activity which is a reserved legal activity is to be determined solely in accordance with the provisions of this Act.

(2)   A person is entitled to carry on an activity ("the relevant activity") which is a reserved legal activity where—

    (a)   the person is an authorised person in relation to the relevant activity, or

    (b)   the person is an exempt person in relation to that activity.

(3)   Subsection (2) is subject to section 23 (transitional protection for non-commercial bodies).

(4)   Nothing in this section or section 23 affects section 84 of the Immigration and Asylum Act 1999 (c. 33) (which prohibits the provision of immigration advice and immigration services except by certain persons).

Offences

14   Offence to carry on a reserved legal activity if not entitled

(1)   It is an offence for a person to carry on an activity ("the relevant activity") which is a reserved legal activity unless that person is entitled to carry on the relevant activity.

(2)   In proceedings for an offence under subsection (1), it is a defence for the accused to show that the accused did not know, and could not reasonably have been expected to know, that the offence was being committed.

(3)   A person who is guilty of an offence under subsection (1) is liable—
   (a)   on summary conviction, to imprisonment for a term not exceeding 12 months or a fine not exceeding the statutory maximum (or both), and
   (b)   on conviction on indictment, to imprisonment for a term not exceeding 2 years or a fine (or both).

(4)   A person who is guilty of an offence under subsection (1) by reason of an act done in the purported exercise of a right of audience, or a right to conduct litigation, in relation to any proceedings or contemplated proceedings is also guilty of contempt of the court concerned and may be punished accordingly.

(5)   In relation to an offence under subsection (1) committed before the commencement of section 154(1) of the Criminal Justice Act 2003 (c. 44), the reference in subsection (3)(a) to 12 months is to be read as a reference to 6 months.

Interpretation

18   Authorised persons

(1)   For the purposes of this Act "authorised person", in relation to an activity ("the relevant activity") which is a reserved legal activity, means —
   (a)   a person who is authorised to carry on the relevant activity by a relevant approved regulator in relation to the relevant activity (other than by virtue of a licence under Part 5), or

(b)   a licensable body which, by virtue of such a licence, is authorised to carry on the relevant activity by a licensing authority in relation to the reserved legal activity.

(2)   A licensable body may not be authorised to carry on the relevant activity as mentioned in subsection (1)(a).

(3)   But where a body ("A") which is authorised as mentioned in subsection (1)(a) becomes a licensable body, the body is deemed by virtue of this subsection to continue to be so authorised from that time until the earliest of the following events—
   (a)   the end of the period of 90 days beginning with the day on which that time falls;
   (b)   the time from which the relevant approved regulator determines this subsection is to cease to apply to A;
   (c)   the time when A ceases to be a licensable body.

(4)   Subsection (2) is subject to Part 2 of Schedule 5 (by virtue of which licensable bodies may be deemed to be authorised as mentioned in subsection (1)(a) in relation to certain activities during a transitional period).

(5)   A person other than a licensable body may not be authorised to carry on the relevant activity as mentioned in subsection (1)(b).

(6)   But where a body ("L") which is authorised as mentioned in subsection (1)(b) ceases to be a licensable body, the body is deemed by virtue of this subsection to continue to be so authorised from that time until the earliest of the following events—
   (a)   the end of the period of 90 days beginning with the day on which that time falls;
   (b)   the time from which the relevant licensing authority determines this subsection is to cease to apply to L;
   (c)   the time when L becomes a licensable body.

20   Approved regulators and relevant approved regulators
(1)   In this Act, the following expressions have the meaning given by this section—
   "approved regulator";
   "relevant approved regulator".

(2)   "Approved regulator" means—
   (a)   a body which is designated as an approved regulator by Part 1 of Schedule 4 or under Part 2 of that Schedule (or both) and whose regulatory arrangements are approved for the purposes of this Act, and
   (b)   if an order under section 62(1)(a) has effect, the Board.

(3) An approved regulator is a "relevant approved regulator" in relation to an activity which is a reserved legal activity if—

    (a) the approved regulator is designated by Part 1, or under Part 2, of Schedule 4 in relation to that reserved legal activity, or

    (b) where the approved regulator is the Board, it is designated in relation to that reserved legal activity by an order under section 62(1)(a).

(4) An approved regulator is a "relevant approved regulator" in relation to a person if the person is authorised by the approved regulator to carry on an activity which is a reserved legal activity.

(5) Schedule 4 makes provision with respect to approved regulators other than the Board. In that Schedule—

    (a) Part 1 designates certain bodies as approved regulators in relation to certain reserved legal activities,

    (b) Part 2 makes provision for bodies to be designated by order as approved regulators in relation to one or more reserved legal activities, and

    (c) Part 3 makes provision relating to the approval of changes to an approved regulator's regulatory arrangements.

(6) An approved regulator may authorise persons to carry on any activity which is a reserved legal activity in respect of which it is a relevant approved regulator.

SCHEDULE 2

THE RESERVED LEGAL ACTIVITIES

Introduction

1   This Schedule makes provision about the reserved legal activities.

2   In this Schedule "the appointed day" means the day appointed for the coming into force of section 13 (entitlement to carry on reserved legal activities).

Rights of audience

3   (1) A "right of audience" means the right to appear before and address a court, including the right to call and examine witnesses.

    (2) But a "right of audience" does not include a right to appear before or address a court, or to call or examine witnesses, in relation to any particular court or in relation to particular proceedings, if immediately before the appointed day no restriction was placed on the persons entitled to exercise that right.

Conduct of litigation

4   (1)   The "conduct of litigation" means—

        (a)   the issuing of proceedings before any court in England and Wales,

        (b)   the commencement, prosecution and defence of such proceedings, and

        (c)   the performance of any ancillary functions in relation to such proceedings (such as entering appearances to actions).

    (2)   But the "conduct of litigation" does not include any activity within paragraphs (a) to (c) of sub-paragraph (1), in relation to any particular court or in relation to any particular proceedings, if immediately before the appointed day no restriction was placed on the persons entitled to carry on that activity.

Reserved instrument activities

5   (1)   "Reserved instrument activities" means—

        (a)   preparing any instrument of transfer or charge for the purposes of the Land Registration Act 2002 (c. 9);

        (b)   making an application or lodging a document for registration under that Act;

        (c)   preparing any other instrument relating to real or personal estate for the purposes of the law of England and Wales or instrument relating to court proceedings in England and Wales.

    (2)   But "reserved instrument activities" does not include the preparation of an instrument relating to any particular court proceedings if, immediately before the appointed day, no restriction was placed on the persons entitled to carry on that activity.

    (3)   In this paragraph "instrument" includes a contract for the sale or other disposition of land (except a contract to grant a short lease), but does not include—

        (a)   a will or other testamentary instrument,

        (b)   an agreement not intended to be executed as a deed, other than a contract that is included by virtue of the preceding provisions of this sub-paragraph,

        (c)   a letter or power of attorney, or

        (d)   a transfer of stock containing no trust or limitation of the transfer.

    (4)   In this paragraph a "short lease" means a lease such as is referred to in section 54(2) of the Law of Property Act 1925 (c. 20) (short leases).

Probate activities

6 (1) "Probate activities" means preparing any probate papers for the purposes of the law of England and Wales or in relation to any proceedings in England and Wales.

   (2) In this paragraph "probate papers" means papers on which to found or oppose—
        (a) a grant of probate, or
        (b) a grant of letters of administration.

Notarial activities

7 (1) "Notarial activities" means activities which, immediately before the appointed day, were customarily carried on by virtue of enrolment as a notary in accordance with section 1 of the Public Notaries Act 1801 (c. 79).

   (2) Sub-paragraph (1) does not include activities carried on—
        (a) by virtue of section 22 or 23 of the Solicitors Act 1974 (c. 47) (reserved instrument activities and probate activities), or
        (b) by virtue of section 113 of the Courts and Legal Services Act 1990 (c. 41)(administration of oaths).

Administration of oaths

8 The "administration of oaths" means the exercise of the powers conferred on a commissioner for oaths by—
        (a) the Commissioners for Oaths Act 1889 (c. 10);
        (b) the Commissioners for Oaths Act 1891 (c. 50);
        (c) section 24 of the Stamp Duties Management Act 1891 (c. 38).

SCHEDULE 4
APPROVED REGULATORS

PART 1

EXISTING REGULATORS

1   (1)   Each body listed in the first column of the Table in this paragraph is an approved regulator.

(2)   Each body so listed is an approved regulator in relation to the reserved legal activities listed in relation to it in the second column of the Table.

Table

Approved regulator	Reserved legal activities
The Law Society	The exercise of a right of audience. The conduct of litigation. Reserved instrument activities. Probate activities. The administration of oaths.
The General Council of the Bar	The exercise of a right of audience. The conduct of litigation. Reserved instrument activities. Probate activities. The administration of oaths.
The Master of the Faculties	Reserved instrument activities. Probate activities. Notarial activities. The administration of oaths.
The Institute of Legal Executives	The exercise of a right of audience. The administration of oaths.
The Council for Licensed Conveyancers	Reserved instrument activities. The administration of oaths.
The Chartered Institute of Patent Attorneys	The exercise of a right of audience. The conduct of litigation. Reserved instrument activities. The administration of oaths.
The Institute of Trade Mark Attorneys	The exercise of a right of audience. The conduct of litigation. Reserved instrument activities. The administration of oaths.
The Association of Law Costs Draftsmen	The exercise of a right of audience. The conduct of litigation. The administration of oaths.

2   (1)   The regulatory arrangements of a listed body, as they have effect immediately before paragraph 1 comes into force, are to be treated as having been approved by the Board for the purposes of this Act at the time that paragraph comes into force.

    (2)   "Listed body" means a body listed in the first column of the Table in paragraph 1 as that Table has effect at the time that paragraph comes into force.

    (3)   Sub-paragraph (1) is without prejudice to the Board's power to give Directions under section 32 (powers to direct an approved regulator to take steps in certain circumstances, including steps to amend its regulatory arrangements).

Law of Property (Miscellaneous Provisions) Act 1989
(Sections 1, 2, 3, 4, 5 and 6)

Chapter 34

An Act to make new provision with respect to deeds and their execution and contracts for the sale or other disposition of interests in land; and to abolish the rule of law known as the rule in Bain v. Fothergill. [27th July 1989]

BE IT ENACTED by the Queen's most Excellent Majesty, by and with the advice and consent of the Lords Spiritual and Temporal, and Commons, in this present Parliament assembled, and by the authority of the same, as follows:——

1.-   (1)   Any rule of law which—

             (a)   restricts the substances on which a deed may be written; execution.

             (b)   requires a seal for the valid execution of an instrument as a deed by an individual; or

             (c)   requires authority by one person to another to deliver an instrument as a deed on his behalf to be given by deed, is abolished.

       (2)   An instrument shall not be a deed unless—

             (a)   it makes it clear on its face that it is intended to be a deed by the person making it or, as the case may be, by the parties to it (whether by describing itself as a deed or expressing itself to be executed or signed as a deed or otherwise); and

             (b)   it is validly executed as a deed by that person or, as the case may be, one or more of those parties.

       (3)   An instrument is validly executed as a deed by an individual if, and only if—

             (a)   it is signed—

                   (i)   by him in the presence of a witness who attests the signature; or

                   (ii)   at his direction and in his presence and the presence of two witnesses who each attest the signature; and

             (b)   it is delivered as a deed by him or a person authorised to do so on his behalf.

       (4)   In subsections (2) and (3) above "sign", in relation to an instrument, includes making one's mark on the instrument and

"signature" is to be construed accordingly.

       (5)   Where a solicitor or licensed conveyancer, or an agent or employee of a solicitor or licensed conveyancer, in the course of or in connection with a transaction involving the disposition or creation of an interest in land, purports to deliver an instrument as a deed on

behalf of a party to the instrument, it shall be conclusively presumed in favour of a purchaser that he is authorised so to deliver the instrument.

(6)   In subsection (5) above—
"disposition" and "purchaser" have the same meanings as in the Law of Property Act 1925; and

"interest in land" means any estate, interest or charge in or over land or in or over the proceeds of sale of land.

(7)   Where an instrument under seal that constitutes a deed is required for the purposes of an Act passed before this section comes into force, this section shall have effect as to signing, sealing or delivery of an instrument by an individual in place of any provision of that Act as to signing, sealing or delivery.

(8)   The enactments mentioned in Schedule 1 to this Act (which in consequence of this section require amendments other than those provided by subsection (7) above) shall have effect with the amendments specified in that Schedule.

(9)   Nothing in subsection (1)(b), (2), (3), (7) or (8) above applies in relation to deeds required or authorised to be made under—
(a)   the seal of the county palatine of Lancaster;
(b)   the seal of the Duchy of Lancaster; or
(c)   the seal of the Duchy of Cornwall.

(10) The references in this section to the execution of a deed by an individual do not include execution by a corporation sole and the reference in subsection (7) above to signing, sealing or delivery by an individual does not include signing, sealing or delivery by such a corporation.

(11) Nothing in this section applies in relation to instruments delivered as deeds before this section comes into force.

2.—   (1)   A contract for the sale or other disposition of an interest in land can only be made in writing and only by incorporating all the terms which the parties have expressly agreed in one document or, where contracts are exchanged, in each.

(2)   The terms may be incorporated in a document either by being set out in it or by reference to some other document.

(3)   The document incorporating the terms or, where contracts are exchanged, one of the documents incorporating them (but not necessarily the same one) must be signed by or on behalf of each party to the contract.

(4)   Where a contract for the sale or other disposition of an interest in land satisfies the conditions of this section by reason only of the rectification of one or more documents in pursuance of an order of a court, the contract shall come into being, or be deemed to have come into being, at such time as may be specified in the order.

(5)   This section does not apply in relation to—
   (a)   a contract to grant such a lease as is mentioned in section 54(2) of the Law of Property Act 1925 (short leases);
   (b)   a contract made in the course of a public auction; or
   (c)   a contract regulated under the Financial Services Act 1986;

and nothing in this section affects the creation or operation of resulting, implied or constructive trusts.

(6)   In this section—
"disposition" has the same meaning as in the Law of Property Act 1925;

"interest in land" means any estate, interest or charge in or over land or in or over the proceeds of sale of land.

(7)   Nothing in this section shall apply in relation to contracts made before this section comes into force.

(8)   Section 40 of the Law of Property Act 1925 (which is superseded by this section) shall cease to have effect.

3.   The rule of law known as the rule in Sam v. Fothergill is abolished in relation to contracts made after this section comes into force.

4.   The enactments mentioned in Schedule 2 to this Act are repealed to the extent specified in the third column of that Schedule.

5.—   (1)   The provisions of this Act to which this subsection applies shall come into force on such day as the Lord Chancellor may by order made by statutory instrument appoint.

(2)   The provisions to which subsection (1) above applies are—
   (a)   section 1 above; and
   (b)   section 4 above, except so far as it relates to section 40 of the Law of Property Act 1925.

(3)   The provisions of this Act to which this subsection applies shall come-into force at the end of the period of two months beginning with the day on which this Act is passed.

(4)   The provisions of this Act to which subsection (3) above applies
are—
(a)   sections 2 and 3 above; and
(b)   section 4 above, so far as it relates to section 40 of the Law
of Property Act 1925.

6.—   (1)   This Act may be cited as the Law of Property (Miscellaneous
Provisions) Act 1989.

(2)   This Act extends to England and Wales only.

Law of Property Act 1925
(Sections 74 and 74A)

Part II Contracts, Conveyances and Other Instruments

Conveyances and other Instruments

Execution of instruments by or on behalf of corporations
74.- [(1)   In favour of a purchaser an instrument shall be deemed to have been duly executed by a corporation aggregate if a seal purporting to be the corporation's seal purports to be affixed to the instrument in the presence of and attested by –

(a)   two members of the board of directors, council or other governing body of the corporation, or

(b)   one such member and the clerk, secretary or other permanent officer of the corporation or his deputy.]

[(1A) Subsection (1) of this section applies in the case of an instrument purporting to have been executed by a corporation aggregate in the name or on behalf of another person whether or not that person is also a corporation aggregate.]

[(1B) For the purposes of subsection (1) of this section, a seal purports to be affixed in the presence of and attested by an officer of the corporation, in the case of an officer which is not an individual, if it is affixed in the presence of and attested by an individual authorised by the officer to attest on its behalf.]

(2)   The board of directors, council or other governing body of a corporation aggregate may, by resolution or otherwise, appoint an agent either generally or in any particular case, to execute on behalf of the corporation any agreement or other instrument which is not a deed in relation to any matter within the powers of the corporation.

(3)   Where a person is authorised under a power of attorney or under any statutory or other power to convey any interest in property in the name or on behalf of a corporation sole or aggregate, he may as attorney execute the conveyance by signing the name of the corporation in the presence of at least one witness [who attests the signature], [   ] and such execution shall take effect and be valid in like manner as if the corporation had executed the conveyance.

(4)   Where a corporation aggregate is authorised under a power of attorney or under any statutory or other power to convey any interest in property in the name or on behalf of any other person (including any corporation), an officer appointed for that purpose by the board of directors, council or other governing body of the corporation by resolution or otherwise, may execute the [instrument by signing it] in the name of such other person [or, if the instrument

341

is to be a deed, by so signing it in the presence of a witness who attests the signature], and where an instrument appears to be executed by an officer so appointed, then in favour of a purchaser the instrument shall be deemed to have been executed by an officer duly authorised.

(5)   The foregoing provisions of this section apply to transactions wherever effected, but only to deeds an instruments executed after the commencement of this Act, except that, in the case of powers or appointments of an agent or officer, they apply whether the power was conferred or the appointment was made before or after the commencement of this Act or by this Act.

(6)   Notwithstanding anything contained in this section, any mode of execution or attestation authorised by law or by practice or by the statute, charter, memorandum or articles, deed of settlement or other instrument constituting the corporation or regulating the affairs thereof, shall (in addition to the modes authorised by this section) be as effectual as if this section had not been passed.

Execution of instrument as a deed
A1-355   [74A. (1)   An instrument is validly executed by a corporation aggregate as a deed for the purposes of section 1(2)(b) of the Law of Property (Miscellaneous Provisions) Act 1989, if and only if –
(a)   it is duly executed by the corporation, and
(b)   it is delivered as a deed.

(2)   An instrument shall be presumed to be delivered for the purposes of subsection (1)(b) of this section upon its being executed, unless a contrary intention is proved.]

General definitions
A1-356   205.-(1)   In this Act unless the context otherwise requires, the following expressions have the meanings hereby assigned to them respectively, that is to say:-

[...]

(ii)   "Conveyance" includes a mortgage, charge, lease, assent, vesting declaration, vesting instrument, disclaimer, release and every other assurance of property or of an interest therein by any instrument, except a will; "convey" has a corresponding meaning; and "disposition" includes a conveyance and also a devise, bequest, or an appointment of property contained in a will; and "dispose of" has a corresponding meaning;

[...]

(xx)   "Property" includes any thing in action and any interest in real or personal property;

(xxi)   "Purchaser" means a purchaser in good faith for valuable consideration and includes a lessee, mortgagee or other person who

342

for valuable consideration acquires an interest in property except that in Part I of this Act and elsewhere where so expressly provided "purchaser" only means a person who acquires an interest in or charge on property for money or money's worth; and in reference to a legal estate includes a chargee by way of legal mortgage; and where the context so requires "purchaser" includes an intending purchaser; "purchase" has a meaning corresponding with that of " purchaser"; and "valuable consideration" includes marriage but does not include a nominal consideration in money.

2   Fraud by false representation

(1)   A person is in breach of this section if he—

      (a)   dishonestly makes a false representation, and

      (b)   intends, by making the representation—

            (i)   to make a gain for himself or another, or

            (ii)   to cause loss to another or to expose another to a risk of loss.

(2)   A representation is false if—

      (a)   it is untrue or misleading, and

      (b)   the person making it knows that it is, or might be, untrue or misleading.

(3)   "Representation" means any representation as to fact or law, including a representation as to the state of mind of—

      (a)   the person making the representation, or

      (b)   any other person.

(4)   A representation may be express or implied.

(5)   For the purposes of this section a representation may be regarded as made if it (or anything implying it) is submitted in any form to any system or device designed to receive, convey or respond to communications (with or without human intervention).

3   Fraud by failing to disclose information

A person is in breach of this section if he—

(a)   dishonestly fails to disclose to another person information which he is under a legal duty to disclose, and

(b)   intends, by failing to disclose the information—

      (i)   to make a gain for himself or another, or

      (ii)   to cause loss to another or to expose another to a risk of loss.

4   Fraud by abuse of position

(1)   A person is in breach of this section if he—

      (a)   occupies a position in which he is expected to safeguard, or not to act against, the financial interests of another person,

      (b)   dishonestly abuses that position, and

      (c)   intends, by means of the abuse of that position—

            (i) to make a gain for himself or another, or

            (ii) to cause loss to another or to expose another to a risk of loss.

(2)   A person may be regarded as having abused his position even though his conduct consisted of an omission rather than an act.

Obtaining services dishonestly

11   Obtaining services dishonestly

(1)   A person is guilty of an offence under this section if he obtains services for himself or another—

(a)   by a dishonest act, and

(b)   in breach of subsection (2).

(2)   A person obtains services in breach of this subsection if—

(a)   they are made available on the basis that payment has been, is being or will be made for or in respect of them,

(b)   he obtains them without any payment having been made for or in respect of them or without payment having been made in full, and

(c)   when he obtains them, he knows—

(i)   that they are being made available on the basis described in paragraph (a), or

(ii)   that they might be, but intends that payment will not be made, or will not be made in full.

(3)   A person guilty of an offence under this section is liable—

(a)   on summary conviction, to imprisonment for a term not exceeding 12 months or to a fine not exceeding the statutory maximum (or to both);

(b)   on conviction on indictment, to imprisonment for a term not exceeding 5 years or to a fine (or to both).

(4)   Subsection (3)(a) applies in relation to Northern Ireland as if the reference to 12 months were a reference to 6 months.

Supplementary

12   Liability of company officers for offences by company

(1)   Subsection (2) applies if an offence under this Act is committed by a body corporate.

(2)   If the offence is proved to have been committed with the consent or connivance of—

(a)   a director, manager, secretary or other similar officer of the body corporate, or

(b)   a person who was purporting to act in any such capacity, he (as well as the body corporate) is guilty of the offence and liable to be proceeded against and punished accordingly.

(3)   If the affairs of a body corporate are managed by its members, subsection (2) applies in relation to the acts and defaults of a member in connection with his functions of management as if he were a director of the body corporate.

The Perjury Act 1911
(Sections 1, 2,5,7,9,15 & 16)

1.   (1)   If any person lawfully sworn as a witness or as an interpreter in a judicial proceeding wilfully makes a statement material in that proceeding, which he knows to be false or does not believe to be true, he shall be guilty of perjury, and shall, on conviction thereof on indictment, be liable to penal servitude for a term not exceeding seven years, or to imprisonment with or without hard labour for a term not exceeding two years, or to a fine or to both such penal servitude or imprisonment and fine.

    (2)   The expression "judicial proceeding" includes a proceeding before any court, tribunal, or person having by law power to hear, receive, and examine evidence on oath.

    (3)   Where a statement made for the purposes of a judicial proceeding is not made before the tribunal itself, but is made on oath before a person authorised by law to administer an oath to the person who makes the statement, and to record or authenticate the statement, it shall, for the purposes of this section, be treated as having been made in a judicial proceeding.

    (4)   A statement made by a person lawfully sworn in England for the purposes of a judicial proceeding-
    (a)   in another part of His Majesty's dominions; or
    (b)   in a British tribunal lawfully constituted in any place by sea or land outside His Majesty's dominions ; or
    (c)   in a tribunal of any foreign state, shall, for the purposes of this section, be treated as a statement made in a judicial proceeding in England.

    (5)   Where, for the purposes of a judicial proceeding in England, a person is lawfully sworn under the authority of an Act of Parliament-
    (a)   in any other part of His Majesty's dominions; or
    (b)   before a British tribunal or a British officer in a foreign country, or within the jurisdiction of the Admiralty of England;

    a statement made by such person so sworn as aforesaid (unless the Act of Parliament under which it was made otherwise specifically provides) shall be treated for the purposes of this section as having been made in the judicial proceeding in England for the purposes whereof it was made.

    (6)   The question whether a statement on which perjury is assigned was material is a question of law to be determined by the court of trial.

2. If any person –
    (1)   being required or authorised by law to make any statement on oath for any purpose, and being lawfully sworn (otherwise than in a judicial proceeding) wilfully makes a statement which is material for that purpose and which he knows to be false or does not believe to be true; or

    (2)   wilfully uses any false affidavit for the purposes of the Bills of Sale Act, 1878, as amended by any subsequent enactment, he shall be guilty of a misdemeanour, and, on conviction thereof on indictment, shall be liable to penal servitude for a term not exceeding seven years or to imprisonment, with or without hard labour, for a term not exceeding two years, or to a fine or to both such penal servitude or imprisonment and fine.

5. If any person knowingly and wilfully makes (otherwise than on oath) a statement false in a material particular, and the statement is made-
    (a)   in a statutory declaration; or
    (b)   in an abstract, account, balance sheet, book, certificate, declaration, entry, estimate, inventory, notice, report, return, or other document which he is authorised or required to make, attest, or verify, by any public general Act of Parliament for the time being in force; or
    (c)   in any oral declaration or oral answer which he is required to make by, under, or in pursuance of any public general Act of Parliament for the time being in force, he shall be guilty of a misdemeanour and shall be liable on conviction thereof on indictment to imprisonment, with or without hard labour, for any term not exceeding two years, or to a fine or to both such imprisonment and fine.

7. (1)   Every person who aids, abets, counsels, procures, or suborns another person to commit an offence against this Act shall be liable to be proceeded against, indicted, tried and punished as if he were a principal offender.

    (2)   Every person who incites or attempts to procure or suborn another person to commit an offence against this Act shall be guilty of a misdemeanour, and, on conviction thereof on indictment, shall be liable to imprisonment, or to a fine, or to both such imprisonment and fine.

9. (1)   Where any of the following authorities, namely, a judge of, or person presiding in, a court of record, or a petty sessional court, or any justice of the peace sitting in special sessions, or any sheriff or his lawful deputy before whom a writ of inquiry or a writ of trial is executed, is of opinion that any person has, in the course of a proceeding before that authority, been guilty of perjury, the authority may order the prosecution of that person for such perjury, in case there shall appear to be reasonable cause for such

prosecution, and may commit him, or admit him to bail, to take his trial at the proper court, and may require any person to enter into a recognizance to prosecute or give evidence against the person whose prosecution is so ordered, and may give the person so bound to prosecute a certificate of the making of the order for the prosecution, for which certificate no charge shall be made.

(2) An order made or a certificate given under this section shall not be given in evidence for the purpose or in the course of any trial of a prosecution resulting therefrom.

15. (1) For the purposes of this Act, the forms and ceremonies used in administering an oath are immaterial, if the court or person before whom the oath is taken has power to administer an oath for the purpose of verifying the statement in question, and if the oath has been administered in a form and with ceremonies which the person taking the oath has accepted without objection, or has declared to be binding on him.

(2) In this Act-
The expression " oath " in the case of persons for the time being allowed by law to affirm or declare instead of swearing, includes " affirmation " and " declaration," and the expression " swear " in the like case includes It affirm " and " declare " ; and

The expression " statutory declaration " means a declaration made by virtue of the Statutory Declarations Act, 1835, or of any Act, Order in Council, rule or regulation applying or extending the provisions thereof ; and

The expression " indictment " includes " criminal information."

16. (1) Where the making of a false statement is not only an offence under this Act, but also by virtue of some other Act is a corrupt practice or subjects the offender to any forfeiture or disqualification or to any penalty other than penal servitude, or imprisonment, or fine, the liability of the offender under this Act shall be in addition to and not in substitution for his liability under such other Act.

(2) Nothing in this Act shall apply to a statement made without oath by a child under the provisions of the Prevention of Cruelty to Children Act, 1904, and the Children Act, 1908.

(3) Where the making of a false statement is by any other Act, whether passed before or after the commencement of this Act, made punishable on summary conviction, proceedings may be taken either under such other Act or under this Act:

Provided that where such an offence is by any Act passed before the commencement of this Act, as originally enacted, made punishable only on summary conviction, it shall remain only so punishable.

REQUIREMENTS FOR LEGALISATION OF DOCUMENTS

Please note that these pages should be used for guidance purposes only. The Author will not be liable for any errors or omissions.

In these pages FCO means Foreign & Commonwealth Office and ABCC means Arab British Chamber of Commerce.

Afghanistan
Apostille from FCO & Consular Legalisation

Albania
Apostille from FCO
No Consular legalisation required

Algeria
Apostille from FCO & Consular Legalisation

Andora
Apostille from FCO
No Consular legalisation required

Angola
Apostille from FCO & Consular Legalisation
Embassy requires Portuguese translations
Commercial documents require backup

Antigua & Barmuda
Apostille from FCO
No Consular legalisation required

Argentina
Apostille from FCO
No Consular legalisation required

Armenia
Apostille from FCO
No Consular legalisation required

Australia
Apostille from FCO
No Consular legalisation required

Austria
Apostille from FCO
No Consular legalisation required

Azerbaijan
Apostille from FCO
No Consular legalisation required

Bahamas
Apostille from FCO
No Consular legalisation required

Bahrain
Apostille from FCO
No Consular legalisation required

Bangladesh
Apostille from FCO & Consular Legalisation

Barbados
Apostille from FCO
No Consular legalisation required

Belarus (Republic of)
Apostille from FCO
No Consular legalisation required

Belgium
Apostille from FCO
No Consular legalisation required

Belize
Apostille from FCO
No Consular legalisation required

Bolivia
Apostille from FCO & Consular Legalisation

Bosnia & Herzegovina
Apostille from FCO
No Consular legalisation required

Botswana
Apostille from FCO
No Consular legalisation required

Brazil
Apostille from FCO, provided the notary is registered with the Brazilian
Consulate

Bulgaria
Apostille from FCO
No Consular legalisation required

Brunei
Apostille from FCO
No Consular legalisation required

Burma (Mynamar)
Apostille from FCO & Consular Legalisation

Cambodia (Royal government of)
Apostille from FCO & Consular Legalisation

Canada
Apostille from FCO & Consular Legalisation

Cape Verde
Apostille from FCO
No Consular legalisation required

Cayman Islands
Apostille from FCO & Consular Legalisation

Chile
Apostille from FCO & Consular Legalisation

China
Apostille from FCO & Consular Legalisation
Documents must be bound together and must not mention Hong Kong or Taiwan.

Colombia
Apostille from FCO
No Consular legalisation required

Costa Rica
Apostille from FCO
No Consular legalisation required

Croatia
Apostille from FCO
No Consular legalisation required

Cuba
Apostille from FCO & Consular Legalisation
Embassy requires Spanish translation

Cyprus
Apostille from FCO
No Consular legalisation required

Czech Republic
Apostille from FCO
No Consular legalisation required

Denmark
Apostille from FCO
No Consular legalisation required

Dominican Republic
Apostille from FCO
No Consular legalisation required

Ecuador
Apostille from FCO
No Consular legalisation required

Egypt
Apostille plus Consular Legalisation

El Salvador
Apostille from FCO
No Consular legalisation required

Ethiopia
Apostille from FCO & Consular Legalisation

Fiji
Apostille from FCO
No Consular legalisation required

Finland
Apostille from FCO
No Consular legalisation required

France
Apostille from FCO
No Consular legalisation required

Gambia
Apostille plus Consular Legalisation

Georgia
Apostille from FCO
No Consular legalisation required

Germany
Apostille from FCO
No Consular legalisation required

Ghana
Apostille from FCO & Consular Legalisation

Greece
Apostille from FCO
No Consular legalisation required

Grenada
Apostille from FCO
No Consular legalisation required

Guatemala
Apostille from FCO & Consular Legalisation

Guyana
Apostille from FCO & Consular Legalisation

Haiti
Apostille from FCO
Nearest Consulate is in Brussels

Holland
Apostille from FCO
No Consular legalisation required

Honduras
Apostille from FCO
No Consular legalisation required

Hong Kong
Apostille from FCO
No Consular legalisation required

Hungary
Apostille from FCO
No Consular legalisation required

Iceland
Apostille from FCO
No Consular legalisation required

India
Apostille from FCO
Technically no Consular legalisation required

Indonesia
Apostille from FCO & Consular Legalisation
Back up documentation required at embassy

Iran
Apostille from FCO & Consular Legalisation
Embassy closed.
FCO and local chamber of commerce.

Iraq (Islamic Republic of)
Apostille plus Consular Legalisation
Also requires ABCC

Ireland
Apostille from FCO
No Consular legalisation required

Israel
Apostille from FCO
No Consular legalisation required

Italy
Apostille from FCO
No Consular legalisation required

Ivory Coast
Apostille from FCO & Consular Legalisation

Jamaica
Apostille from FCO & Consular Legalisation

Japan
Apostille from FCO
No Consular legalisation required

Jordan
Apostille from FCO & Consular Legalisation

Kazakhstan
Apostille from FCO
No Consular legalisation required

Kenya
Apostille from FCO & Consular Legalisation

Korea (Republic of)
Apostille from FCO
No Consular legalisation required

Kuwait
Apostille from FCO & Consular Legalisation
Commercial documents require ABCC.

Kyrghystan
Apostille from FCO
No Consular legalisation required

Latvia
Apostille from FCO
No Consular legalisation required

Lebanon
Apostille from FCO & Consular Legalisation

Lesotho
Apostille from FCO
No Consular legalisation required

Liberia
Apostille from FCO
No Consular legalisation required

Libya
Apostille from FCO & Consular legalisation

Luxemburg
Apostille from FCO
No Consular legalisation required

Madagascar (Republic of)
Apostille from FCO & Consular Legalisation

Malavi
Apostille from FCO
No Consular legalisation required

Malaysia
Apostille from FCO & (Usually N.P. Acceptable)
Consular Legalisation

Malta
Apostille from FCO
No Consular legalisation required

Mauritius
Apostille from FCO
No Consular legalisation required

Mexico
Apostille from FCO
No Consular legalisation required

Mongolia
Apostille from FCO & Consular Legalisation

Morocco
Apostille from FCO & Consular Legalisation

Namibia
Apostille from FCO
No Consular legalisation required

Nepal
Apostille from FCO & Consular Legalisation

Netherlands
Apostille from FCO
No Consular legalisation required

New Zealand
Apostille from FCO
No Consular legalisation required

Nicargua
Apostille from FCO
No Consular legalisation required

Nigeria
Apostille from FCO & Consular Legalisation

Niue
Apostille from FCO
No Consular Legalisation required

Norway
Apostille from FCO
No Consular legalisation required

Oman
Apostille from FCO
No Consular Legalisation required

Pakistan
Apostille from FCO & Consular Legalisation

Palestine
Apostille from FCO & Consular Legalisation

Panama
Apostille from FCO
No Consular legalisation required

Paraguay
Apostille from FCO & Consular Legalisation

Peru
Apostille from FCO
No Consular legalisation required

Philippines
Apostille from FCO & Consular Legalisation

Poland
Apostille from FCO
No Consular legalisation required

Portugal
Apostille from FCO
No Consular legalisation required

Qatar(State of)
Apostille from FCO & Consular Legalisation

Ras Al-Khaimah
Apostille from FCO & Consular Legalisation (UAE)

Romania
Apostille from FCO
No Consular legalisation required

Russian Federation
Apostille from FCO
No Consular legalisation required

Rwanda
Apostille from FCO & Consular Legalisation

San Marino
Apostille from FCO
No Consular legalisation required

Sao Tome
Apostille from FCO
No Consular Legalisation required

Saudi Arabia
Apostille from FCO & Consular Legalisation

Senegal
Apostille from FCO & Consular Legalisation

Serbia
Apostille from FCO
No Consular legalisation required

Seychelles
Apostille from FCO & Consular Legalisation

Sharjah
Apostille from FCO & Consular Legalisation (UAE)

Sierra Leone
Apostille from FCO & Consular Legalisation

Singapore
Apostille from FCO & Consular Legalisation

Slovak Republic
Apostille from FCO
No Consular legalisation required

Slovenia
Apostille from FCO
No Consular legalisation required

South Africa
Apostille from FCO
No Consular legalisation required

Spain
Apostille from FCO
No Consular legalisation required

Sri Lanka
Apostille from FCO & Consular Legalisation

Sudan
Apostille from FCO & Consular Legalisation

Sweden
Apostille from FCO
No Consular legalisation required

Switzerland
Apostille from FCO
No Consular legalisation required

Syria
Apostille from FCO & Consular Legalisation
Embassy is closed until further notice.
ABCC is all that can be done.

Tadjikstan
Apostille from FCO & Consular Legalisation (Russia)

Taiwan
Apostille from FCO & Consular Legalisation

Tanzania
Apostille from FCO & Consular Legalisation

Thailand
Apostille from FCO & Consular Legalisation

Tonga
Apostille from FCO
No Consular legalisation required

Trinidad & Tobago
Apostille from FCO & Consular Legalisation

Tunisia
Apostille from FCO & Consular Legalisation

Turkey
Apostille from FCO & Consular Legalisation
Document must also be stamped at local chamber of commerce if going to embassy

Turkmenistan
Apostille from FCO & Consular Legalisation

Uganda
Apostille from FCO & Consular Legalisation

Ukraine
Apostille from FCO
No Consular legalisation required

Ummal-Qaiwan
Apostille from FCO & Consular Legalisation (UAE)

United Arab Emirates
Apostille from FCO & Consular Legalisation
Embassy will not accept bundled documents or foreign documents

United States of America
Apostille from FCO
No Consular legalisation required

Uruguay
Apostille from FCO
No Consular legalisation required

Uzbekistan
Apostille from FCO
No Consular legalisation required

Venezuela
Apostille from FCO
No Consular legalisation required

Vietnam
Apostille from FCO
Consular legalisation required

Yemen
Apostille from FCO & ABCC & Consular Legalisation

Zaire
Apostille from FCO & Consular Legalisation (Congo)

Zambia
Apostille from FCO & Consular Legalisation

Zimbabwe
Apostille from FCO & Consular Legalisation

THE HAGUE APOSTILLE CONVENTION, 1961

CONVENTION ABOLISHING THE REQUIREMENT OF LEGALISATION
FOR FOREIGN PUBLIC DOCUMENTS
(Concluded 5 October 1961)
(Entered into force 24 January 1965)

The States signatory to the present Convention,
Desiring to abolish the requirement of diplomatic or consular legalisation for foreign public documents,
Have resolved to conclude a Convention to this effect and have agreed upon the following provisions:

Article 1
The present Convention shall apply to public documents which have been executed in the territory of one Contracting State and which have to be produced in the territory of another Contracting State.
For the purposes of the present Convention, the following are deemed to be public documents:

a)   documents emanating from an authority or an official connected with the courts or tribunals of the State, including those emanating from a public prosecutor, a clerk of a court or a process-server ("huissier de justice");
b)   administrative documents;
c)   notarial acts;
d)   official certificates which are placed on documents signed by persons in their private capacity, such as official certificates recording the registration of a document or the fact that it was in existence on a certain date and official and notarial authentications of signatures.

However, the present Convention shall not apply:
a)   to documents executed by diplomatic or consular agents;
b   to administrative documents dealing directly with commercial or customs operations.

Article 2
Each Contracting State shall exempt from legalisation documents to which the present Convention applies and which have to be produced in its territory. For the purposes of the present Convention, legalisation means only the formality by which the diplomatic or consular agents of the country in which the document has to be produced certify the authenticity of the signature, the capacity in which the person signing the document has acted and, where appropriate, the identity of the seal or stamp which it bears.

Article 3
The only formality that may be required in order to certify the authenticity of the signature, the capacity in which the person signing the document has acted and, where appropriate, the identity of the seal or stamp which it bears, is the addition

of the certificate described in Article 4, issued by the competent authority of the State from which the document emanates.

However, the formality mentioned in the preceding paragraph cannot be required when either the laws, regulations, or practice in force in the State where the document is produced or an agreement between two or more Contracting States have abolished or simplified it, or exempt the document itself from legalisation.

Article 4

The certificate referred to in the first paragraph of Article 3 shall be placed on the document itself or on an "allonge", it shall be in the form of the model annexed to the present Convention.

It may, however, be drawn up in the official language of the authority which issues it. The standard terms appearing therein may be in a second language also. The title "Apostille (Convention de La Haye du 5 octobre 1961)" shall be in the French language.

Article 5

The certificate shall be issued at the request of the person who has signed the document or of any bearer.

When properly filled in, it will certify the authenticity of the signature, the capacity in which the person signing the document has acted and, where appropriate, the identity of the seal or stamp which the document bears.

The signature, seal and stamp on the certificate are exempt from all certification.

Article 6

Each Contracting State shall designate by reference to their official function, the authorities who are competent to issue the certificate referred to in the first paragraph of Article 3.

It shall give notice of such designation to the Ministry of Foreign Affairs of the Netherlands at the time it deposits its instrument of ratification or of accession or its declaration of extension. It shall also give notice of any change in the designated authorities.

Article 7

Each of the authorities designated in accordance with Article 6 shall keep a register or card index in which it shall record the certificates issued, specifying:

a) the number and date of the certificate,

b) the name of the person signing the public document and the capacity in which he has acted, or in the case of unsigned documents, the name of the authority which has affixed the seal or stamp.

At the request of any interested person, the authority which has issued the certificate shall verify whether the particulars in the certificate correspond with those in the register or card index.

Article 8

When a treaty, convention or agreement between two or more Contracting States contains provisions which subject the certification of a signature, seal or stamp to certain formalities, the present Convention will only override such provisions if those formalities are more rigorous than the formality referred to in Articles 3 and

Article 9
Each Contracting State shall take the necessary steps to prevent the performance of legalisation by its diplomatic or consular agents in cases where the present Convention provides for exemption.

Article 10
The present Convention shall be open for signature by the States represented at the Ninth Session of the Hague Conference on Private International Law and Iceland, Ireland, Liechtenstein and Turkey.
It shall be ratified, and the instruments of ratification shall be deposited with the Ministry of Foreign Affairs of the Netherlands.

Article 11
The present Convention shall enter into force on the sixtieth day after the deposit of the third instrument of ratification referred to in the second paragraph of Article 10.
The Convention shall enter into force for each signatory State which ratifies subsequently on the sixtieth day after the deposit of its instrument of ratification.

Article 12
Any State not referred to in Article 10 may accede to the present Convention after it has entered into force in accordance with the first paragraph of Article 11. The instrument of accession shall be deposited with the Ministry of Foreign Affairs of the Netherlands.
Such accession shall have effect only as regards the relations between the acceding State and those Contracting States which have not raised an objection to its accession in the six months after the receipt of the notification referred to in sub-paragraph d) of Article 15. Any such objection shall be notified to the Ministry of Foreign Affairs of the Netherlands.

The Convention shall enter into force as between the acceding State and the States which have raised no objection to its accession on the sixtieth day after the expiry of the period of six months mentioned in the preceding paragraph.

Article 13
Any State may, at the time of signature, ratification or accession, declare that the present Convention shall extend to all the territories for the international relations of which it is responsible, or to one or more of them. Such a declaration shall take effect on the date of entry into force of the Convention for the State concerned.
At any time thereafter, such extensions shall be notified to the Ministry of Foreign Affairs of the Netherlands.
When the declaration of extension is made by a State which has signed and ratified, the Convention shall enter into force for the territories concerned in accordance with Article 11. When the declaration of extension is made by a State which has acceded, the Convention shall enter into force for the territories concerned in accordance with Article 12.

Article 14

The present Convention shall remain in force for five years from the date of its entry into force in accordance with the first paragraph of Article 11, even for States, which have ratified it or acceded to it subsequently.

If there has been no denunciation, the Convention shall be renewed tacitly every five years.

Any denunciation shall be notified to the Ministry of Foreign Affairs of the Netherlands at least six months before the end of the five year period.

It may be limited to certain of the territories to which the Convention applies.

The denunciation will only have effect as regards the State which has notified it. The Convention shall remain in force for the other Contracting States.

Article 15

The Ministry of Foreign Affairs of the Netherlands shall give notice to the States referred to in Article 10, and to the States which have acceded in accordance with Article 12, of the following:

a)   the notifications referred to in the second paragraph of Article 6;

b)   the signatures and ratifications referred to in Article 10;

c)   the date on which the present Convention enters into force in accordance with the first paragraph of Article 11;

d)   the accessions and objections referred to in Article 12 and the date on which such accessions take effect;

e)   the extensions referred to in Article 13 and the date on which they take effect;

f)   the denunciations referred to in the third paragraph of Article 14.

In witness whereof the undersigned, being duly authorised thereto, have signed the present Convention.

Done at The Hague the 5th October 1961, in French and in English, the French text prevailing in case of divergence between the two texts, in a single copy which shall be deposited in the archives of the Government of the Netherlands, and of which a certified copy shall be sent, through the diplomatic channel, to each of the States represented at the Ninth Session of the Hague Conference on Private International Law and also to Iceland, Ireland, Liechtenstein and Turkey.

BIBLIOGRAPHY

1.   The Faculty Office website

2.   The Legal Ombudsman Website

3.   The National Archives Website

4.   Foreign and Commonwealth Office Website

5.   Cheeswrights Website

6.   The General Notary by Tony Dunford, The Notaries Society 1999

7.   Brookes Notary by N P Ready, Sweet & Maxwell 13th Edition

8.   The Notaries Society Website

9.   The Scriveners Society Website

10.   HCCH Website

11.   The Civil Law Notary- Neutral Lawyer for the Situation, Peter Murray, Verlag C.H.Beck Munchen 2010

Notes

SPG Charity
Make the difference...

We all dream for a better tomorrow. SPG Charity supports various registered charities in India and UK creating a healthy society for the future. SPG Charity believes that money should not be an obstacle for people in need.

Get involved and make a big impact with a small contribution
You can make the difference

We believe that no-one should have to face a crisis alone, we provide the vital key for building a better tomorrow - whoever they are. None of our work would be possible without the generous support of people like you, and in these uncertain times we need your help more than ever.

SPG Charity is funded completely by charitable donations. Please consider donating generously to SPG Charity.

Account Name: SPG Charity
Bank: HSBC
Account Number: 91586963
Sort Code: 40-28-03
or send a cheque payable to **SPG Charity** to
219 Bramcote Lane, Wollaton, Nottingham, NG8 2QL, UK